In The Lands Of Black Lions And White Bears

My Life In Ethiopia And Canada

By

ALEMAYEHU AMBO

First published by AuthorHouse 04/14/04

ISBN: 1-4140-7191-4 (e-book)
ISBN: 1-4184-3379-9 (Paperback)

Printed in the United States of America
Bloomington, IN

This book is printed on acid free paper.

IN MEMORY OF MY PARENTS

ACKNOWLEDGEMENTS

I am grateful to my wife Shewaye Feyissa, who supplemented our income through her work during the writing and publication of this book. I am also grateful to my dear lifetime friend Abebayehu Tegene who sacrificed his time to read the manuscript and give his comments, always encouraging me to go on with the book.

CHAPTER ONE

Deep in south-western Ethiopia, a region of virgin forests and coffee bushes, rivers echoed from all directions. Bananas, oranges, papayas and pineapples grew wild. Cattle and wild animals abounded. People survived well enough with a minimum of effort. Tradition predominated in all aspects of life, including medicine and worship. There was no formal religion. There were no schools, no health centres, and no amenities at all. Nevertheless, nature had provided full bounty to this part of the world. A place there known as Angsho[1] gave coffee to humankind.

In 1935, Italy again invaded Ethiopia.[2] At the time, a large family living in Angsho was preparing for the wedding of its youngest son, 28-year-old Ambe. Although there was no formal religion, there were rituals to be carried out. Thus Ambe had been circumcised. He was the family's favourite son and not required to do hard work. Usually, he spent his time roaming around the village.

One day, Ambe had travelled quite a distance from home when he came across a desperate-looking man standing in front of the police station. His cattle had been impounded for destroying somebody's farm. Ambe barely

---

[1] Ethiopia was governed under three major administrative hierarchies: the province, the *awraja* and the *woreda*. Angsho was in the Kefa Awraja and in the Gesha Woreda.
[2] The invasions had begun in the 18th century as a way for Italy to get control of Ethiopia's resources. The invaders had penetrated the hinterland in 1887 but were defeated at the Battle of Dogali. They tried again in 1889, only to be defeated at the battle of Adua. The 100,000 militiamen mobilized by Emperor Menelek bitterly defeated the 25,000 Italian troops. The invaders had concentrated on the northern part of the country; the southern part was not affected except in so far as to mobilize against the invasion.

knew the man, but he listened to him because Ambe was a compassionate person. He was also curious. The man explained to Ambe that he had no money to pay the fine and asked him to bail his cattle out. Ambe said that he had no money at hand. The man asked him if he would at least wait at the police station until he could take his cattle home and come back with the money. After thinking about the matter for several minutes, Ambe decided to bail the cattle out. However, the man did not come back that day or the next. Ambe was jailed. He waited. He began to worry about himself, his parents and his forthcoming marriage. Days went by and Ambe still waited. Word of the invasion spread and the villagers thought that Italian troops would soon be in Angsho. The police chief ordered a general mobilization, including prisoners. Those mobilized were to go to the capital, Addis Ababa, a city more than 600 kilometres away.

The journey started one week after Ambe was jailed. He was confused, stunned and helpless. Along with a fellow prisoner by the name of Muleta, a man about Ambe's age, he began the long journey on foot. The police were on horseback. They crossed the jungles of Gesha, spending the night in grass-covered huts and sharing food with the hut's inhabitants. Ambe wouldn't remember anything – not the area he covered through, not even the direction he travelled. He was completely lost. He had no formal education and knew neither the days of the week nor the months of the year.

After some hard travelling, they arrived at the town of Bonga, the administrative capital of Kefa Awraja. Close by in the small village of Baha, there is Saint George's Church and a monastery of the Tewahedo Church. They stayed at Bonga to rest for a few days and then went on. They crossed the wide rivers of Gojeb and Gibe and the forests of Kefa and Shewa Provinces. They slept little. They had many bad days but finally reached a small place called Dabo Gojo, not far from Addis Ababa. Ambe would never remember how long the journey had taken. By the time he arrived at Dabo Gojo, the group was in disarray and he was no longer a prisoner.

In Dabo Gojo, Ambe met an old man, Habte Michael, who gave him shelter. Habte Michael was an Orthodox Tewahedo Christian and so advised Ambe to be baptised. Ambe agreed and was baptised, with Habte Michael as his godfather. From that day on, Ambe thought of Habte Michael as his father. In time, Ambe moved to Addis Ababa but kept strong ties with Habte Michael's family and thought of the sons as his brothers and the daughters as his sisters.

Addis Ababa was already an occupied city. The Italians had a strong garrison at Yeka, the eastern gate leading to the city centre, and Ambe settled there. Saint Michael's Church, the oldest Orthodox Tewahedo Church in Addis Ababa, had been founded at Yeka. Most of the Italian soldiers were conscripts from Eritrea, an Italian colony at the time. Addis Ababa was completely foreign to Ambe. Nothing was the same as in Angsho. The food, the language and the people were all different. Muleta was the only person he knew who spoke his language. Ambe had been accustomed to eating root crops and maize porridge while the people of Addis Ababa ate mainly *injera*[3] served with different kinds of sauces.

Ambe found work, washing clothes for the Italian soldiers. They were cruel to the local people and especially given to harassing and beating the women. They spat in the faces of women who were fetching water from the local spring. Once, Ambe was accused of defaming the occupation forces and was held without food and water in a very small room, where he was beaten for more than three days. He spoke neither Amharic, the official language of Ethiopia, nor Italian, the language of the occupier. Whatever he said was misinterpreted.

It took him a long time to mix with people. There was no one to help him in case of misfortune and the consequences of a miss-step were very harsh. Gradually, but bitterly, he began to adapt to his new circumstances. He would go to small bars to drink *tella*, the local beer. He learned some Amharic but never mastered it for his mother tongue was Keficho[4] and not related to Amharic in any way.

[3] *Injera* is popular Ethiopian bread, similar to chapatti, and made from the flour of a grain called *teff.*
[4] Keficho belongs to the Omotic language family and Amharic to the Semitic. It is thought that the ancestors of the speakers of Omotic languages have been in southern and south-western Ethiopia for many years. Amharic belongs to the Semitic family as does Arabic and Hebrew. Amharic uses the Geez script, derived from South Arabic script. The script has been in use by the Ethiopian Orthodox Church for at least 1,500 years. The Geez script and that used for Arabic are the only non-Roman scripts in Africa.

* * *

Aldad was born and brought up in Waka[5] Town and was the youngest child in the family. Her mother was from Kefa Awraja and her father from a small place called Kucha in Gamo Gofa Province, the southern province of Ethiopia bordering Kenya. Her mother adored her and her father, who was much older than her mother, treated her with great affection. Aldad drank milk fresh from the cow. During the morning and evening cow milking, Aldad was there to take her share in her small clay pot. Her father begot her in his old age and so died when she was very young. Her mother was a famous conjurer, much admired for her miracles. When the clouds got heavy with unwelcome rain, people would call on Aldad's mother to drive away the rain cloud. Sometimes it worked and sometimes it didn't. If it didn't work, people cursed Satan and not Aldad's mother. Unfortunately, she too died when Aldad was young. Shortly after, and according to local tradition, Aldad married a young man. She begot a baby boy, but he died in infancy. Aldad didn't stay long with her husband. She divorced and was taken on as a cook by the local administrator.

News of the Italian invasion had disrupted the life in Kulo Konta Awraja too. As the invasion expanded to southern Ethiopia, the administrator of Kulo Konta Awraja decided to mobilize conscripts to advance against the invaders. He had decided that Aldad would travel with them as his cook. His force was large, but had no guns. The conscripts armed themselves

---

[5] Waka is the administrative centre of Kulo Konta Awraja, which lies towards the south and borders Kefa Awraja. The people of Waka speak Wolaitigna, part of the Omotic family.

5

with spears, swords and machetes and moved towards Addis Ababa. They crossed Omo River, one of the longest rivers in the country. They advanced on Wachemo commonly called Hosanna Town, 250 kilometres west of Addis Ababa. There were no roads to speak of and no transport between Addis Ababa and Hosanna.

Except for a very few people on horseback, they made their way on foot through the forests. Aldad had a very hard time walking. Sometimes, the administrator took care of her – she was, after all, his cook. They walked through the village of Mareko, commonly called Butajira, and then through Melka Konture.[6] Then, they crossed the village of Alemgena and finally reached Addis Ababa. By the time they arrived, Addis Ababa was fully controlled by the Italian forces, so the people from Kulo Konta slipped away in the city. Aldad was alone and had nowhere to go. She went from house to house until she finally met a woman who helped her settle at Yeka. She started to work at fetching water from a nearby spring for her neighbours. She was harassed and intimidated by the Italian soldiers and thus decided to quit. Next, she baked *injera* and sold it to the households nearby.

A woman named Mamite was selling *tella*, a local beer. Mamite was very popular in Yeka and many men, including Ambe, frequented her house. Aldad sold *injera* to Mamite and so was also a frequent visitor. Ambe had

---

[6] Melka Konture is a prehistoric archaeological site dating from the early Stone Age and thought to be more than one million years old. Close to Melka Kunture, there are rock-hewn churches believed to have been built in the 13th century.

noticed Aldad many times. One day he asked Mamite about her and she told him that Aldad was a woman by herself who survived by selling *injera*. Ambe decided that he wanted to know Aldad.

Ambe and Aldad met through Mamite and in time they married and rented a ramshackle house. Both came from deep within the county and had no prospect of going back. They had no property and no relatives around. They had lost the past and had no idea what to expect from the future. They were, however, heartened by the people around who had come from the same background. There were many people who had come from Kefa, Sidamo and Gamo Gofa provinces under similar circumstances. Some of them worked as servants for landlords who lived nearby.

Aldad kept selling *injera,* but Ambe shifted to cutting and selling firewood. The most common tree was eucalyptus, a species imported from Australia. The trees were tall and large with roots ranging all over the place under ground. The trees had to be chopped down, cut into logs one metre in length, and then into pieces small enough for burning. The work required at least two people and they were paid one Birr[7] per cubic metre of firewood. They worked for days in the forest and lived under canopies made of tree branches. To earn 10 Birr per week was to do very well. Enough for a piece of bread and a glass of *tella* would often be the most Ambe would get. Worse yet, the work stopped during the rainy season because the roads

---

[7] One Birr was equivalent to about US $ 0.40 at the time. It has been devalued several times, however, and in late 2003 was worth about US $ 0.15.

would be too muddy for travel and the firewood itself would take too long to dry. During the rainy season, Ambe would borrow money at exorbitant interest rates and hope to pay it back when the next dry season came.

Aldad was not making much money either. She had to pay for flour and then she would make dough with flour and water and yeast. It would take some time for the dough to ferment and to bake the bread. The price for *injera* was low and her profit per day was not more than the value of two *injeras*. Because of that, she too shifted to selling firewood, but mainly from tree branches.

In the beginning, she would carry the firewood on her back, which was very tiring. She would walk into the forest and collect her wood and then carry it back to her place. Early the next day, she would begin her walk towards the markets. On the way, those who wanted to buy it would stop her and bargain for the price. Sometimes she ended up without buyers and dumped it. Other days, she had to sell at a loss. This went on until they managed to buy a donkey. Socially, however, life was much better now. Most of the people in the area were poor and co-operated with each other in order to survive. Under the traditional practice of *debo*, they came together in groups to build houses and fences at no charge to the owner. In turn, the owner provided a free lunch and *tella.*

People formed *mahbers,* traditional associations named for angels and saints. They met at one of the member's houses once a month[8] on the saint's day and ate *injera* and drank *tella*. They ate and drank in turns, with first one and then the next taking a piece of bread on *mesob* and *tella* in a small jar. And they always had a drawing of the saint from the last month's house. When in difficulty or beset by a problem, people called on angels and saints. The members shared fortune and affliction alike. Ambe and Aldad had wanted to take part, but hadn't had the money for even the meal and drink.

Similarly, through the *equb,* people came together to solve financial problems. Every week on Sunday, people would go to Mamite's house and contribute an agreed-upon sum of money. Of those who contributed, the one with the most pressing financial problem would get the first collection. The next week, the one with the next most serious problem would, and so on until they all got their money back. The last person, of course, would lose the benefit of his money's earning power, but the purpose was not to make money but to share and solve problems. Sometimes, too, they would have a free draw and the next week a sale of some kind. After every round of *equb* was over, glasses and dishes were bought with the money earned at the sales and distributed amongst the members. Ambe and Aldad joined in and used the *equb* to buy more draft animals and household furniture.

---

[8] Ethiopia has 13 months of sunshine – 12 months of 30 days each and one month of five days (six in a leap year). The New Year falls on September 11th or 12th, depending on whether it's a leap year. The calendar differs between seven and eight years from the Gregorian calendar. This discrepancy comes from differences between the Ethiopian Orthodox and the Roman Catholic Churches following their separation. Almost every day of an Ethiopian month is named for an angel or a saint.

Ambe and Aldad begot their first child – a daughter – after they had been married one year. They were tenants of a landowner and, through the *debo*, had built a house. The house was not far from where they had lived before. The land belonged to a lady with three grown-up children. Ambe had agreed to pay her five Birr each year.

Many of his kind made similar agreements and moved to the new place. However, Ambe had to spend most of his time in the forest and could not help Aldad in handling the child. What seemed to be good fortune became bad luck. The child was not properly fed and cared for and thus became very sick. Sometimes, Aldad had to go to collect firewood and left the child alone in the house. "Unfortunately," some would say, they begot another daughter two years later. That child was pronounced dead by a local doctor few days after her birth. Ambe and Aldad had no money to take her for treatment and so were very troubled. In desperation, they took the body to Saint Mary's Mahber and she miraculously recovered. They were so happy that they joined the *mahber*.

After the second child was born, Ambe decided to stay closer to the family and worked nearby. The second child became totally dependent on him and sucked at his breast when he was at home and Aldad was busy or away from home. That daughter did that for a year and a half. A third daughter was born two years after the second. Ambe started complaining to God for a boy. However, the children at hand were barely surviving – they had little food and poor care and were all sick. The first child died soon after the third child was born. During her burial, the house caught fire while people were cooking and it burned to ashes. The second child was barely saved and the third was found dead. Ambe and Aldad were devastated. They had no money and nobody to help them. They had hoped that their children would help them when they were old, but now two of them were gone in one day. When in trouble, Ambe would call on Saint George of Baha and Aldad would call on Saint George of the Lydia. Ambe and Aldad considered saints as God and made no distinction between angels and saints or between God and angels and saints.

Ambe prayed and prayed to Saint George of Baha for a boy. Aldad got pregnant again. However, they still didn't have enough income to feed even the two of them. The only surviving child was not doing well either. But in spite of their wretched life, they wanted more children, especially boys. When it came time for the fourth child to be born, Aldad's labour was very hard. The child had come from the wrong direction. There was no clinic around, but there were traditional doctors. Finally, the child – a boy – was born but with no sign of life. Weeping with disappointment, they put the body aside. Ambe went outside and complained bitterly to Saint George of Baha that he had never asked for a dead boy. After half an hour, the baby sneezed again and again. Ambe and Aldad ran to him and found him alive.

That child was me. The time was 1946; five years after the emperor had come back from exile. After two years and ten months, Ambe and Aldad had another son. He was the last child. Emaye, as I called my mother, named me Alemayehu – meaning My Happiness and My World. She named my brother Negussie – My King. My sister was called Tirfu – The Survivor.

Abaye, as I called my father and Emaye had seen what the Italian occupation had done to the country. The enemy had publicly murdered the head of the Ethiopian Orthodox Tewahedo Church when he refused to collaborate with them. On February 19, 1929, Marshal Grazziani, Mussolini's general and the Italian viceroy to Ethiopia invited the people of Addis Ababa to the compound of the emperor's palace. The marshal was going to deliver a propaganda speech there. There was a large crowd. While the marshal was delivering his speech, two pro-Ethiopia Eritreans tried to assassinate him by throwing grenades. That day, in retaliation, the Fascist soldiers burned down house after house and killed over 10,000 people. Blood streamed through the streets of Addis Ababa. Throughout the city, vultures hovered over the corpses of men, women and children. Flames from the burning houses lit up the sky. It was a bad day for the people of Addis Ababa and Emaye and Abaye had witnessed it.

However, it was not easy for the occupiers to prevail. The massacre rather gave new strength to the resistance movement and Ethiopian patriots fought back until the five-year occupation ended. They expected nothing from the Italians but to fight them whenever they could. Eventually, in 1941, the British army together with the Ethiopian patriots drove the occupiers out.

After end of the occupation, many Italians soldiers stayed behind. Some had married Ethiopian women and had begot children; they didn't want to forsake their families. Some of them had set up construction companies and commercial businesses and were making profit. Those integrated who themselves had no problem stayed in Ethiopia. Despite their ruthlessness, the people of Addis Ababa extended magnanimity and both lived in peace afterwards.

CHAPTER TWO

When I was five years old, Emaye took me to the nearest priest school. The school was connected to the Ethiopian Orthodox Tewahedo Church[9] and the teaching materials were the product of that. Priest schools marked a crossroads for students. One road would lead to becoming a deacon and then a priest. The other would lead to modern schools, taught in English and French. At the time, to choose a modern school would be to betray the Ethiopian Orthodox Tewahedo Church. Being Roman Catholic or Protestant was as different as being Moslem, Hindu or Buddhist. Likewise, going to a modern school was to abandon the Ethiopian Orthodox Tewahedo Church.

There were about 30 of us at the priest school and we were all from the same village. We studied in one room and the teaching was mostly oral, with lots of shouting. First we had to learn the Geez alphabet, then its combinations, then how to read. The seniors would call out the symbols of the alphabet

[9] Ethiopia was well known to ancient writers. It appears in the Bible about 40 times. According to the Kebre Negest (The Glory of the Kings), Ethiopia had a good relationship with Israel. Biblical sources say that the relationship began in the time of Moses and continued throughout the era of the New Testament. According to many historians, a Christian philosopher from Tyre, a man named Meropius, had his ship founder along the coast of the Red Sea. It cost him his life. However, his two guards, Frumentius and Aedesius, washed ashore, were found, then taken to the royal palace in Axum. Eventually, Frumentius became the king's private secretary and Aedesius the royal cupbearer. After serving the king for some time, the two men returned to the Mediterranean through Egypt. While in Egypt, Frumentius contacted the bishop of Alexandria and asked him to send missionaries to Axum. He emphasised that the people there were ready to receive the Gospel. The bishop appointed Frumentius as the first a*buna,* or bishop, of the Ethiopian Orthodox Church. Frumentius became known as the *Abuna Salama,* the Bishop of Peace. He succeeded in converting the Ethiopian king Ezana, and Ethiopia became a Christian country in the second quarter of the fourth century. Since then, the Orthodox faith has flourished. Geez was the language of the Church and Amharic the official language, evolved from it. Geez and Amharic used the same script.

and the juniors would shout back the symbols. People walking nearby could hear us. Sometimes, the teachers wouldn't be around.

Our teacher would give us orders before we left school for the day. Each day, he told us to wash our parents' feet that night. He said he would walk around our houses and peep through the doors to check who was washing and who wasn't. The next day, he would stare at us and would pick out those he thought had not done it. The punishment was to be beaten with a strap. He was good at that. To avoid punishment, we begged our parents to let us wash their feet. Most of the time, I washed and kissed Abaye's feet, but Emaye refused to let me wash hers.

The priest would take us to the forest to collect firewood and brush for his house. The brush was full of thorns and scratched our barely clothed bodies. Sometimes, we spent the whole day in the forest. My parents were paying for my education, but wasn't worth it. Abaye would bring home written things and ask me to read to him. It could be in Italian, Arabic or any other language – he could not read at all and had no way to know which language he was looking at. I couldn't read what he brought home. I could have cheated and pretended, but I had no intention of doing that. Then one day he said, "I will not send you to English school."

After I spent a year in the first school, Emaye took me to another priest school. It was near the biggest market in the village and was a little further away than my first school. The area was very busy on Wednesdays and

Saturdays, the market days. I didn't go to school on Saturdays. That school was even worse than the first one. The priest was a young man who was fond of beating his students. The method of teaching was similar to the first – lots of shouting. Parents neither monitored nor complained. Sometimes, we would cut class and spend the day playing elsewhere. For a clock we had the bell at Saint Michael's Church. It normally rang at noon. When I wasn't in school, I used to listen for it and then go home. Sometimes, I got tricked – the bell might ring to call priests to prayer or when someone died. When Emaye found out that I was not in school, she beat me.

Field hockey was popular during the Christmas season. We spent a lot of time searching the forest for the right stick. Three days before Christmas, the priest asked us to bring our sticks the next day and play hockey on the field in front of the school. I was very happy. At the time, I had the best stick and was eager to play with my friends. I went to school early the next day. Most of the other students were early too. We decided to play until the priest came. After half an hour or so, the priest arrived. He was furious that we had started without him. He ordered us to hand over our sticks. Then he called his housemaid and told her to chop the sticks into firewood. I lost my best stick ever. I hated that man!

I also lost my appetite for that school. My father was not happy either, for my learning had not improved at all. Some students cheated on their parents and pretended that they could read when they could not. Their parents were illiterate and so couldn't check. Even so, these students managed to get into the English school. I didn't and I never knew why. My mother knew that I had no interest in my school. Next, she took me to Saint Michael's Church and handed me over to the third priest.

He was an older man and his left arm was lame. The school was inside the church compound. It was big and there were many students. We sat in circles and, as always, shouted. The priest was unpredictable and would lose control for no reason. Once, he threw stones randomly at students, bloodying some. Fortunately, he did like some of us and I was one of his favourites. Those he liked stayed after school for extra lessons. Before we left for home, he would ask us to massage his feet and to sing to him. We would sing about what a great teacher he was and wish him a long and wealthy life and wish for knowledge and wisdom for ourselves. I was one of his best students.

As elsewhere in Ethiopia, our village had three social classes. Those at the top were very few, but they were extremely rich and had lots of land in town as well as in other provinces. One landlord had more than 6,000 hectares in Bale Province. People of that kind abounded in Addis Ababa. It was said that five percent of the people held 85 percent of the land in the country. Those people had such wealth and power that the poor did not see them as human beings like themselves. The poor rarely even saw the rich. The second class had some land and a reasonably stable income. These people had established connections with the wealthy as well as with the poor. The third class comprised the poor and my family belonged to that class.

Two families in the village had some income and had managed to acquire radios. I thought that the rich had radios too, but there was no way of knowing for sure for they lived behind heavily protected walls. The two radios were identical and took two or three minutes to start. First, their lights would begin to glow till they were red. Then the sound would start. The families that owned them were considered rich and we envied them. One of the families had a monthly income of 125 Birr, while the second family ran a *tej* business, selling of local wine. Ethiopia had public radios too, but that was in the city centre and far from our village.

Older people believed that radios were the work of Satan. Like other poor families, my family believed in superstitions. Emaye visited conjurers and would spend the night at the conjurer's if one of us got sick. Every year on May 1st[10] the poorer villagers baked bread, roasted grain and made coffee underneath a big fig tree that grew near our house. Then people would gather around the tree and share the food and drink. First, a small portion of the food was thrown and coffee was splashed, both to appease evil spirits. Then we would all be fed. We had to eat it all there – none was to be taken home, for evil spirits would attack those who left with food or drink. I was extremely careful to comply.

When I was seven years old, Emaye thought that it was time to take me to an English school. By then, she had two donkeys to help her carry her firewood

[10] May 9th on the Gregorian calendar.

and she was also counting on me to help her. On the other hand, she didn't want me to lag behind. There were two English schools not too far away. The first one was about three kilometres west of our village, towards the centre of the city, and was called Kokebe Tsiba, or "morning star." It was both an elementary and secondary school. The elementary grades ran from one to eight and the secondary from nine to 12. The other school was east of us, about six kilometres away. It was called the Dejazmach Wondirad School and it had only the elementary grades. It had been named after our landlady's father, a famous patriot during the Italian invasion. The school was closer to the forest where Emaye collected her firewood and she wanted me to get in there so I could help her after school.

Early one morning, she took me to Dejazmach Wondirad School. When we reached the gate, she asked the campus guard to show us the director's office and he took us there. We entered the office and he treated Emaye with respect and kindness. He asked her to buy me a uniform to wear for special occasions and to bring me back as soon as she could. The uniform would be kept at the school. She agreed and thanked him and we left to collect firewood. The uniform would cost her about five Birr, quite a lot in terms of what she earned, and she would not be able to buy it right away, so she decided to keep me with her in the forest until she got the money.

When my mother had collected enough firewood to sell, she would divide it into four bundles and load two on each donkey. First, she would have to cover the eyes of the donkeys with cloth to keep them standing still. Next, she would pick up a bundle, balance it against one side of the donkey, and tell me to hold it there with my chest and face. Then she would have me grab a rope in each hand. She would then go around to the other side of the donkey and pick up the second bundle, hold it there, and tell me to throw the two ropes to her so that she could tie them together. I would stand with my face and chest against my bundle until she had tightly fastened the ropes and stabilized the load. She would do the same with the second donkey and then we went home. The next day, she would wake me up early in the morning; we would load the donkeys and together go to sell the firewood. Ehte as I called my sister, stayed at home and cooked food while Wondime as I called my younger brother, went to a priest school. Till the holidays and the rainy season came, Abaye worked in forest.

Life was difficult. When our father was at home, we would all eat from the same dish, all seated around it. If there was not enough food for all, our parents would eat little and leave the rest for us. Wondime and I would clean the dish and thank God for the food and for having given us the best parents and ask Him to them alive and healthy. After supper, we would sit around the fire and enjoy Abaye's jokes. He would tell joke after joke and we would laugh and laugh, our laughter growing so that even the neighbours could hear us. Ehte was a good laugher – she would laugh at anything and Abaye would scold her for that, but the way he did it brought even more laughs.

Once Abaye had borrowed some money from a man he knew. However, he found it very difficult to pay it back. The man came for the money many times, but to no avail. Sometimes, he would spend the night at our house and Abaye would ask me to wash his feet. I did. One day, he came during the day when none of us were home except for an old woman who was cleaning up after the donkeys. He stayed for a while, then left. When Abaye came home from work, he discovered that his pants were missing. The woman told him that the man visited the house during the day and Abaye guessed that he had stolen the pants. He was very upset. We kept quiet around the fire for a very long time. Wondime was late that day and Emaye was worried. Abaye said, "Forget about him. I have even lost my pants." That broke the ice and we all laughed except him. Finally, when he went to bed and pulled back the blanket, the sheet was gone too. He said, "He has also taken the sheet. I wish Satan would do the same to him."

Emaye and I spent most of our time in the forest. There were many kinds of fruit there, so we would eat them, then quench our thirst with fresh water from a nearby spring. The worst part was going to and coming from the markets. The donkeys would run on the way back and Emaye had a hard time keeping up with them. One day, the donkeys got into the middle of a street and blocked a small Volkswagen that was passing by. The driver stepped out of the car and came towards us. He asked Emaye if the donkeys were hers, and when she said yes, he slapped her face twice and left. That was too much for me, but I was too young to do anything. Such cruelty was common from the rich and even policemen had no power to stop them. A landlord in our village, a man with royal blood, was famous for running the only traffic light in Addis Ababa at the time. He would drive right through it and no policeman dared to do anything. Fortunately, accidents were not common for there were very few cars in the city.

I grew older and Emaye started to regret keeping me away from the English school. For three years, I stayed out of school, but when I was 10 years old, she took me back to my last school. It still had the same director. He recalled the last experience and refused to let me in. Emaye fell at his feet and said she was sorry. He helped her up. Many times he had seen us walking behind our donkeys and admitted me on the spot. My mother left me at the school and headed to the forest. After school, I ran to her and we loaded the donkeys and went home together. Wondime enrolled in that school the following year.

Emaye started to lose her strength and could not lift the bundles of the firewood. It became my turn to do that part of the work. She would say, "If you lift the bundle, I will give you money for your books." I tried and failed many times until I finally succeeded. Our loading routine was the same, but with a different commander. I would lift one bundle and hand it to Emaye to hold it against the donkey. Then I'd go to the other side and lift the second one and tie the ropes. My brother kept the donkeys from moving, so we didn't have to cover their heads any more. Emaye was relieved and felt she had real help. She once said, "I am the farmer and you are my oxen."

When I was in grade one, our Amharic language teacher asked us to make paper stars. I didn't know why. I took the cover from an exercise book that I found lying on the ground. It had the emperor's picture on it. I cut a beautiful star. I was very happy and took it to the teacher. He looked pleased until he turned the star over and saw that the emperor's picture had been on the back. He got mad and beat me until he was tired. I was lucky that he was an old man. I was confused and shocked and said nothing. He gave me zero for my mark and would have given me two zeros if he could have.

The teachers mocked and beat students for nothing. They beat us for laughing, for failing to answer questions, for being slow to respond. Once, the oldest student in class failed to give the right answer. The teacher then asked the youngest student and she answered correctly. The teacher then had her say to the older student, "Dad, the answer you gave as … was wrong. The right answer was…" The oldest student never came back to class. Parents never challenged the school and the director was scared of the teachers and even praised them.

In 1957, I was in grade two. That year, Emperor Haile Selassie's son, Prince Mekonnen was killed in a car accident 48 kilometres south of Addis Ababa. All of Ethiopia was shocked. The emperor was highly regarded, especially by older people, who called him *These Nevus* – The Sun King. They believed that if he died, the sun would fail to rise.[11] When his son died, the women of Addis Ababa dressed in black, the men, including students, put black ribbons on their jackets and businessmen wore black ties. National

---

[11] *Haile Selassie* means The Power of Trinity and he was known as the Emperor of Ethiopia, Lion of Judah, King of Kings and Elect of God.

mourning was declared and all public entertainment, including music at weddings, was banned for 40 days. A flyer with his picture on it was distributed in his memory. I managed to get one, which I put in my exercise book. Our class monitor was sitting beside me. He pulled out the flyer and said that I had punched a hole through one of the prince's eyes. I had seen no hole. The class monitor took me to the director – he was recently appointed – and he got angry and every morning for three days straight he beat me in front of the whole school.

He was one of the cruellest persons I have ever met, not only because of what he did to me, but he was harsh with all students. If a student was late, he would be turned away. And if a student was late three times, he would be expelled. The last hour of the school day was a study period, but with no observer except the director. He would walk very quietly from class to class, as if in his bare feet, then suddenly open the door wide to catch students talking or standing. Those who were caught were beaten bitterly.

Ehte, my sister, got married that year, a few days before the prince died. The wedding was grand by our standards. I never found out how my parents managed to get the money for it, but I thought that they had borrowed it. Abaye bought a big bull for 40 Birr. Food grains were plentiful at the feast and more than ten times cheaper than they are today. Guests brought some money and the amount got written down. My father kept that record for many years. Whenever he was invited to a wedding, he would ask me to check the record to see how much the host for the coming wedding had contributed to my sister's wedding. When my sister left for her new home, Wondime and I cried bitterly and followed the wedding car until people turned us back. She delivered a son, but he died within a year. Her husband was as old as Abaye and I had disagreed with the marriage for that reason. My sister had told him my views, so he has hated me for that ever since. He was a nice person when sober, but wild after alcohol. He would invite people for parties at his house, then get drunk and, brandishing a big stick, would chase everybody out. They begot a boy two years after the death of the first son who was named Kassahun. Later, they divorced and my father adopted Kassahun and made him his namesake.

Once, Saint Mary's Mahber was held at our house. The members had come to eat *injera*, drink *tella* and enjoy the occasion. My sister was divorced from her husband and was at home. However, her husband had been invited and had come early, though non-members would usually come after members had left. He had his lunch, drank enough and was ready to leave, but when he looked for his hat, it was not there. No one knew that my sister had left with it. He yelled for his hat but to no avail. He got mad and overturned the tables. He was ready to fight anybody who looked at him. The members didn't want to interfere – it was a family affair – and so left early and disappointed. Neighbours couldn't be invited to the house because the house was in disarray and he was fighting with anybody who came in the house. It was an embarrassment for my family. My parents had spent precious resources only to see them wasted. They cursed themselves for their misfortune.

The road to Dejazmach Wondirad School was made of asphalt and was the only surfaced road leading away from the city. There were very few vehicles on it apart from some trucks that used it at night. We would walk in groups in the middle of the road. Most of the time, ten of us would walk single file, with the boy on one end talking to the boy at the other end, and the road would be full of noise. Mario was a truck driver who drove between Addis Ababa and the nearest north-eastern town, Debre Berhan. He was Italian. He drove through early in the morning two to three days a week and threw us candies as we walked along the road. He was popular with the students. Whenever students saw his truck, they shouted, "Mario! Mario!" Then he threw candies all over. Most of the time, I wasn't lucky enough to get any since I had to load firewood for Emaye. However, I did manage to get some a few times. The candies were not wrapped. He threw a lot at once and we would run into the bushes to find them, something that sometimes took a lot of time.

Wondime and I couldn't afford to have lunch at the school. After school, we would run to the forest to Emaye, who most of the time brought something for us to eat. We would eat, drink from a nearby spring, load the firewood, and then be off home. That was what we did every day, every week and every month of the school year. When school term ended, we took charge of all the work in the forest and for the market while Emaye would take vacation and cook. One day at school, I had left the campus at lunchtime to see the surroundings. When I returned, after half an hour, Wondime was looking for me. I asked him why and he said a friend of his had given him five cents and he wanted to buy roasted grain and share it with me. We did that and had a very good lunch. Whatever we managed for lunch, we shared.

One day, we went to Emaye after school as usual. She had not brought any food. We were very hungry and had expected something. We felt sorry for Emaye and understood that she had nothing to bring. She had something else in mind. She had lost 25 cents at home and thought we had stolen it. She had been asking students from our village if we had had lunch that day. If we had, she had calculated that it would have been paid for with the stolen money. We loaded the donkeys and headed for home. We were very hungry and so walked fast to reach home and eat something. When we reached home, Ehte said that we shouldn't expect to eat anytime soon. We were bewildered. After we unloaded the donkeys, we were confined in the kitchen. Emaye started beating us, questioning about the money, but we had no idea what she was talking about. She beat us for hours. Emaye was very cruel that day. We had no food until late that evening. When we went to the forest on the third day, Emaye embraced us and cried bitterly. She said, "My boys, I was cruel to you for something you never did. I am very sorry." The money was found at home, underneath one of the beds. She gave us the money for lunch.

Our house was topped with grass. It was not well roofed since that required money and expertise. During the rainy season, inside the house was as damp as the field outside. My brother and I slept on a wooden bed that had tree leaves as mattresses. When we had fresh leaves, the night seemed but an hour long. Our roof wasn't strong enough to protect us from the rain. One wet night, the roof was extremely weak and the rain poured straight into our bed. We couldn't sleep at all. The next day, Abaye put his overcoat over the top of the roof, right above our bed, and it was much better that night.

We were good at school. Wondime was one class behind me. We were among the top five in our respective classes. After exam papers had been handed back, Abaye asked me what I had scored. When I told him I had scored 95, he asked about the balance. He expected 100 every time and in all subjects. My father was good at maths. I helped my nephew learn his multiplication tables. When I would ask him what X times Y was, if he couldn't answer, Abaye would call out the result. The school knew about our efforts at home and once gave us prizes in front of all the other students. We got determined to go on with our education.

On the weekend and during the school break, we sold firewood at the markets, to give our mother a break. She had a large family of customers in town. The grandparents lived in a compound with their three married daughters. Two families of relatives also lived in the compound. The place was crowded with children. On holidays, they would kill cows, share the meat amongst themselves and, in turn, dine together at the different houses in the compound. The grandparents were very nice to us. Whenever Wondime and I went there, they would invite us into their house. The man would call us to come and sit by him and would ask his wife to bring us food. While we ate, he would ask us how we were making out at school and express his appreciation for our help to our parents and for our efforts at school. Other families did the same. Sometimes, all the families would invite us, but we couldn't handle them all. There was another family; however, that Emaye had problems with. One day, our donkeys got in their garden and the man called me "a donkey following a donkey." She got furious and decided not to sell firewood to that family any more. Other families tried to soften her heart, but she had decided. Henceforth, we never sold them firewood again and we never entered their house.

One day at school, a friend, my brother and I were roaming around at lunchtime. We went to a place that sold bread and roasted grain, just to look, because we couldn't afford to buy either. We met another friend on the way. He was the most mischievous boy in our village. His nickname was Diablos – Devil. He asked us if we had had our lunch and we said no. He took us to one of the bread sellers and asked her to show him all the bread she had, so he could choose the best. He took one without her noticing and hid it under his jacket. Next, Diablos took us to another place and did the same thing. He didn't buy from anybody and cheated two. The three of us shared the bread for lunch. Diablos also had contracted with a lady to supply him with bread every day. He had said that he would pay her at the end of every month. At the time, the price of a piece of bread was ten cents. He ate 20 pieces of bread every month – worth two Birr – but paid her with 20 units of five cents and the woman thought even that was too much.

Once, Diablos was with a friend in downtown Addis Ababa. They went into a musical instrument shop. He asked the seller for harmonica. The seller showed him some but Diablos asked him to show him some more. The man brought out all the harmonicas he had. Diablos quietly put one in his friend's pocket, without his friend seeing him. They left the shop without buying anything. After they had been walking for a while, Diablos took the harmonica from his friend's pocket and started playing with it. His friend was furious – but that was how Diablos was and everybody knew that. He would eat lunch in restaurants, wash his hands, then slip out without paying the bill, and nobody would say anything since he would pretend to be someone who had paid even larger bills. In case he was asked, he would just say, "Sorry, I forgot."

There was an abandoned flourmill in our village, once the property of Italians. It had a staircase with seven steps and sidewalls from the main road led to the mill. My friends and I would sit there after school and tease one another. When a boy would join us for the first time, we would ask him for to be a judge – to settle disputes between two friends. If he agreed, he would sit on the highest step. The plaintiff and the defendant would approach him to present their cases. Then, one would take one of the judge's legs and the other would take the other leg, and they would drag him to the bottom of the staircase.

Shune was the biggest tease of all the boys in our village and known for that at school too. His friends cursed him and so did his classmates and the villagers. He was short and slight, but he talked a lot. Saturdays, during the rainy reason, he would be busy fooling passers-by by arranging mud and wrapping it with the leaves of false banana to look like butter bought at the market. When nobody was looking, he would lay his slabs of "butter" by the side of the road and then hide himself in a ditch to watch. A passer-by would spot the "butter," check to see if anybody was looking, then pick it up and hide it under his or her clothes, and walk away fast. He was also busy on Saturdays tormenting bus riders who had their hands sticking out the window. Everybody cursed him – if cursing could have hurt anybody in that village, Shune would have been the first to be hurt. One day, Shune, his brother Alemu and I went to steal green chickpeas from a public farm close by. As we were collecting chickpeas, the watchman saw us and ran towards us. We also ran, but the watchman caught Shune, hoisted him on top of his head, and headed towards the guardhouse. Shune knew he was in trouble and made his escape by peeing on the watchman's head. The man threw him down on the green and began wiping off his clothes and Shune ran fast for freedom.

A bully from another village used to harass and intimidate us. He was too strong and too big for any of us to challenge him physically and would beat us up whenever he wanted. We knew that we couldn't go on that way, so we prepared sticks to teach him a lesson he wouldn't forget. One morning, ten of us hid behind a bush and waited for him. After some time, we saw him coming and the boldest of us went to challenge him. When the bully advanced on our friend, we were all over him in no time and beat him bloody. Then we left. Henceforth, he was very nice to us and even helped us out when we needed it.

Buhe is a children's holiday in Ethiopia and is similar to Halloween. However, on *Buhe,* children sing special songs, make noise with special straps and collect loaves and money; instead of wearing costumes, begging treats and playing pranks as they do in North America and in the British Isles. Saturday was the big market day in our village. Farmers would come by horse and by mule from all directions. Horsetails were used for the tips of the noise-making straps we used on *Buhe*. One time, my friend Abera, Wondime and I went to the market to get horsetails for our straps. When we reached the market, we found many horses and mules tied to poles by the bars. Abera went up to one horse and pulled some hair from its tail. The horse kicked out with a rear leg and knocked him down. Abera was unconscious. Wondime and I pulled him aside and waited until he came to his conscious. We waited for the owner of the horse to come and decided not to leave without seeing him. Finally, he came out of a bar and I approached him and explained what had happened to my friend. He was very sorry and asked me how he could help. I asked him to buy us candies. With five cents, he bought 12 candies and gave us all of them. Then we carried Abera to his house and went home with all the candies. It took him long to fully recover.

When I was in grade five, another student in our class was from our village. He never mixed with us, not in the village and not at school. He lived in a broken family. Just before exams in the first semester, he missed class because of illness. We felt very sorry for him. He came for the exams with his head tightly wrapped with lightweight cloth. We said he should postpone his exams, but he insisted and sat them anyway. He stood first in class and first in the second semester. We became suspicious about his illness. We understood later that he had been "ill" to have an excuse to stay at home and study. We didn't admire him or want to copy him because of his dishonesty. He didn't advance beyond elementary school and later he joined the military because of his family problem.

Some teachers in Dejazmach Wondirad School considered themselves politically progressive and wanted the government to change. However, Emperor Haile Selassie was very popular among the adults. A majority of them had suffered during the Italian occupation and so considered him to be both liberator and messiah.

Germame Neway was an aristocrat who was educated in the United States. After his return to Ethiopia, he was appointed governor in Jijiga Awraja near the Somali border and then in Wolaita Awraja in southern Ethiopia. It was said that he had revolutionary tendencies and that the emperor didn't like it. His older brother, General Mengistu Neway, commanded the Imperial Bodyguard and was one of the emperor's favourites. I had seen the general while he was leading a military exercise a ways from my school. He was tall, had bright eyes and heavy moustache and looked good. During the exercise, he observed the guns being fired in the distance and stripped the ranks from those officers who missed their targets. He promoted those who hit their targets.

In 1960 when I was in grade seven, the Imperial Bodyguard, under the leadership of Mengistu and Germame, organised a coup d'état while the emperor was on a state visit to Brazil. The rest of the military opposed the coup. People couldn't believe it happened, for the emperor was very popular with the masses, although not with the intellectuals. One afternoon our social studies teacher came to our class and declared, "The crown prince has become the new king." I was confused by his obvious happiness since almost everybody was loyal to the emperor. My parents – all the people in my village – were very angry about the coup. I told what the teacher had said to the villager who loved the emperor most and she cursed him all day. Older people liked the emperor for his role in expelling the Italian invaders, though his actions remain controversial among the intellectuals because the emperor left the battlefield and went into exile. In Ethiopia, leaders are expected to stay close to the troops during wartime and to provide direction and moral guidance – leadership is the most decisive factor in winning wars.

When the coup happened, there was shooting in the city centre and a lot of people took refugee in our village. The crown prince spoke on the radio, declaring that he had become the new emperor. However, the coup didn't last long and many soldiers from the Imperial Bodyguard died as a result. Others went to jail. The leaders massacred many top officials. The emperor returned from Brazil in few days and the people received him jubilantly. Our new landlord, Girma Yayehyirad, was a relative of Mengistu and Germame and was suspected of sheltering them, so our village became the target for air bombardment by the government. Fortunately, the men were seen out of the city. A shootout took place. Mengistu was wounded, while Germame was alleged to have committed suicide. Two others were killed. The soldiers brought the dead bodies to Addis Ababa and hung them in the city centre. People poked the bodies with sticks and cursed them for what they had done. Later on, the general was court-martialled, sentenced to death and was hanged.

As I understood later, the country had lost a chance for change. The Haile Selassie government was autocratic and was subjugating those who lived in the countryside, especially the people of southern Ethiopia, depriving of their lands and thus of their livelihoods. Had the coup d'état succeeded, some sort of land reform could have pacified those in the countryside and the intellectuals. Germame was believed to be radical and could have brought at least a modicum of political and economic change. People's consciousness could have changed, preparing them for radical changes to follow.

Dejezmach Wondirad School gave me a hard time about hygiene. One day each week, the school randomly checked our clothes, nails and hair. There was a river adjacent to the school compound and we went there once a week to wash our feet and cut our nails. Students with very poor clothes and unclean hair were sent home. Those with long nails were beaten. My problem was poor clothes – I couldn't afford otherwise.

The school also had gardening for students. Each of us got a small plot to grow vegetables and tree saplings. Some students were keen at that and made money by acquiring more plots and selling the saplings. Wondime and I had no time for that because right after school was when students attended their plots and we had to go and help Emaye. Some students didn't do well in class but were good at gardening. They repeated classes, but didn't mind because they made money by staying in school – 500 Birr or more every year. The most I made was 11 Birr, of which Emaye shared half.

During the rainy season, the traffic police wouldn't allow us to travel on the asphalt road when we went to market. As a result, we went along a muddy path and the donkeys would get stuck. From November through January, the ground was covered with dew. We had no shoes and our feet became so cold that sometimes we cried as we walked. The traffic police were corrupt and wanted us to pay a bribe to travel on the asphalt road. We couldn't afford that. We eventually decided to start our journey at six in the morning, to avoid the mud and the traffic police. We never thought of having good sleep at the time.

Haile Selassie I Secondary School was half a kilometre away from Dejazmach Wondirad School. Many elementary school students wanted to go there. It was sponsored by foreign governments and was well managed.

Students from well-to-do families and those sponsored by the government boarded at the high school and the poor attended as day students. On one occasion, the Imperial Bodyguard's band was asked to play for the staff and students of the high school. The concert was arranged for nighttime and we decided to try our luck. There were no streetlights and it was beautiful to walk in the moonlight. They wouldn't let us into the hall. We tried many times but to no avail. Finally, we sat in front of the building, by the main door. A teacher, Roseless would come out from time to time, to chase us away. Then, when he came out unexpectedly, Abera – the boy who had been kicked by the horse – ran fast and saw a shadow that he thought was a ditch. He ran to jump over it, but landed in a real ditch filled with stones and gravel. His legs bled and hands were torn. We pulled him out, but there was no candy this time.

One day in August, the weather was terribly wet in Addis Ababa. I had finished my National Elementary School Leaving Examination that June. That morning, I had left early for the forest, hoping to return soon to play soccer with my friends. I met my classmate, Chane who was walking to town and he congratulated me on passing my exam. He had the newspaper with him and showed me my registration number and the mark I had scored – over 90 percent. I was very happy and thanked him for the news and continued on my way. I broke the news to my parents that night while we were sitting round the fire. Abaye asked me what I scored and I told him it was 94 percent. As usual, he asked me what happened to the other six percent.

Completing elementary school was a great success for me. I had targeted grade six, half of high school completion. Many students dropped out of the school, especially the children of farmers – they were needed to work the land. Students could be in their 20s and in grades one and two. When I entered the school at the age of 10, I was among the younger students in my class. One student in our class was older than many of the others. He had reached grade four in two years, but his father had asked him to leave school – he had expected him to complete high school in 12 months, a class per month. However, the boy was determined to finish high school and left home to live with relatives. At the time, those who completed their elementary education had many opportunities – a chance to join Ethiopian Air Force, or the Ethiopian Navy, or take a one-year teacher-training course, or a health dressing program, or become a telephone operator, and so on. Despite the opportunities and the financial problems at home, I decided to go on with my high school education.

CHAPTER THREE

While in grade eight, we were given a form and told to select three high schools. I had picked Bahir Dar Polytechnic School as my first choice, the Commercial School of Addis Ababa my second choice and Addis Ababa Technical School as my third choice. None of them worked. Instead, I was assigned to Haile Selassie I Secondary School next to my elementary school. I had chosen those schools because I had a strong desire to get a job after finishing a high school. I wanted to help my parents.

My high school had students from different parts of Ethiopia. It was boys' school – no girls admitted. I was in the day school program. The school was meant to keep boys from affluent families from getting spoiled in town. There was no public transport between the school and the city centre. The boys would be dropped off at the school on Monday and picked up on Friday. There was no place to go to in between, except to class and to the library. I met students from different backgrounds. Many of the boarding students were the sons of ministers, high ranking military officers, parliamentarians and landlords. My world and theirs was quite different. They talked about nightclubs, the food they ate and the beauty of places they had spent previous night. It was beyond my imagination, then and in the future.

I was better off financially in high school. The government paid ten Birr a month to needy students and I was qualified for that. Through an *equb* with my classmates, I saved five Birr a month or 50 Birr by the end of the school year. I gave four Birr per month to Emaye and shared the balance with Wondime. The 50 cents in my pocket sufficed me to buy lunch for a week. I managed to buy clothes for Wondime and for me with the money I saved through the *equb*.

A classmate from the aristocracy became close to me. His name was Gizaw. He was good in class and very broad-minded and up-to-date on current events. He knew I was poor but doing well in class and so he liked me. He never liked the rich and fought with those who exalted themselves. His clothes were few and most of them were old. He told me that his father was a crown-councillor to the emperor and was also a parliamentarian who owned land all over the country. His sister had been married to the emperor's most favoured son, the one who died in a car accident when I was in grade two. He told me that he didn't fit in well with the rest of his family and had a single room where he spent most of his time. I later understood that his father begot him from a lower-class woman and so his brothers and sisters discriminated against him. But his father liked him and brought him articles from the parliament and he enjoyed reading them.

Gizaw was good in history and general knowledge but poor in maths. On October 24, 1962, United Nations Day, we were all given questions to answer about the UN. From grade nine on, Gizaw was at the top of the school. He was a well-versed individual. He also told me that he had advised his father many times to share his land with the poor but his father laughed at him. Gizaw was very radical. One day at lunchtime, the two of us were watching soccer. Most of the students playing were from the rich families. Gizaw said, "You know what I would do if I had the power? I would have these boys ground into powder and use them as fertilizer."

In 1962, many American Peace Corps volunteers came to Ethiopia as teachers. I was in grade nine. We had two of them in our class, Tilley and Hoyt and they were good teachers. Gizaw never liked them – he was against capitalism. One day, he delivered a speech in English class. His words were beyond what we could understand. However, we somehow managed to understand his message. He compared President Eisenhower of the United States and President Khrushchev of the Soviet Union with respect to their attitude towards Africans. He stated that the former was wearing a swimsuit when he received our emperor at the White House, while the latter travelled to Moscow International Airport to welcome the emperor. Gizaw finished his speech by denouncing the American government. The English teacher, Ms Hoyt got nervous – it was only two months after her arrival from the United States and the incident was her first experience with dissent. Henceforth, the Peace Corps volunteers at the school hated Gizaw and he couldn't qualify for American Field Service Program, although he spoke and wrote good English.

One of the Peace Corps volunteers had prepared a letter to a friend in the United States, criticising the type of food the boarding students ate. Some students discovered the letter before he mailed it and took it to the director – an Englishman – and asked him to take action. He refused. The students were militant and confronted the director and it took some time before the matter subsided. This same man was a lousy teacher and always sat on a table while teaching. One day, some students put a piece of hot iron on that table. The man sat down without looking, then bounced like a tennis ball when he felt the heat. Some students were very cruel.

Tilley, my geography teacher, was very unassuming. He would go to local bars and drink *tella* and he would get travel on open trucks – he would just ask the driver for a ride. He was different from his colleagues.

There were many Indian teachers at the school. They taught all types of subjects. My grade nine maths and history teachers were Indians. The former was very smart and the latter wrote a lot. In addition, the history teacher required a copy of her lectures when giving exams and we had to cram everything. The history teacher in grade 11 was also Indian and an interesting man. During his lectures, he was always saying, "India is the land of milk and honey!" Sometimes, he'd begin, "India is the land of milk and…" and students would loudly call out "honey!"

At the end of every school year, the school gave awards to students who performed exceptionally well in their classes. Old graduates of the school who held high positions in the government would hand out the awards. When I finished grade nine, the minister of foreign affairs, His Excellency Ato Ketema Yifru handed out the awards and the minister of industry, His Excellency Lij Endalkachew Mekonnen did it in grade ten. I got awards both times and felt very gratified. For students like me, it was a real encouragement to us to further our education.

Wondime joined me the year I was promoted to grade ten. He was paid stipend too. He also gave four Birr per month to Emaye and she felt better off financially. The money we gave her covered her monthly expenses for chillies, the most important ingredient in preparing the sauce for *injera*. We were better clothed now and I managed to buy a watch. We continued helping Emaye in the forest.

One day, Wondime and I were coming home after selling firewood. The donkeys were running fast and it was difficult for us to keep up with them. A private traffic policeman tried to stop them, but he couldn't. He yelled at us and told us to take the muddy path instead. It was difficult to catch the donkeys and the policeman followed us. At last, we restrained the donkeys. He insulted us and threatened to beat us. Wondime said, "I may get educated and become your boss – as a lieutenant – one day." The policeman became furious and ordered us to go to the nearest police station. We left the donkeys tied with a rope outside the police station and went inside. A corporal was sitting there. The private policeman said, "This boy said that I would be promoted to corporal for putting him in jail." Wondime had never said that. We watched the corporal get mad at us. After an hour, a lieutenant arrived. The corporal said, "This boy said to the private that he would be promoted to lieutenant for putting him in jail." We got scared and felt helpless. After another hour, the lieutenant colonel – the chief of the area – arrived. The lieutenant went over to him and said, "This boy said to the private that he would be promoted to lieutenant colonel for putting him in jail." We thought we were finished. The lieutenant colonel took us to his office. He queried us about our education and our family background and we told him about school, about classes and about our parents. He listened patiently. Finally, he reprimanded Wondime, advised us to be serious at school and let us go. We couldn't believe that and headed home fast.

Once, our landlord, Balambaras Girma had prepared a wedding feast for his granddaughter. The feast started well in advance of the wedding and he gave orders to his guards and servants not to stop tenants and their families from enjoying the festivities. We began to go there two weeks before the wedding day. As soon as we got home from school, we would unload the donkeys, drop our exercise books and go straight to the landlord's compound. We were provided with food and drink and would stay there until late at night. The wedding day was special – there had never been such a wedding anywhere in the area. There were hundreds of guests. Three big tents were raised and the area was filled with cars, as though all the cars in town were there. The cars were fancy, too, and guests dressed in sophisticated clothes. We tenants were treated with food and drink even before the guests left. Some tenants got drank and fell in the ditch. One got so drunk that he walked over the whisky glasses, breaking many of them. That made the landlord angry and ordered his guards to beat the man. When things went wrong, the landlord could be very cruel. I went home early – before the same thing happened to me.

One Easter, Wondime and I went to the landlord's house to deliver a gift from our parents. The wife accepted the gift and had us served food and drink. We had just started to eat when we came across a half-eaten cow bone. It was normal for the rich to do that when treating the poor to food. However, it was hard for us to continue eating. We were poor but not that poor. We had never looked for handouts and had never taken food unless invited. We had seen that Emaye respected the rich, but she never accepted their bad behaviour.

Another crown councillor to the emperor had his house adjacent to our landlord and he was an in-law to our landlord. He was very rich, with land throughout the country. His wife and he were known in the village for loving money. His wife counted the *injera* before she left the house – she suspected her servants of stealing it. Whenever the husband went to church, he never used the main gate but instead went in the back door, to avoid beggars. When a panhandler would beg him for money, he would give ten cents and if one complained, he would take the coins back. He never deposited his money in a bank but hoarded it at home. From time to time, his grandsons would air the money for him. Eventually, they stole thousands of Birr and left the country. Everybody in the village felt happy about that since they hated him for stinginess.

I had a very close friend by the name of Teshome. He was from my village. He was born in Arsi, the closest southern province to Addis Ababa. His father had died and his mother was not around. His aunt brought him to the city and abandoned him because they didn't get along. Someone had given him shelter, but he had no food. Every year after the harvest, his mother would send him some money. However, Teshome was generous and in a few days he would be empty-handed. The stipend for grade nine had helped him a lot. When we were promoted to grade ten, things changed. Now a student had to score an average of 60 percent to qualify for the stipend. Unfortunately, Teshome narrowly missed the cut-off point. Life became very difficult for him and he stopped coming to school.

His friends and classmates were worried about him. Teshome and I approached a Peace Corps teacher, Goldberg for help. Goldberg was willing to help him out with ten Birr per month, provided that Teshome would clean the teacher's house twice a month. He agreed and I volunteered to help him. Every second Saturday, we would go to the house. It was a very big house with many rooms. We washed the floors and waxed them until they shined. It was very tiresome, but Teshome needed the money to survive. In addition, Teshome got his stipend back – the director had helped him with his studies and he became even better off and would invite us for lunch sometimes.

One day after I'd finished grade ten, I was playing soccer with friends. The director called us all into his office. He told us that some of the students who had completed high school had left for other provinces, so the administration required that other students stand in for them and receive their certificates from the emperor. I did not have the proper clothes and my trousers had holes in the knees. The director gave each of us a name – the student I was given was Wuhib – then he took us to the Grand Palace for the ceremony. My heart was beating fast until Wuhib's name was called and I managed to receive the certificate from the emperor. I had a heavy heart. Fortunately, Wuhib didn't get high marks, for the emperor was asking questions of those who had done very well.

One morning when I was in grade 11, the director of the school broke down during the flag-raising ceremony. He sobbed that Belgian soldiers had massacred 4,000 Congolese civilians. After we went to our classes, students like Gizaw began to say that we shouldn't be silent about what had happened. They insisted that we ought to demonstrate and many boarding students agreed. Placards were prepared and handed out to us. We left the compound in a procession, with Gizaw as our leader. He walked alone at the side of the road like a military commander. First, we went to the Belgian Embassy, about seven kilometres from the school. As we approached, the guards opened the gates for us. We went into the compound. The ambassador walked out of his office and greeted us. Gizaw stepped up on a bit of raised ground in front of the building and delivered a powerful speech. At the end of his speech, he shouted slogans and we shouted them after him. Then he came down. The ambassador defended his government's position. He said that the people of the city had rioted and killed officials, including the mayor, and that things got out of control, so the soldiers had no choice. We left the compound peacefully and proceeded to the American Embassy.

We saw the American ambassador's limousine on our way and yet we continued our march shouting our slogans. When we reached the American Embassy, the guards refused to let us into the compound and told us the ambassador had gone out of town. We insisted that they let us in, but they refused. Finally, they agreed to let in two students to represent us and deliver a letter. When they opened the gate, we pushed hard and, within a few seconds, everybody was in. We refused to leave the compound until the ambassador talked to us. He came back after two hours. Gizaw was furious with the ambassador's arrogance. He gave a speech that harshly denounced the American government. "Down with capitalism! Down with imperialism!" The ambassador defended his government's position and we left the compound peacefully and returned to school the way we had come.

I had a side-business during my vacations while I was in Haile Selassie I Secondary School. I bought firewood with my own money, chopped it and carried on my head to market. In addition, I saved some money during Buhe. With the money I had earned from the firewood and Buhe, I bought drawings of flowers for the Ethiopian New Year, September 10th or 11th, depending on the leap year. On the New Year's Day, I distributed the drawings to families in the village and collected money, which I used to buy exercise books for the coming school year. I did that from the time I was in elementary school till I completed grade 11.

One high school in Addis Ababa was named after the emperor's grandson, Prince Bedemariam Laboratory School. It had grades 11 and 12. Students going to grade 12 were picked from high schools across Ethiopia after passing an entrance exam. The school prepared students for the Education Faculty of Haile Selassie I University. Students who were admitted to the high school had to commit themselves to becoming professional teachers in Ethiopian high schools. The school had free boarding and gave pocket money of three Birr per month. They had advertised at my high school. I thought about it very seriously. Abaye was always talking about people who had finished high school and started work to help their parents. I knew he was telling me indirectly that I should finish and find work, but I had a strong desire to further my education. I decided on the latter and passed the exam. I knew that was a great disappointment to my mother. However, Wondime had grown up and was helping her a lot.

I completed grade 11 in 1965, a very bad year for the whole nation because of the poor harvest. The rainy season was even worse for us. Abaye had so many debts that nobody was willing to lend him any more money. We had almost nothing to eat. I remember a day that we did manage to have lunch and my nephew Kassahun, five years old at the time, said, "It is good we had our lunch. Can we have something for supper too?"

However, the situation was not so bad for me. A woman in our village asked me to teach her maths and English in the evening and I agreed. The arrangement was for two days a week and the payment was five Birr per month. After the lesson, she usually invited me for supper. Her husband came home late after work and also came home drunk most of the time.

He was a mechanical engineer, educated in Germany. When he entered the house drunk, she ordered him like a small child, telling him to go straight to bed and he complied with no complaint. They had a very big and very beautiful house, an affluent life by Ethiopian standards. They were materially well off but unhappy. The woman always looked dispirited. Our house was the reverse. We were really poor but – amazingly – very happy. And we laughed long and hard before bed.

I completed grade 11 at Haile Selassie I secondary school in June 1965. Haile Selassie I Secondary School was well established and one of the top high schools in the country. It was meant for the children of the rich, including the royal family, and some of us were there by chance. Prince Sahle Selassie, the emperor's youngest son, attended the school. A story about him says that soon after he started school, he had a problem with the food. As a result, the palace arranged to bring him food, but without the knowledge of the emperor. As soon as the emperor found out, he ordered the practice to stop. I had seen some families bringing food for their children. The day students that earned a 60-percent class average survived on the ten-Birr stipend. We never cared about the wealthy, they never cared about us and we had no problem between us.

I didn't make friends with the rich students. The only time I talked to them was before class, while we waited for the teachers, and during class. I talked a lot with students from Eritrea, particularly with a student named Yitbark. He didn't speak good Amharic, but what he said was full of humour. One day, he raised a point about the Eritrean soldiers who had fought for the Italian invaders while Eritrea was a colony. He said, "You people condemn our soldiers for their actions during the invasion. You are the ones who sold us to Italy. Let us say you had a cow and you sold it to somebody. If that cow got into your farm and ate your crops, would you sue the owner or leave it free, considering that the cow was yours once upon a time?" I said that I would sue the owner. He said, "You do that because it is not yours any more – and that was what happened during the Italian invasion. The soldiers were not Ethiopians because Eritrea had been sold to Italy." It made sense to me, except that we didn't actually sell them and those soldiers were very cruel and some of those who stayed behind behaved very badly.

September 1965 came and it was time for me to leave my parents for the Laboratory School. On the day I left, Abaye went with me to the bus station. When the bus drove up, he pulled out a tied-up handkerchief from his pocket, untied it and gave me the only 50 cents he had. I told him I could pay for the bus. He insisted and I accepted and said good-bye, with tears in my eyes. I felt I was running away, leaving them alone in a precarious situation.

We were 215 students in the Laboratory School. The dormitories were at the back of the Haile Selassie I University Campus and the classes were at the southern part of the compound. One hundred ten of us were assigned beds in the largest dormitory. Students came from all over Ethiopia. Those from the province of Eritrea stood out. At the time, the people of that province were hoping to secede. The Eritrean students I met at Haile Selassie I Secondary School had similar feelings and were bitter against the government and the rest of the Ethiopian people. The Eritreans at the Laboratory School lined their beds up in a row. They considered the rest of us unfriendly. If one of us had an argument with one of them, the rest stood behind their man, no matter what. However, most people in the rest of Ethiopia didn't know the differences between the Eritrean highlanders and the Tigreans in the northern part of the country since they had the same feature and spoke the same language. Tigrean students were sympathetic to the Eritrean students, while the latter looked down on them. I wondered why the Tigrean students submitted to them so much – Tigray is the cradle of Ethiopian civilization.

Most of the teachers, including the school's director, were Americans. Some had come from other countries and had been assigned to the school through the United Nations. It was a well-organized school. Classes were arranged in accordance with the interests of the students. I focussed on maths and physics. We had activities like debates and sports. I was good in athletics, soccer, volleyball and basketball. The food was excellent. I felt guilty about enjoying the food while my family was barely getting enough to eat. I hated going home empty-handed. The three Birr they gave us was for laundry and personal hygiene, so it was difficult to save anything for them.

A student whose bed was close to my bed was named Abiy. He was from a rich family that owned coffee plantation in Illubabor Province, western Ethiopia. Once, his mother sent him 750 Birr. I wished my parents had never left their birthplaces – there they had plenty of coffee bushes and could have been like Abiy's parents. He gave me his stipend every month. I thanked him a lot for his generosity. I saved that for my family and visited them every three months.

While I was in the Laboratory School, Wondime worked in a drive-in theatre as a bartender after school and earned some money to support our family. One night, a man didn't get his change from the bar service. The man, a professor at Haile Selassie I University, complained to the management and was asked to identify the person on the spot, but he couldn't do it because it was dark. He came early the next day and stood by the gate to watch the bartenders arriving for work and identify the thief. Wondime arrived late, after helping Emaye in the forest. The professor picked out Wondime as the man who kept his change and argued that my brother's late arrival was an indication of his guilt. He had him arrested. At the police station, some criminals stole his shoes almost as soon as he was inside. Emaye didn't know what had happened to him and pleaded with Saint George of the Lydia. She was crying the whole night. He spent the night in jail and was set free the next morning because of insufficient evidence. He walked home barefoot.

Students in the dormitory of the Laboratory School divided themselves into three groups: Eritrean students who could not go along with the rest of the students, anti-Eritrean students and those in the middle. I was in the middle. One day on the soccer field, a fight broke out between two students. Both students were of Eritrean origin. One was straight from Eritrea while the second one was from another part of Ethiopia, Welo Province. The anti-Eritrean students stood with the latter. It was diffused for the moment.

Another day, after supper, there was a big fight between the Eritreans and the anti-Eritreans and some students were hurt. One of the Eritrean students was hospitalized. As a result, the Eritrean students insisted that they wanted to go home. They were approached by the dean of the education faculty and urged to change their minds. They remained adamant. Finally, the administration said they could leave, but they would have to pay for their own transportation. They changed their minds and stayed. However, the problem didn't end there.

Two students had come from Gondar, in northern Ethiopia, where people pride themselves on their rich history.[12] One Saturday morning, they left by the back gate for Merkato, the biggest market in Addis Ababa. It was the first time they had left the campus. On the way back, they took a bus that passed by the university's main gate that they thought was of another university. They didn't want to ask people for pride – they are Gondares. They travelled all the way to the bus terminal with no sight of the gate they were looking for. Then they tried going back, but they still couldn't find the gate. It got dark. Totally confused, they spent a night in a hotel. They took a taxi back to the university the next day.

[12] In the 17th century, Gondar was the centre of the Kingdom of Ethiopia.

Another student from Harerghe Province bullied the students in his dormitory. When he quarrelled with a dorm mate, he would jump right at him – like a paratrooper. Everybody was scared of him. The students in his dorm laughed when he laughed and kept quiet when he was in a bad mood. An Eritrean student in our dormitory tried the same thing. One night, he said he was in a mood to go to sleep early and then turned out the light. We were dismayed. However, another student from Harerghe Province turned the light back on. The bully turned out the light again. But this time, the second student went to the first and told him that he would put his eyes out if he turned the light out a third time. From then on, peace prevailed.

Education was good at the Laboratory School – we had competent teachers, enough books and good food and the environment was conducive to learning. There were eight sections and I was in Section E. I took maths, physics, biology, geography, Amharic and English classes. My maths teacher was an Italian. Americans taught me physics, biology and English. The geography teacher was from the United Kingdom and the Amharic teacher was Ethiopian. There was very good laboratory for biology. Typing class was held one afternoon a week. I found it very interesting – the mix of students was educational in itself. I met very nice students from other parts of Ethiopia and a few are still my friends. Getaneh bought a land and built a house near my place to be close to me and I am the godfather to Tesfaye's son. There were many good students – those who came from other parts of Ethiopia were the brightest in their provinces. For encouragement, the school organized dinners for the top students. Unfortunately, many students weren't interested in teacher training. Teaching was not a financially rewarding profession and so was looked down on. Those who wouldn't sign up with the faculty of education had to pay 550 Birr to change faculties.

Once, the geography teacher arranged a trip to one of the Rift Valley lakes. The trip was voluntary and transport and food were provided. I decided to go. The destination was Lake Awasa, 278 kilometres southwest of Addis Ababa. We started our journey at eight in the morning, travelling south for 73 kilometres and then southwest along the five Rift Valley lakes for 205 kilometres. We reached our lake at four that afternoon. We had not eaten on the way and were very hungry. The teacher was an Englishman who behaved like a soldier. He cared about going forward, not about food. By then, we needed to eat at least a piece of bread. He said that would be provided after pasta had been cooked. We waited for an hour and a half. While the cook was draining the water from the pasta, the pasta flowed out with water, right into a ditch. Some students tried to recover the hot pasta and were rewarded with burnt fingers. What a trip!

The year ended successfully and I was qualified to enter university the coming year. I rejoined my family at the end of the year and resumed helping my mother in the forest. The rainy season was as terrible as usual. One afternoon, as Wondime and I were walking home, following the two donkeys, a heavy rain came out from nowhere. We had no place to run for shelter – there weren't even any trees. We saw a Volkswagen coming towards us. The driver held his head in his hands in surprise when he saw us. That was our life.

Life was no easier now that I had finished high school. However, I was determined to continue my education. Tadesse Mengesha, a student in our village who had graduated from university encouraged me. His father was selling chickens – carrying them from far away on his shoulders – and his mother sold *injera*. There were six children in the family with Tadesse as the eldest. He had graduated from Haile Selassie I University and was supporting his family. People talked about and admired him. What he did motivated students from poor families. We believed we could beat poverty through education.

CHAPTER FOUR

In September 1966, I joined the faculty of education at Haile Selassie I University, with a major in mathematics and minor in psychology. I knew my parents were disappointed although they said nothing. Emaye had never commented on my furthering my education, but Abaye had spoken indirectly about it many times. However, they both wished me good luck.

At the time, I had no income with which to support them. I had heard a story that reminded me not to forget them. A poor Ethiopian farmer had his son at the university in Addis Ababa. He was very proud of him and would send him whatever he had managed to save. One day, the father decided to visit his son and travelled to Addis Ababa. His clothes were old and muddy. It took him a long time to find the university and when he did find it he was very tired. At the gate, he told the guards that he was there to visit his son. A student heard him say his friend's name and went to get him. The poor man sat on a rock in front of the gate, waiting for his son. The son came but was not happy to see his father. He didn't even want to greet him. The father was disappointed, gave him the money and left. The son's friend asked him about the man. The son said that he was his father's servant, who was sent to deliver the money. It was pitiful to know that happened to a father who had talked so proudly to his neighbours about his son. I didn't want to be that boy.

Iyassu was a good friend of mine at the Lab School. He was born and brought up in Nazareth Town, 100 kilometres south-east of Addis Ababa but his parents had come from Eritrea. He didn't go to the university although he was qualified for. Instead, he had joined the HVA (Ethiopia) Sugar Factory as a trainee mechanic. He came to visit me at the university. We had supper together at the university cafeteria and after supper, I escorted him out of campus. We left the compound through the main gate by Sidist Kilo Square and headed towards Nazareth School that was located 300 meters south, leaving Haile Selassie I Hospital on the right. There was no street light and the area was very dark. Before reaching Nazareth School, we turned east towards the direction of Saint Mary's Church. We couldn't see anything and anybody, just felt the two of us. As we reached the German School, Iyassu gently put a paper money in my right hand and said goodbye. We shook hands and went to our respective ways. As I was walking back, I thought a lot about the paper money he dropped into my hand. I believed it was one Birr but prayed if it would be five Birr. I walked fast to check it by the light at the hospital. I saw it but was not green like one Birr and neither yellow like five Birr. It was red like ten Birr but the light was not enough to check the number. I ran to my dormitory and saw it under the bright light – it was ten Birr. I couldn't believe it. Ten Birr at the time is equivalent to 300 Birr today. What a concerned friend he was! I came to know him in the Lab School and he was an Eritrean from Nazareth and I was Kefa from Addis Ababa. The two places of our origins were far, far apart, in space and culture and yet we made good friends.

One of the advantages of the Laboratory School was that it accustomed us to the university system of education. Classes were conducted along similar lines and some of the courses were held in the faculty of arts building. However, I started losing interest in staying in the faculty of education because it had such low prestige in the university community. Students who had entered the university after studying at the Laboratory School were very bright but not appreciated because their profession would be teaching. I had passed the Ethiopian School Leaving Certificate Examination, which qualified me to enrol in other faculties. So, a friend of mine, Tesfa and I started approaching other faculties. They were willing to take us, provided that the faculty of education would release us. However, we didn't have the money to pay.

At the time, the Pentecostal Church had a presence within the university community. Some strong emotions were involved and loud praying. I had been attending Pentecostal services every Friday evening. They were held close to the faculty of science. Cookies and tea were served afterwards and some students went just for that. One Friday, the service lasted a bit longer. In the middle of it, a student raised his hand and asked for his cookies – he said he had to leave early to study for an exam the next day. He was asked to stay a little longer but left early and without any cookies. He never returned.

Near the end of the first semester of the first year, Yilma, a friend of mine from my village, came to visit me. He told me that the excise tax department of the ministry of finance had posted an advertisement for grade 12 graduates. The pay was 300 Birr per month. As well, a 40-percent desert allowance and 50 Birr per month for housing were being considered. That was a lot of money – a university graduate would earn 500 Birr per month. I was tempted and sat the exam. The department needed ten people and I stood fifth. Yilma stood first. There was still the interview to do.

I thought seriously about the consequences of leaving the university. If I were determined to further my education, I might be able to return. If I returned, I could shift to another faculty – I wasn't happy in the faculty of education. However, if I stayed in university and something happened to my parents, my regret would last a lifetime. I decided to sit for the interview. The interview was at 9:00 in the morning and I had an exam between 8: 30 and 11:00 that same day. I didn't want to miss my exam either. I did my best in half an hour and left for the interview. I did well in the interview and was accepted. I also passed my exam, but just barely.

That job taught me about nepotism. The two people who stood seventh and eighth on the qualifying exam were from the same area as the director. They were assigned to Addis Ababa, while the rest of us were designated to Asab, 800 kilometres away. In addition to being remote, Asab was one of the hottest parts of Ethiopia. I had no choice. Worse yet, by the time we were ready to leave, our pay had been cut by 100 Birr per month and the desert allowance by 40 Birr. What cheats! It stimulated me to return to the university. I talked with my family about how to distribute my pay. We agreed that 60 Birr per month would be about right for my parents, my brother would get 15 Birr, and the balance would be for me.

Eight of us left for Asab. The journey took two days. Yilma had also been assigned to Asab and made the journey with me. It was my first time so far from home and I left with lots of uncertainties. I knew it was my responsibility to support my parents. However, I wasn't sure I would manage to return to university and so was deeply sorry for quitting. The whole journey was filled with contemplation. The first day we travelled along the highlands of Welo Province and the weather was fine. However, the second day was long and hot.

The lowlands are very dry. The lowland at Danakil lies below sea level and has a temperature of more than 50° C. Along the road were mirages of vast shining sands. It is home to the Afar people. Sometimes, we saw three or four of them sitting by the road.[13]

We reached Asab on the third day. We stayed in a hotel for few days. I met one of my high school teachers Mr. Roseless, a man from Finland. He had also taught my friend Yilma. We knew he loved beer and drank 20 or 30 bottles at a time. To avoid being cheated, he kept the empty bottles under his

---

[13] According to Afar tradition, when people travelling in different directions meet, they sit and exchange information. The eldest starts, telling in detail what he has seen on his way. Each talks in turn until the youngest has finished. There are no interruptions. It is meant to protect travellers against the unexpected.

chair until he had paid the bill. The two of us bought him 16 bottles of beer and he was extremely happy.

The first Ethiopian refinery was established in Asab and had become operational just before we arrived. The Soviet Union built it as an economic development project. The Soviet Union had also set up a polytechnic institute in the town of Bahir Dar in north-western Ethiopia. Compared to the United States, the Soviet Union carried out significant development work – the Soviet Union, of course, was interested in launching the communist ideology in Ethiopia. Except for offering academic fellowships and training technicians, the Americans were not doing much to counteract the Soviets. Crude oil was imported and refined at Asab. Four oil companies operated there: Mobil, Shell, Agip and Total. Our job was to record the amount of oil distributed to these companies and to determine how much was taxable and how much was duty free. I was appointed the provisional boss but got no extra pay for that.

The eight of us rented a villa. It had fans but no air conditioners. We hired a maid to cook and clean for us. The weather was terrible – constant wind. There weren't many trees to be seen and no fresh vegetables to be found. *Injera* and bread spoiled in a day and there was not enough space in the fridge to store it. Asab was ramshackle city and the port was not well developed. I had diarrhoea day after day, a very bad experience. My roommates started fighting over petty matters. They would go to the bars as friends but return as enemies. I would often go to church and when I came home I would have to settle their disputes – except for one, Kenaa the others more or less listened to me. Yilma was the most pugnacious of them all. He had quarrelled with everyone except with Gutema and me. I knew his behaviour and his mother had asked me to cool him down as much as possible. Our families were very close and he listened to me.

It was a Sunday afternoon. One of the boys had brought his girlfriend to the villa and we were playing cards. Another was in bed. When he woke up, he saw the girl and said she had been his girl friend. The two fought over her and one of them was beaten terribly. That night, he retaliated and the villa was in total disarray when I got home from church. Friends had to step in and settle the problem. That was routine.

The 1967 Arab-Israeli War broke out. Ibrahim was anti-Israel, but hard-line Christians in the villa supported Israel. Although the emperor claimed to be the Lion of Judah, he sympathised with the Palestinians and had received refugees in 1948 when Israel declared its independence. However, the point of the 1967 War looked to be the destruction of the state of Israel and Ethiopian Christians[14] did not favour that. The argument in our house was very emotional and looked to lead to the second Arab-Israeli War. It seemed that my roommates had many reasons to fight and few to reconcile. They

---

[14] Nonetheless, Ethiopia is among the few countries in the world where Christians and Muslims live amicably, especially Orthodox Christians and Muslims. When the former built churches, Muslims would be there, and when the latter built schools and health centres, the Christians would be there. Any problems between the two are instigated by foreign elements, usually those hoping to control the source of Ethiopian rivers.

quarrelled in the office as well as at home and because of that our work was adversely affected.

I decided to change residence and convinced Yilma to move out of the house with me. Gutema hadn't quarrelled with him yet and he moved out with us. We managed to get a reasonably priced house. However, the two started fighting shortly after, which became very disturbing for me both at home and at the office. I asked the head office to send a senior person to serve as the boss. The head office agreed but was slow to act. Finally, they sent someone who had completed grade eight and was getting paid half what we were. We couldn't take him seriously and things got even more messed up.

There were many things to see and do in the area. The Afar people drank liquor made from palm trees. They made holes in palm stems and drained out a dark, oily liquid. I drank a little but felt drunk. They liked it and drank a lot without feeling drunk. They said it helped to keep them from getting thirsty when they were in the desert. It was expensive though.

A beach ran along the coast of the Red Sea. The Soviets working at the refinery used to enjoy themselves at the beach. Once, a group of Americans came to the beach, carrying cases of cold beer. They had no swimming trunks and so cut off their pant-legs and swam into the sea. The Soviets stared at them in surprise. After the Americans had finished swimming, they opened the beer and offered to everybody, including the Soviets. I took the

Americans for cowboys and they acted accordingly. They never cared about anybody or anything. I liked them though.

In August 1967, Gutema and I received letters transferring us to Massawa, the Ethiopia's second port on the Red Sea. Massawa was even further away from home and a four-day trip by bus from Asab. The first day was to Desie Town, where we had spent a night on our way to Asab. The next day was a hard trip through the mountains and valleys where Ethiopian forces engaged the Italian army during World War II. We had to go about 350 kilometres and it took us the whole day, much longer than to go the 400 kilometres from Addis Ababa to Desie. I met a young Japanese man on the bus who spent the whole time denouncing the Americans because of what they did to Hiroshima and Nagasaki. He worked for a Japanese tire manufacturing company and was there to observe and report on the terrain and surfaces of Ethiopian roads.

We reached Asmara, the capital of Eritrea, the northern province of Ethiopia. Eritrea had been a colony of Italy between 1895 and 1952. Then the British had made Eritrea a protectorate for ten years. We were there not long after the British left. Asmara was a well-planned and well-laid-out city and was very clean with good restaurants and hotels. The shops had smart suits, shoes and sweaters. There were well-kept cinema houses. The main road was named after Emperor Haile Selassie I. During the Italian occupation, local people were strictly forbidden from entering the cinema zone. Cinemas for locals were on the outskirts – those along the main road were meant for the Italians.

We rented good hotel rooms for six Birr per night. Food was good and clean and reasonably priced. We visited the excise tax department for the region and were introduced to the man who would be our boss at Massawa. We spent the rest of the day exploring the town. We had our pictures taken on top of the municipal building – lovely views around. After two nights in Asmara, we left for Massawa.

Asmara is about 3,000 metres above sea level, while Massawa is at sea level. The distance between them is 115 kilometres by road. We rode along very steep escarpments and noticed drastic changes in altitude and temperature. Many passengers threw up on the way to Massawa. There were fruit and vegetable farms along the way, with good restaurants to rest in. It took us three hours to reach Massawa. It is a port city and very beautiful. As one approach it, the road on the left runs to the naval base, while the road on the right runs to the Agip fuel depot and then to a village called Hargigo. Another road runs to the island of Tiwalet and then crosses to the main island where the port is. The islands are connected with man-made structures. Another island lies further into the sea and isn't connected to the mainland. The houses by the port were very old. Ships came from all parts of the world. Massawa had very beautiful scenery.

Gutema and I spent about a week in a hotel and then rented a house. Massawa was much better than Asab. Houses were good and rents cheap. Asmara was close, so we could go there on the weekend. Nearby farms brought in fresh vegetables and fresh fruit every day. There were plenty of bars for cold drinks and ice cream. However, the heat was terrible – it was much hotter than Asab, but there was a breeze. The house rented for 50 Birr for two rooms. My pay had been increased by that amount per month and I was getting handsome over-time too. My new boss was an excellent person – unassuming, humble, kind and honest. Within few days in Massawa, I knew I could resume my university education. After expenses, I could save 250 Birr per month.

Massawa was hottest from June to September, with daily temperatures of more than 40° C. At times, it reached 49° C. Sunstroke was common. Sometimes, even the leaves on the trees were still and we could see no waves on the sea. I used to take five showers a day – at six in the morning before going to work, at one in the afternoon, after work, at five in the evening after a nap, at seven after a walk, and again at ten before going to bed. Each time, I changed my shirt. I set cold water aside early in the morning since it was impossible to use water direct from the tap during the day.

We hired a housemaid to cook and wash clothes. However, none stayed long. They left for no reason, but a replacement was available in no time. They had established an employment insurance scheme on their own. As soon as a maid lost her job, the association paid her until the next job. That was smart, but the lazy ones survived on the backs of diligent workers. The government didn't have such a scheme.

Once, the newly appointed director at the headquarter came to visit us. He was the son of an aristocrat. He came to my office at Agip Depot and, as he entered my office, I stood up to greet him. He approached my table and I stretched my two hands – one to shake hands, the other as a gesture of respect. He ignored me and went to the Italian manager and shook his hand instead. I was embarrassed that I had been so naïve.

I received a letter from Wondime. He had started the university in September 1967. Emaye had stopped going to the forest to collect firewood. However, Abaye had never stopped working. He was not the type of person who would give up work, even if he had enough money. He was happy since expenses at home were taken care of and he no longer had to dread the rainy season. He had enough money to enjoy doing things with his friends. He was also good at managing money, while Emaye was the opposite. She was the most generous person I ever knew. Even when we were desperately poor, she shared whatever she had with her neighbours – they were desperate too. She would tell us, "Cooked food is wasted if it isn't shared." She had constant fights with Abaye about her poor management of money.

In July 1968, I went to visit my family, after a year and half away. They had improved the house. Now it had a corrugated iron roof, electricity, and potable water at the door. Life was much better for them. Wondime had quit

69

university and joined the Ethiopian Airlines as a trainee mechanic. Abaye was going to the forest as usual, but his responsibilities at home were much reduced and carried out at his discretion. I was very much encouraged. I bought a gold necklace for Ehte and went back to work after a month.

Gutema told me that he had met a girl back home and they were getting serious. She was in grade 11 at the time. He had worked for a while at the malaria eradication service before he joined the department. According to Ethiopian custom, it was common for the husband to excel his wife in education and income. In my friend's case, she was advancing in education and was determined to go further, while he had no plan for that. I was a bit puzzled. Anyway, he left to become engaged. He spent all the money he had saved and called me to send him some money for his return to work. He came back on time. After that, his behaviour completely changed. He was not friendly to me any more. Whenever she sent him complaining letters, he would get upset and stop talking to me. I knew his problem was not with me, but I felt very uncomfortable. At the end of her school year, she came to visit him. He left his room for her and joined me. She spent a month with us, but they never kissed. He handled her like something fragile and she behaved like a baby. In the first place, he should have known her better before the engagement. I knew he was going to lose her.

I have never agreed with traditional marriages. When I was in grade four at Dejazmach Wondirad Elementary School, a girl in my class – her name was Yeshi – was very intelligent both academically and in craftsmanship. She was very well liked. Her marks were in the 90s and the tablecloths she made were excellent and admired even by her girlfriends. By the end of the year, she was among the top five in the class. When the school closed in June, we went our own ways. School opened again in September, but Yeshi was not there. I heard that she had got married to a private policeman during the vacation, under pressure by her parents and relatives, which was a crime. In a few years, she became the mother of three children and looked devastated. If she had continued with her schooling, she could have succeeded in her education and would have become a role model to other female students.

I knew quite a few people in Massawa. I was still going to a Protestant church. I had met some teachers and was visiting them and they were visiting me. One day, Eshetu, an elementary school teacher that I had never talked to before, came to my place. I barely knew him and had heard he was from Addis Ababa, near my village. He looked depressed and took him some time before he spoke out. He said that he loved a girl from the area. She was living with her father in a broken family. Her mother lived in Sudan. The two had agreed to get married in the future. After the end of the academic year, he was to go on vacation to Addis Ababa and she wanted to go with him. However, neither her father nor he had agreed to that idea. When he left for Addis Ababa without her, she disappeared from home. The father looked for her in many places but couldn't find her and then he committed suicide.

When her mother heard the news, she came from Sudan. She had Eshetu called from Addis Ababa and asked him to marry her daughter. He had spent all his money during his vacation and didn't know what to do. Therefore, he came to me to borrow 500 Birr. That was a lot of money for a person I didn't really know. In addition, I had decided to go for vacation in six months and to go back to university if accepted. I told him I had to think about it and said bye. I consulted his colleagues and all rejected the idea outright. He came back three days later. He looked desperate and I felt sorry for him. I told him I was leaving in six months. He said he would pay me 100 Birr per month and finish it before I left. He said he would sign on that. It took me some time to decide. Finally, I said, "I understand the seriousness of your problem but, I don't know you. In addition, I have my own problems. However, I will give you the money and I don't need any written agreement. God is our witness." I gave him the money.

The next month came, but there was no money. I said to myself, "You can't blame anybody but yourself." Some of Eshetu's colleagues said, "We told you so!" I passed by his place to check if he was in the neighbourhood and he was around. However, I neither contacted nor asked him for the money. The next month, he came with 100 Birr and said he was sorry for not showing up the previous month. He paid me back every month after that, although he wasn't on time. He was short by 100 Birr. I asked him to pay the balance to Gutema and left for home. I have not seen him since. By the end of the year, I received the last 100 Birr through my friend. He taught me a real lesson: there are people who are very close but disappointing and others so far away but encouraging and responsible. I blessed their marriage.

I went to the university and reapplied to return. I was accepted and so resigned from my job. I requested vacation pay. The director of the day was new. He asked me why I was leaving. I told him I was going back to the university. He said, "It is a wise decision instead of remaining a clerk all your life." With pleasure, he signed the paper for my vacation pay, shook my hand and wished me good luck. He was not a feudal person like the previous director.

When I was in Massawa, Gutema told me that his fiancée was going to the United States on the American Field Service Program. I had heard about students who had gone on that program and returned with superficial, even odd, characters and I had commented about that. He told me that her parents wanted her to go. She went. During her stay in the US, he was sending her money from his savings. He had showed me receipts for 5,000 Birr. She returned after a year. By then, he had been transferred to Addis Ababa and had rented a nice four-room house not far from the centre of the city. He had bought a beautiful sofa and other good furniture too. When she arrived, he went to the airport with a friend who had a car and picked her up and took her to his place. She walked from room to room, then said, "How can you live in a house with no shower?" None of her relatives had showers – very few houses in the whole country had showers at the time. That was the beginning of the end of their relationship.

She began to avoid him and he got frustrated. He had expected a promotion and that had not materialised. He wrote a book and borrowed money to publish it. The book did not sell well and he couldn't pay his debt. That led to a court case. One day, I met him while I was taking a walk and he asked me to lend him 100 Birr, but I did not have that much money at the moment. After a few days, I heard he had committed suicide. I felt very sorry for his misfortune.

CHAPTER FIVE

When I left my job to return to university, I had saved 3,500 Birr for my parents. Wondime was in training at Ethiopian Airlines. He boarded at the training school and was paid 20 Birr per week in pocket money. He agreed to give me half of that and never to touch our parent's money except to cover their monthly expenses. The money I had saved was transferred to his account. Wondime was half way through his training; so we thought that the money would suffice our parents until he graduated.

I was totally committed to my education. My first day back at the university, I met a friend from my village who was in law school. He told me that the university had been disturbed because one of its students who was on university national service had been assassinated. I asked him the name of the victim and he told me it was Hagos. Hagos had been a very good friend of mine at the Laboratory School. We were in the same class and he was bold and outspoken and enjoyed arguing with people. When arguing, he never listened to his opponents but instead kept lambasting them with his words. I asked him once why he was doing that and he said, "If I listened to my opponents, I would get angry and lose my temper and the points I want to make in my argument. The best tactic is to put my words into their ears." I heard that he had been very outspoken, especially in classrooms, against the government while he was on national service. At the time, student movements were very strong in Ethiopia and the government was trying to break that spirit by eliminating the student leaders. In this case, as well, the government was alleged to have assassinated him.

Gizaw, of my previous high school, had been gunned down in Addis Ababa the year before. As I heard it, he had run for the presidency of the University Students Union when he was in his third year and had lost marginally. Then, he withdrew from the university in order to come back the following year and run again – fourth-year students didn't qualify for the office. After he withdrew, I had seen him around my village in Addis Ababa, late one day when I had come for vacation. He looked tense and was surrounded by his friends. We briefly shook hands and went our own ways. He looked as though he was very suspicious about something, but I wasn't aware of his situation. He returned to the university the following year and resumed his political struggle and did get elected as president of the association. One evening, while he was walking with his girlfriend, he was shot dead from a passing car. The government was alleged to have been responsible for that too. Gizaw had developed a strong hatred for the wealthy and the aristocrats and was bitter when he talked about them. If he had had the power, his revenge could have been catastrophic for those people, which wouldn't have helped the country.

By the time of my return, the university's academic program had been changed: arts, physical science and life science streams had been established for first-year students. After completing first year, students would choose their specialities, based on their first-year results. I was assigned to the arts stream because I had only taken maths courses before I withdrew. Most of my friends from the Lab School were now in fourth year. I was a bit lonely. However, I rented a house with Tesfa, an old friend from the Lab School who had just returned from work like me. He had left the university for a year. He was a gentleman. Nobody would fight with him. During an argument, he would stick to his points and if his opponent got emotional, he would say, "Your argument could be right, but I feel mine stands strong." He would never utter a word after that. I admired him of his conduct.

This time I had handsome pocket money from my brother and no pressure to support my parents. I visited my parents often and whenever I went home, I would see Emaye standing in front of the house, stretching her hands towards the sky, praying for us. She would beg the Almighty to call her before He called us and would kiss the ground many times. She never understood religion in general and Christianity in particular but believed that there was a Creator and prayed to him in the name of saints and angels. I didn't know whether her prayers would be heard, but I knew that she was doing it from the bottom of her heart. She was a wonderful believer in the Almighty.

I completed my first year with better grades. At the end of the year, I met Belete, a classmate from my previous high school who had finished his second year in biology. He said he was quitting. He wanted to study medicine but did not get accepted. He told me that he wanted to go to Poland to study medicine but had no money for a plane ticket. Then he decided to travel by surface transport, first to Eritrea, then to Sudan and Egypt, and finally across the Mediterranean. I told him there was no surface transport between Ethiopia and Sudan. He said he would do it, even on foot. He asked me to contribute to his transport and I gave him 50 Birr. Belete wrote to me after two years. He had travelled to Asmara by bus, 1,080 kilometres, and then by bus to the border with Sudan, another 400 km, and then on foot into Sudan. He was jailed in Sudan for illegal entry and was released after a week. He took a train to Alexandria in Egypt and was hired as a labourer on a vessel up and sailed to the port city of Marseilles in France. While in Marseilles, he contacted a friend in Norway and was told he had a better chance of getting in medical school there. He went to Norway and enrolled in medical school. That was quite a lot of determination.

I stayed with my parents after the university was closed for the year. Teshome, a close friend of mine in my village was married to a relative of a *tej*[15] seller who owned one of the two radios in the village. She was from the ruling Amhara ethnic group. One day, Teshome had gone to visit her. Her girlfriend was there too. The *tej* seller wasn't wearing her gold necklace that day and her girlfriend asked her about it. The *tej* seller said that she had stopped wearing it after Tirfu, my sister, wore it and that the gold had lost its value ever since. She was right – gold necklaces are not meant for the poor. Social exclusion was very common at the time, with the people from the ruling class looking down at everybody else. As well, the Amharas

---

[15] *Tej* is an Ethiopian wine made from raw honeycomb and hops.

considered themselves to be the best, followed by the Tigreans, Oromos, and so on. The grassroots Amharas didn't benefit from the system except in name and were rather thought of as exploiters by the other ethnic groups.

During my second year, I applied to study statistics and I was accepted. Around the time we were registering, I met up with Wossen, a friend from first year, and asked him what he was going to be studying and he said he was quitting. I knew he had been applying to different universities in the United States. He had applied to more than 50 universities but was not successful. I admired his tenacity – it was a lot of research to be doing and time and money to be spending while he was a student. Finally, he had applied to universities in Oregon and Idaho and he got lucky. Fourth-year history students at Oregon University had picked Ethiopia as the topic for their senior essay. Wossen was asked to facilitate their visit and to help them. So he quit university and worked with the group. After they returned to the US, their university sent him a grant and an air ticket and he left for US the next year. After many years, he wrote me a letter. He said that he had two BAs, two MAs, and a Ph.D., joking that one BA and one MA were for his dad and his mom. I admired his tenacity.

Statistics was interesting and I was also studying economics as a minor. I made seven new friends, most of them much younger than me. The eight of us formed a group – we ate together, walked around campus together, sat and talked together. I found it very interesting. We were all from different places and different ethnic backgrounds. Gurmu was an Oromo from Legedadi.

Tegene and Teferra were Amharas from Arsi and Gamo Gofa Provinces, respectively. Debesai was an Eritrean and had come from Asmara. Feyissa and Yoseph were Gurages, from Sodo and Sebatbet respectively. Bekele was Hadiya and had come from Hosanna. I was Kefa but born and brought up in Addis Ababa. However, we neither noticed nor talked about our differences except to laugh about and to tease one another. It was one of the best times of my life.

The first semester went fine. I performed well in class. However, because of student political activities, there was no guarantee that we would have a second semester. Students were expressing their dissatisfaction with the government by boycotting classes and by demonstrating in the streets of Addis Ababa. Student leaders were calling for "land to the tiller" and advocating for socialism and communism and praising Mao Tse Tung, Che Guevara and Fidel Castro. This was the time that the Soviet and Chinese political ideologies were spreading in many countries. They had many followers, especially amongst junior university students, in the high schools as well. The government had been trying to silence the movement through police brutality and by imprisoning student leaders. Students boycotted during the second semester as expected.

Eventually, the university administration gave an ultimatum: students had to go back to classes. Traditionally, third- and fourth-year students would register, while first- and second-year students would boycott and were usually dismissed. Our group didn't go to class and so faced dismissal.

Three of us had a big fight with four third-year statistics students from Eritrea. They attacked one of our friends and the two of us stepped in to protect him. Most of the Eritrean students weren't interested in university activities – they considered themselves Eritreans, not Ethiopians. The three of us were attacked not only by the four Eritreans but also by all the Eritreans on campus. The Tigrean students sympathised with the Eritreans, while the rest remained neutral. Stones flew at us from all directions and I was hit on the head and legs and my face was covered with blood. The campus was in chaos. Eventually, the four ran away, jumping over the fence when one of our friends joined us. Finally, the university was closed to first-year and second-year students. I had quit my job to get a university education but it did not seem promising. I left the campus and went back home to think about my future.

I started looking for a job. Zeleke, a teacher I knew, had promised to find me one. One day, he called and told me that he had got one. I was very pleased and met him the next day. He told me that my work would be to collect anti-government leaflets from the campus and that I'd be paid 20 Birr per month. Even at my most desperate time, I had never done anything like that. I declined politely and asked him for another job. After a week, Zeleke called me again and we met at his place. He said my pay had been raised to 30 Birr per month but the job would remain the same. I thanked him a lot and left for good.

I intensified my search for a job, but it was not easy. I went to my old employer but there was no work for me there either. I applied to few other places but did not succeed. By the end of May, I managed to get a job at Agip (Ethiopia) Ltd. as a clerk, with pay of 190 Birr per month. It was permanent. However, work was not interesting and the pay was low for my level of education. I worked there for three months and quit when the university reopened. A crash program was organized to enable us finish the last part of the second year. It was very bad. Some of the expatriate professors had left the country and were replaced with newcomers. I did very poorly but survived because of my past performance.

At the end of my second year – in 1971– some friends in my village set up an association to help each other in times of sickness, death or even when one of the group had financial problems. It was our form of social insurance. The government had no such scheme. It was called the Association of Eastern Shola Youths. There were 50 of us in the beginning, but the number went down due to poor communication – our jobs had left us scattered all over the country. It still exists under the same name, with 20 members, 40 including spouses. The majority of us are now over 50 years old and enjoying the word "Youth." Members meet once a month and families meet every three months for lunch. It has become the envy of the village. Those who have left the country still make their monthly contributions and still send congratulatory cards when somebody has success and condolence cards in times of grief.

Third year started well. According to university regulations, third- and fourth-year students had to reside off campus and so eight of us rented a house. The university gave us each 20 Birr per month for rent, but we had to pay only 13.5 Birr per head. On payday, we liked to go to the Venus Nightclub and did so with the rest of the stipend. Drinks were expensive at nightclubs, so we would go to a bar and share four bottles of wine between us at 0.75 Birr each, then go to the Venus and pay two Birr each at entrance and spend the rest in there. By the time we left the Venus, the money would be gone – no more nightclubbing for us until the next month.

In my third year, I had my worst professor. He was supposed to lecture on economics for four hours a week but most of the time he didn't show up. Whenever he came, he would sit for a while then drag himself up to get a piece of chalk. Sometimes, he was too lazy to get the chalk and instead wrote with the dust. When he was supposed to be invigilating our second-year exam, he left us alone in a large classroom and disappeared. Students joked about him, saying that he never marked exam papers. They said that what he did was to take the papers to his bedroom and toss them at the ceiling – those that landed on top of the cupboard were As, those on the dressing table were Bs, those on the bed and chairs were Cs and those on the floors were Ds and Fs, depending on where they landed.

Class boycotts again started in the middle of the second semester of my third year. It was very upsetting. Leaders of first- and second-year students were militant; they wanted everybody out of class and dragged out those who refused. The struggle was meant to be for democracy, but what was happening was the opposite. When student co-operation weakened, they mobilised high school students who were more militant. We third-year students wanted to continue our education but had a hard time.

Tegene, my close friend, was president and I was treasurer of the Statistics Students Association (SSA). It was set up to help in times of trouble on campus. This time, the University Students Union of Addis Ababa called representatives of the different associations to a meeting at its Sidist Kilo office. My friend went, representing SSA. They met on the main campus and agreed on strategies to help needy students. The meeting ended late in the afternoon. The government had been aware of the meeting and had sent a force to apprehend the student leaders. As the first group left the meeting place, they were surrounded and taken to jail. In the meantime, Tegene had stayed behind to wait for a friend Tilahun. When Tilahun still wasn't ready to leave, Tegene left the room alone. He was a very suspicious person and so sensed that something had gone wrong. Instead of his usual route, he made his way through the brush and reached the department of statistics in Arat Kilo. The security force had come back and had apprehended the rest in the meeting room, including Tilahun.

Tegene was the only person who wasn't jailed. Students took him for a spy who gave information to the security force. However, his close friends knew that he was not such a person. The security police had a list of the representatives who had attended the meeting, so Tegene didn't come back to class. We signed him in. After a few days, the security force called his cousin – his guarantor – and asked him to hand over Tegene. His cousin told them that Tegene was attending classes – he knew we were signing for Tegene. Then they told Tegene's cousin to tell him not to worry but to continue with his classes. Tegene remained suspicious and did not appear on campus. We continued sign in for him in every class.

One day, Tegene went to visit a female cousin and told her the entire story, including about the security officer who had interviewed his guarantor. She asked him for the name of the officer and he gave it to her. The officer was a major and was one of her neighbours. The female cousin knew the officer's wife very well and talked to her. While Tegene was there, the major's wife called her husband at his office. The major told his wife that they had not apprehended Tegene yet and were still looking for him. His wife yelled at him and warned that the worst would happen between them if he did apprehend Tegene. She told him that she at least wanted to live in peace with her neighbours. Finally, the major called Tegene and asked him for a deal. He said he would let him go free, provided he told him the whereabouts of two statistics students, Abebe and Tenaye. Tegene didn't know their whereabouts, they were fourth year students. Then the major knew that his wife had been serious and set Tegene free. Almost a month after the meeting, Tegene came back to class. Those jailed stayed in jail until the end of the academic year.

After students completed their third year, they had to take part in the national service program. Students were deployed to different high schools in the country to teach for a year. With students from other departments, I was assigned to Mendefera High School in Eritrea. I knew that part of the country and the people because I had worked there. I also had an Eritrean friend, Debasai. I was pleased with my assignment.

Tegene and Suker, the shortest in our group, were assigned to Debre Tabor High School in the Province of Gondar. Traditionally, the people of Gondar contended for power with the central government. Thus, our friend Teferra said that the Gondares would even feel bitterer this time and would complain that the government of Shewa had sent them one person cutting into two.

Mendefera was a pretty town and the people were excellent. Abebe, Yimam, Belay and I rented a house in the centre of the town. Our neighbour was a driver for a government office. He was a very quiet person. Every evening, we would see his wife washing her four-year-old son's feet in front of their house. She was very kind and full of joy. We later learned that they were newly married and that the boy was her stepson. Where I come from, it would have been unusual for a woman to treat her stepson with such love. Abebe was a language teacher at the high school and so asked his students to write a composition on a stepmother. None of them wrote anything negative. It would have been just the opposite where I come from.

I started teaching grade 11 maths. The first one and half months went fine. However, things did not go right after that. Rebels in the province were fighting for independence. The students in the high school were influenced by them and so boycotted classes. They stayed away for quite a few days. While that was happening, teachers would go to the school and spend the day talking and playing table tennis or other games. One day, I went to school, cycling there as usual, to check for students. They hadn't come. On my return, they were just coming out of the nearby forest – I guessed from a meeting – and the road was very crowded. While I was cycling on the shoulder of the road, I heard angry voices talking in an insulting tone. I didn't understand what they were saying or whom it was directed to since I didn't speak the language. I continued cycling to my place. After a while, I heard two students talking to each other in Amharic and I figured out that the students had been talking about me. I felt very angry with them for considering me to be part of the government system – I had no access to it whatsoever and no say in it at all.

I went straight to Gaber's place. I had known him at the Lab School and he was now teaching history at the Mendefera High School after graduating from university. I told him the whole story and asked why they did that to me. He laughed at me and that made me even madder. He said that I was a fool for not understanding what the students thought about people from southern Ethiopia. He said that he had had the same mentality before he went to the Lab School and then to the university. Before, he thought that all the southerners were one ethnic group, Amharas and that all were exploiters.

After mixing with people in the south, he understood the Ethiopian social hierarchy and had come to know that the leaders from north were also exploiters. He said that if the Amharas were considered the top exploiters in the country, then the Tigreans were next, especially the Eritrean Tigreans. I appreciated his arguments and left.

Students were not coming to the school any more. For fear of political repercussions, the government had no interest in moving us to another area. To avoid idleness, we started reading books and playing cards. When we played cards, we would save half the winners' money to buy refreshments. We bought chicken and beer and enjoyed ourselves. During lunch and supper, Yimam was in the habit of coming back to eat again after he had finished and washed his hands. He would be the first to announce that he was full. However, on his way back from washroom, if he saw that someone was still at the table, he would sit down and begin a new meal. He did it again and again, until everyone had left.

Belay could sleep anywhere anytime. When we went to the hospital to visit a sick friend, he slept there like the dead until we left. When went to visit someone in the neighbourhood, he had no time to talk but went straight to sleep. He told me that once at a wedding in his home village he had slept in the open, wearing a cotton blanket. He never noticed that a cow had eaten the blanket and left him half-naked.

Abebe enjoyed being fed by others and never liked using his own hands. Once he hurt his right hand and had to wear a bandage. He enjoyed that since we had to feed him. He wore that bandage for a long time.

One day, I received an urgent letter from home. It stated that Emaye was seriously ill and that I had to go home. Usually, that kind of letter is an indication that someone is about to die and I interpreted it that way. That same day, I left for Asmara to catch the next day's flight to Addis Ababa. I flew to Addis Ababa early in the morning and the flight took 55 minutes. Then I took a taxi to my village. Usually, when somebody dies, women put on scarf-like overdresses. I didn't see that. I didn't even see anybody around that I knew. I went home along a narrow road from the main street, expecting to see a tent in front of our house with mourners inside. I didn't see that either. It was very quiet. I was scared to enter the house. After few minutes, I went in and saw Emaye lying on her bed. Groaning, she called my name. I kissed her cheeks and felt relieved. I sat and cried for a while. She soothed me. Usually, she feels very confident when I'm around but desperate when I go away. In three days she recovered fully and I returned to my assignment after a week. I took a bus since it wasn't urgent – the students were still boycotting classes. I arrived back on the third night.

While in Mendefera, Habte – he was another teacher in the school – and I had started to learn to drive. Our instructor wouldn't allow us to change gears by ourselves. We had never changed gears freely but he recommended that we take the test. The oral test went fine. On the day of the practical test, the instructor took us to the site early, drove along the designated route and explained which gear to change and where. Habte did the exam first and his driving looked fine. Gebrai, another young man, tried next but couldn't start the engine because of his nervousness. We learned that he was taking the test for a job and appreciated his problem.

Now it was my turn. The instructor sat right behind me. When I started the car, I hadn't released the handbrake and the examiner told me to start again. It was a place where, according to the instructor, I was supposed to change to second gear. I thought I was lost. I started again, in first gear, and changed to second after a little while. The car was Fiat 600 and old and the three of us were heavy. There was a traffic light ahead and if I stopped there, I would have to start all over again and then drive up a steep hill. It was hard to get up the hill and manage the gears as instructed. Fortunately, the traffic light showed green and I drove at full speed up the hill. Then, the examiner asked me to back into a garage. I backed in and knew I was in when the instructor pressed my back.

We wouldn't know our results until two weeks later. We were on our way to visit the north-eastern part of the province when we checked. I found my name at number 14 under those who had passed. I showed it to Habte and he congratulated me. He said he had passed too – at number 13 way below mine – and I congratulated him. However, I saw two number 13s and I asked him what was going on. We looked carefully and saw "failed" in the middle. Habte's name was there, right after Gebrai. Habte became very angry and said "I don't mind failing. But how could they put my name under Gebrai, who never even started the engine?"

We began our journey the next day. The first 90 kilometres on the way to Keren Town was farmland. The remaining 270 kilometres were through deserts and Stone Mountains. The towns of Akordat, Barentu and Haikota were on the way, but we didn't stop, except for lunch at Akordat. Keren is famous for its oranges and was well placed and very clean. After crossing Akordat and Barentu, we finally reached Tessenei Town, which is famous for its cotton plantation. The politics in the area seemed tense – heavily armed soldiers searched all passengers for arms. The town was shabby and ramshackle, with no decent hotels or bars. There was nothing to see except open fields. We rented beds in a hotel, but slept in the open for it was very hot inside. The cold Melotti Beer was excellent though.

The next day, we went to see the border with Sudan. The Ethiopian border guard took us to the other side and the Sudanese border guards greeted us. They were very kind. There were no chairs in the room, so they invited us to sit on their beds and they gave us cold water. The Ethiopian border guard put it well: "There is a saying – 'out of world's 100% of kind-heartedness, 99% is in Sudan.'" The area was barren and hot, in the middle of nowhere, and with guards on both sides. We also travelled to Humera Town, in Gondar Province, a town famous for its soybeans and cotton. Settlements along the road looked poor and it was very dry there. We passed Omhajer, a village that looked deserted. Humera was across Tekeze River that flows to Sudan.

The town was very crowded with no planned streets and poor-looking houses. Labourers had come there from highlands of other provinces. It looked like a place that sent its resources to the "master" country. We spent two nights in Humera, returned to Tessenei and then to Asmara.

We also travelled to see the obelisks in Axum, the ancient political and religious capital of Ethiopia. It is 150 kilometres west of Mendefera. Buses travelled between the two towns. The road was good and the journey was too. The obelisks stand on a massive stone base and have been there since an Ethiopian king converted to Christianity in the 4th century AD,[16] according to many historians. We also visited Saint Mary's Church of Zion, where the true Ark of the Covenant is believed to be. Axum had played a role in the traditions of the Muslims too. It is believed that in the fifth year of the Prophet Mohammed's mission, his followers were persecuted in Saudi Arabia and were offered asylum by the Ethiopian Christian king of the time and they freely exercised their religion. They lived in Ethiopia until they felt it was safe to return. Brotherhood and sisterhood between Christians and Muslims still exists in Ethiopia.

We finished our visit and returned to Mendefera the same day. After our return, we heard that some university students had tried to hijack a plane but were killed by anti-hijackers. It was sad news for the university community since those killed were the most prominent student leaders.

[16] The obelisks are among the most important monuments of the ancient Ethiopia. There are massive ruins – monolithic obelisks, royal tombs, ancient castles and giant stellae – dating back many centuries.

Our neighbour's new bride gave birth to a baby boy while her husband was away travelling for a week. We visited her at the hospital. When she got home, we bought a goat for her to slaughter – she would have been desperate without her husband around. He came at the end of the week and thanked us. We told him that he deserved it for his kindness and good neighbourliness.

A policeman we knew in Mendefera invited us to his wedding. He had come from southern Ethiopia and needed us. The bride lived in Asmara and so we had to travel 54 kilometres and return the same day. Five cars were ready for the journey. We reached Asmara early in the afternoon on Sunday. A big tent was planted in the middle of an asphalt road. We entered the tent to find music playing and people dancing. A separate place had been reserved for us and we sat there while guests were eating lunch. There were two big barrels beside us and I had no idea what was inside. The best men handed over the jewels and clothes that had been bought for the bride to the elderly on her side. They were sitting, lined up, opposite us. They checked everything, passing each item from one person to the next, to see if the bridegroom had met his obligations. Finally, the people on bride's side announced the missing items and the best men committed themselves to bring them in few days.

The bride's family gave their approval and we were permitted to eat and drink. The two barrels in front of us turned out to be filled with local beer and exclusively arranged for us. Waiters brought *injera* on trays and sauces in clay bowels. The waiters put some *injeras* in the bowels and stirred with spoon. They put the remaining *injeras* on trays, then emptied the food from the clay pots on the top of those *injeras*. That way of serving food wasn't common in our area. However, we enjoyed eating the food and drinking the beer. We all left the tent and headed for Mendefera. We arrived at Mendefera late in the evening, with the bride at hand, spent the evening at the groom's place.

The school year ended and we hadn't done any teaching. We went back to university life in September 1973. As usual, eight of us rented a villa. The university gave us the same stipend and we spent it as we had the last time – once a month we would go to a nightclub and spend the rest of our time on campus. One night, Debesai came home drunk. He laid on his bed, staring at the ceiling, then said, "Oh! The earth is rotating at its fastest speed!"

The first semester went well. At the beginning of the second semester – February 1974 – however, elementary school teachers began a boycott in opposition to a draft sector program that would benefit the rich and to the detriment of the poor. Actually, they had started earlier. The boycott spread to the high schools and won support from teachers there. Gradually, university students got involved and boycotted classes. Next, it spread to labour unions and the civil service. Eventually, disgruntled non-commissioned military officers came up with their own demands and apprehended their senior officers. By then, the dissatisfaction had spread throughout society and the prime minister, Tsehafi Tizaz Aklilu Habtewold resigned. Everybody was stunned for the country had never experienced such political upheaval. It looked like a mountain was about to cave in.

Lij Endalkachew Mekonnen was appointed as the new prime minister. He tried to calm the situation and wanted the university to resume classes. We fourth-year students were eager to finish our education and leave the area. However, things got worse. A military commission was set up to silence the leaders of labour unions and teachers' associations. However, the population was dissatisfied and determined and the government had run out of ways to manipulate. The old political machinations no longer worked.

Muslims demonstrated for their rights. More than 30 percent of the population follow Islam, but no Muslim holiday was observed in the country. Ethiopia was called a "Christian Island" – a wrong and divisive statement. Along with Muslims, Christians, students and workers participated in the demonstration. It had the effect of unifying people.

There were demonstrations all over Addis Ababa. One day, we started a demonstration at the main campus. We went towards Piazza, the city centre, then down to the National Theatre. We passed the American Library at Piazza and turned left towards Churchill Road. The head of the demonstration was near the National Theatre and the tail near Piazza, making it more than two kilometres long. I was near the Arada Post Office when the shooting started. We split up. I followed some students into the post office – there we would be shielded by the high rows of mailboxes. I cannot imagine how we managed to jump over the mailboxes but we did it. However, we found it difficult to do the reverse after the chaos was over. We looked for a door and managed to set ourselves free.

One day, Tegene was walking towards Piazza with a friend. Demonstrating students were moving towards Piazza while police trucks were headed there from the opposite direction. The two friends were trapped in the middle. Tegene's friend opened the door of a parked car and got inside. He sat there reading a newspaper while my poor friend stood confused. Tegene was apprehended, loaded on a truck with some others and taken to a police station, beaten on the way. He was arrested for anti-revolutionary activities. When the station's commander came, Tegene was accused of distributing anti-revolutionary leaflets that he was supposed to have carried in his back pockets. Fortunately, my friend's pants had no back pockets and he was released. He came in on Monday, wearing dark glasses with bruises all over his face. That happened to many university students.

The new prime minister tried to entice the student leaders to end the boycott. However, things were now beyond their control, even if they had agreed. Student demonstrations near the prime minister's office became a daily event. Finally, his office decided to declare the university closed. I went back home.

The time between June and September 1974 was extraordinary. The military committee calling itself the Derg had got rid of the state machine and several important individuals and it had nationalised royal corporations. That was unprecedented in Ethiopia – those on top had been untouchable. Gradually, those close to the emperor and the powerful were jailed. Those who ran to the bush were hunted down and apprehended and those who resisted were killed. On September 12, 1974, the emperor was removed from power, arrested at a military camp. The Derg made itself the head of state and picked a popular general, Michael Andom, as its leader. Ethiopians were astounded. However, union and student leaders and others denounced the Derg for making itself head of state. Nonetheless, the new government held full power.

Nothing was said about reopening the university. Instead, it was rumoured that the Derg was developing a strategy to get rid of students from senior high schools and higher educational institutions. There was going to be a national development campaign, *Zemecha* and students would be sent to rural Ethiopia. It was another setback to my education. However, I wasn't worried about my parents since Wondime was working. He was giving me enough pocket money as well.

Three months had gone by since the emperor was deposed. It was early morning in November 1974. My brother and I had slept in the same bed. When I turned on the radio, I heard the constant beat of a military drum. It was strange and I waited for an announcement. When the announcement came, it started by explaining what some anti-revolutionary elements had done against the interests of the population. It went on to elaborate their actions and concluded by stating that 60 ex-government officials and military officers had been executed. General Andom, the two prime ministers and almost all prominent officials of the emperor, including some soldiers, had been executed. I was shocked and sat dumbstruck. My brother woke up when he heard the names being read and couldn't believe it. We were apprehensive. The Derg had been advocating that the country be developed without bloodshed. Now it shocked the whole nation by massacring the most prominent officials. It would prove to be a very bad precedent.

I left home to see what was happening on the streets. Soldiers were patrolling in jeeps armed with machine guns and mortars. They looked wild and the people looked shocked. The street was very quiet although there were many people. That was the point that we saw the true picture of the military government. It was rumoured that those who had been massacred were buried in a mass grave. Except during the Italian occupation, I had never heard of such a thing. The situation was very scary.

The Derg continued nationalising state and private proprieties, including insurance companies and banks. It had stated that its ideology was Ethiopian socialism, something no one in the country had heard about before. It seemed that some of the intelligentsia was behind the Derg. It was rumoured that the total number of the soldiers in the Derg was 120 and the public was anxious to know who the real leader was.

* * *

Five months had gone by since the emperor had been deposed. *Zemecha* was proclaimed. The objective would be to enhance the political consciousness of the farmers and this would be accomplished by the deployment of senior high school and university students. The campus of the faculty of engineering was designated as the headquarters for the campaign. Additional offices were to be set up at the provincial, *awraja*, and *woreda* levels. In turn, the *woredas* would open smaller units as needed. The average number of students at the *woreda* level was estimated to be 100. The required number of uniforms was issued and a big procession of participants was performed. The names of the core military leaders, including Mengistu Hailemariam and Atnafu Abate, were revealed and the latter were seen to be emotional when observing the procession. I didn't participate in the procession but watched it from the roadside and it was very big.

Zemecha was now officially underway. One evening, I was ironing my clothes and heard a radio announcement giving the names of participants, the places they had been assigned to, and when their work was to commence. I heard my name read and found out that I had been assigned to Munessa Woreda Station in Arsi Province. I felt that my future was unravelling and I was confused. It had already been stated that those who did not take part would be considered to have betrayed Ethiopia and would not be readmitted to the university. I had no choice and regretted leaving my job at Agip

(Ethiopia) Ltd. I could have stayed there and pursued my education through evening classes.

The deployment began in January 1975. I was not worried about being lonely since four students from the department of statistics were going to the same place. Munessa Woreda Station was a little more than 200 kilometres from Addis Ababa. However, the point of the campaign worried me a lot since the Derg wasn't to be trusted. Wondime gave me enough pocket money to get by. Emaye, with tears in her eyes, wished me good luck. Abaye couldn't speak, but I understood he wished me good luck too. I left home as I had many times before and took a taxi to Janmeda and waited to be deployed. Small buses, each with a 25-passenger capacity, had queued at Janmeda, the largest open field in Addis Ababa. I met my fellow campaigners and got into the bus that read "Munessa Woreda Station." Campaigners for six stations in Arsi Province left together. We headed south towards the Rift Valley. The highlands of Addis Ababa lie 3,000 metres above sea level and the Rift Valley about 2,000 metres. The valley has great potential for economic development – particularly in terms of inland transportation, hydropower and agriculture. There are nine lakes, ranging from the northeast to the southwest, and more than five big rivers flowing into and away from adjacent ridges and all these bodies of water could contribute to the prosperity of the nation and to the benefit of local communities. However, no thorough studies have been carried out and its potential remains unfulfilled while people continue to suffer.

Most of the high school students we encountered seemed unexcited and were rather quiet. We passed Akaki, a village 25 kilometres south of Addis Ababa, and then Debre Zeit Town, 48 kilometres south and the base for the Ethiopian Air Force. Lake Hora is at Debre Zeit and a palace for the former emperor was there too.

Lake Hora is also known for its Irecha ceremony. The Oromo's are the largest tribe in Ethiopia and are monotheists. For them, Waqa or God is the law-giving force of nature. About the time of the Ethiopian national holiday, Meskal – the time of the finding of the True Cross – September 27th or 28th – the Oromo's hold a ceremony under very old sacred trees. The most respected elders gather. Animal blood is poured on the roots of the trees and the trunks are anointed with butter and scents. Then food, including coffee, *tella* and roasted meat, is shared beneath the shade of the trees. During the ceremony, participants pray to Waqa or God for health, fertility, favours, good fortune and prosperity. It is known that the Irecha celebrated at Lake Hora is one of two such rites and is named Melka Irecha. The second, Terara Irecha, is celebrated on a mountaintop.

After Debre Zeit, we headed further south and arrived at Modjo Town, 73 kilometres from Addis Ababa. Modjo is surrounded by farmland and cattle grazing as the herdsmen watch over them. The scenery was breathtaking and the air so fresh that it was bewitching. At Modjo, one group of campaigners branched off towards the southwest, along the lakes of the Rift Valley. The rest of us turned east towards Nazareth, known as Adama by the Oromos, and one of the most important cities in the country. Nazareth is in a strategic spot within the Rift Valley, with vehicles coming in from north, south, east and west. The Koka hydropower station, the Wonji sugar factory and the famous resort area of Sodere are nearby.

At Nazareth, we turned south towards Asela Town which was designated as the regional campaign centre. Then we crossed the Awash River and then headed to Dera, a village 25 kilometres from Nazareth. Dera was dry and surrounded by bush and desert plants. We passed Dera and reached Iteya village, 50 kilometres from Nazareth and known for its grain. Iteya and its surroundings had been producing a huge volume of wheat and were owned by the famous landlords of the Ras Biru family. The area had become the centrepiece of university political discussion because of the evictions of farmers. The second group left us at Iteya. We continued on to Asela, 25 kilometres away, riding past heavily cultivated lands and beautiful scenery. While in Addis Ababa, I had heard about the beauty and productivity from my friend Teshome, who came from the area.

We travelled southwest, towards Asela and the regional centre for the campaign. Thirteen kilometres before we arrived at Asela, the third group branched off to the right and went to the campaign station at Ogolcho. That area is still highly productive. When we neared the regional centre, the campaigners from the high schools started singing passionately, telling the people that we had come for them. However, the people looked rather confused and unenthusiastic.

People in that part of the country had been the most maltreated by the previous government. Most had been evicted from their lands and those who remained were tenants. Agriculturally, the region was one of the richest in the nation and had the advantage of proximity to Addis Ababa. But the government had harshly subjugated the people and the farmers did not trust anyone coming from Addis Ababa, including us. We continued our journey. The campaigners were still singing when we reached Asela Town. We got a warm welcome from high school students who had been assigned to go with us and they joined in singing. We were served lunch at the regional centre.

Asela Town was also the headquarters of the Chilalo Agricultural Development Unit (CADU), financed and given technical support by the Swedish International Development Agency (SIDA). Sweden has been providing aid to Ethiopia since the 1950s and that aid included educational, healthcare and agricultural programs for people in rural areas where poverty is most profound. The unit focussed on training farmers and supplying them with agricultural inputs.[17] SIDA pushed for land reform there, but the government was not keen on it. The regional campaign centre had set up its office in the CADU compound.

We set off again, this time with more students. After ten kilometres, we branched off the main road and went towards the west. After crossing the

---

[17] Agricultural inputs typically range from fertilizer, herbicides, insecticides and fungicides, to seeds and stock, to farm machinery and so on. This is not to say that Sweden provided each such item.

Ketar River, we reached a plateau that had a vast mechanised farm on the right and Lake Ziway, one of the largest lakes in the country, lying beyond. The farm was owned by a man called Tedella and was famous for its productivity. There were no trees around, so we had a clear view of the lake. The lake itself is known to be 1,600 metres above sea level, covers about 50,000 hectares and is about ten metres deep. The lake has many islands, including Lakidembel – where the Ark of the Covenant is believed to have been when Axum was invaded by rebels in the 13th century. The view was astounding. We saw no significant traditional farming and not many local people around, indicating that there had been evictions here too. We continued our journey for about 40 kilometres, noting both traditional and mechanised farms.

As we approached Kersa, a village and our campaign station, we noticed that people had gathered on each side of the road to welcome us. The high school students on the bus leaned out the windows and people greeted them. Not everyone seemed jubilant, however. The mass killing had shocked the nation and they thought we were like the Derg. Most of the villagers were traders and the peasants were not to be seen. The few we did see looked wretched and very sad.

We entered a compound surrounded by a wooden fence. There were houses on the right and a tent on the left. The houses were connected and had two large and three small rooms. The two large rooms would be the boys' dorm, one small room would be for the girls, and another small room would be shared by the captain who commanded the station and by the administrator. The fifth was for office use. The kitchen lay between the houses and the tent was meant for dining and meetings.

A meeting was held that night after super. The captain read out the rules and regulations. He told us that we would be working with the peasants, digging and cleaning wells, teaching basic education to farmers and – after land reform was proclaimed – working on the formation of farmers' associations. He also read out the names of the students in each dorm. Boys could not go near the girls' dorm after eight in the evening. He also told us that our shelter was temporary and that we would move to the permanent dorm which was under construction. I was assigned to the biggest dorm. We had a mattress, a blanket and two sheets. The dormitory looked like the one at the Laboratory School, but there were no beds.

Sleep-talking was very common and I did talk in my sleep. One night, soon after we arrived, one of the high school campaigners got up in the middle of the room and gave a lecture on his girlfriend and how much he already missed her. Some talked about Tejbets – the local wine bars in Addis Ababa and the jokes they had learned. Some talked in Amharic, others in Afan Oromo and some in Tigrigna and some in English.

The make-up of the campaigners was very mixed. We were university and high school students, urban and rural, children of landlords and tenants, mature and very young. I was the oldest in the group and was chosen to be the secretary. Most campaigners, including the university students, respected and listened to me because of my age. Three substations had been made ready and another three would be opening soon. The captain nominated two girls and ten boys for a special trip and I was one of them. A date was set to begin.

Teferra – he had been my roommate in Addis Ababa – was very humorous. He teased Girma, a high school student from Asela, calling him a goat. One morning, Teferra had waked up early. He lay on his back and was yawning so much that tears flowed. Girma got up from his mattress and sat on Teferra's stomach. Girma looked at his face and asked him why the tears. Teferra said that he was deeply sorry that a man had been created like a goat and so was crying for him.

Before we left for our visit to substations, the captain had gone to the regional centre to attend to some administrative matters. He was to return before we left. However, he did not return that day and was still not there at eight that evening. We were worried about him and about the trip. The administrator and I discussed the matter. We thought that if he didn't come, the boys would go and the girls would stay behind. We would be in remote areas and it could be dangerous. The girls were not happy, but I did not want to take responsibility if anything bad happened to them. There were two firearms at the station and I decided to carry the rifle with me, although I had never fired one before. The rifle was cocked and ready for shooting. We thought it should be disabled but neither of us knew how to do that. Finally, we decided to fire a shot close to the floor, so the sound wouldn't scare the students or anyone else who might be around. The administrator did fire the rifle, but he didn't do it close enough to the floor, so it didn't muffle the sound. Students and the villagers surrounded the office and demanded to know what had happened. We tried to calm them, but they were very tense and it took us a while to pacify them. After midnight, I heard the sound of a car approaching. The gate was opened and the car came in. I waited. I heard the captain's voice, was relieved that the girls could go with us and went back to my mattress.

The captain woke us up at five the next morning. I welcomed him and he teased me for thinking about leaving the girls behind, but he also appreciated that I had thought about them. He asked the 12 of us take food and drink with us. We left at six. The first trip was to Waji Genbo, a very remote village. We rode through forests with monkeys leaping from tree to tree and horses enjoying the wilderness. We were told that the hyenas weren't daring enough to bite the horses – the horses would chase them away. There were rivers and brooks all around and their sound was very pleasant. The water was clean and we could clearly see the bottom. We also saw snakes – by the water, in piles of stone and in the brush – but they weren't dangerous. The campaigners from the area showed us lands that belonged to landlords in Addis Ababa who had never seen the place. Their tenants would spend days delivering the crops to them. During that time, they had to feed and shelter themselves. Those with relatives would have places to stay. Those without had to sleep by side of the road. Some landlords were compassionate and would provide shelter, but getting food depended on the generosity of harsh housemaids. Somewhat similarly, the farmers would feed the tax collectors during the period they stayed in the area. They were also paid a per diem. They would stay until they felt they had been well treated by the tenants – even if they had finished collection earlier.

The first six hours were not tiring. The air was fresh and dense forests blocked the sunlight. We took a break in the middle of the day, had our sandwiches and drank river water. It was fresh and we enjoyed it. We rested for an hour and resumed our journey. The next trip was a bit tiring, but we managed it anyway. We reached our destination at five that afternoon.

Guest rooms had been arranged. Local people had also prepared supper and drinks for us. We spent the evening talking to the farmers. Most of the people who approached us were landlords. The tenants were shy. We organized a meeting of the farmers the next day and the captain explained to them that we were there to help the tenants not the landlords. He expressed the government's deep concern for their sufferings under the previous regime. They did not seem impressed. The land, after all, was still in the hands of the landlords. The captain also told them that a group of campaigners would be there very soon and that they had to be prepared to work with them. When I read their faces that time, I saw some signs of encouragement and eagerness for a better future. We visited the surrounding areas and talked to the farmers personally. The place had no school, no health centre and no other amenities.

We spent two nights in Waji Genbo and left early next morning for Degaga, a village to the southwest. The trip involved going down a lot of steep hills and walking over stones and was very tiresome. The land was covered with forest and the area was very fertile, with fresh rivers flowing everywhere. The fertility was amazing in a country so known for starvation. We travelled less than the first day but were dead tired, mainly due to the terrain. I was concerned about finishing the journey and did not enjoy the trip at all. By the time we reached our stop, I was totally exhausted. Elementary school students and villagers there greeted us with chanting and dancing. By rural standards, it was a well-populated place. There was a forestry plant in the area and it had many employees. We were provided with a room to rest in and stayed indoors that afternoon since we were very tired.

There were many landlords in the area, many of them "Neftegnas" from another part of the country. Normally, Neftegnas are thought to be Amharas from central and northern Ethiopia, but from what I saw in Arsi, the Oromos from Shewa have settled in significant numbers, depriving the indigenous people from their ancestral lands. The local people were poor tenants who looked hopeless, having been pushed to the margin and beyond by previous governments. We didn't see many tenants in town. Most of those who received us were landlords, teachers and students.

When we woke up the next morning, we saw two men dragging a big sheep into our room. We asked them what it was for and they said it was for us to slaughter. We refused to take it, suspecting they were doing it in anticipation of favours. They insisted and we said we had to discuss amongst ourselves first. We held a meeting at which some said it wouldn't change their minds whether we ate it or not, some said we should not eat it, and some remained in between. After a very long discussion, we decided to take it and it was slaughtered. It was big and really good and it took days to finish eating it.

The area was rich in agricultural and forestry products. The forest was dense and the trees so tall that it was difficult to get out once in. There were wild and fierce bulls roaming the forest – they scared even the wild animals. Someone showed me the 400 hectares of agricultural land that my landlady had owned. She had never seen it, but her tenants delivered the crops to her door every year. We visited the surrounding areas and talked to the people *en masse*, in groups and individually. We also talked to the teachers since they could play a role with the campaigners who would be following us. We spent three nights and left on the fourth day.

Next we went to Meti, a small village to the northeast. It took us only an hour and a half. It was a relatively dry area. The people looked poorer and had not prepared so much for our arrival. We talked to people and visited some places. We spent a night in a grain store, sleeping on the paved floor. I couldn't sleep due to the roughness of the surface, but some students slept like the dead and were snoring the whole night, which I really envied. We spent the night and left early next day to Kersa, our station.

We went to Kersa on Thursday, March 4, 1975. We had walked for about two hours and now it was eight in the morning and time to listen to the news. The captain turned on the radio. After the news, we heard the sound of military drum being beaten and we thought something serious was coming. It was the proclamation of the land reform. The captain put the radio in the middle of us, got his gun ready and patrolled. All land in Ethiopia had been nationalised. A farmer could not hold more that ten hectares and a farmer's association would be established for every 800 hectares of land. The change was radical and a big blow to the landlords. It was obvious that implementing the proclamation would be a challenge. We knew what to face and were ready for it. We resumed our journey and reached Kersa in two hours.

March 6, 1975, was a Saturday. It was a big market day, with farmers and landlords coming in from the surrounding areas and buyers coming from afar. We had been preparing to hold a land proclamation rally by the market and when the market was busiest, we arrived, singing and shouting slogans and dancing around the market. The landlords looked very angry and the tcnants looked tense but happy. Neither group was sure that land reform would actually happen. The landlords were against it and the peasants shyly supported the change. It was difficult to predict the outcome since the landlords had sons who were part of the Derg regime. However, there were some radicals from the land-owning families, including from the aristocracy.

The first three groups of ten campaigners each were dispatched to Gumguma, Munessa and Egu substations – all two hours travel from Kersa. The groups were comprised of campaigners from Addis Ababa and Arsi and had university as well as high school students. All campaigners started organising peasant associations, cleaning wells, and making sure that grain traders weren't exploiting farmers at the market. The grain traders were known to cheat peasants when they weighed their crops. The sons of grain traders were assigned the task. The government had deployed experts on land distribution to different parts of the country. The person assigned to our area was knowledgeable about the place – he had been born and brought up there. He was Oromo from Shewa originally.

One day, I went with two other campaigners to organise peasants' associations in the area within two hours' distance of Kersa Station. The task took us the whole day since some farmers refused to be grouped with farmers they had problems with and we had to talk with their leaders to convince them. The day went by and we decided to spend the night in the forest. Some peasants living in the highlands have two huts, one in the highlands for the summer and another in the lowlands for the winter, so we managed to find an empty hut to spend the night in. We were sitting around a fire, warming ourselves, when two farmers came to us, dragging a sheep. We asked them what the sheep was for and they said it was for us. We refused to take it, but they insisted. However, we had seen how poor the peasants were and knew that they could not afford it and thus decided not to accept it. Finally, they took back the sheep. After an hour, they came back with food. While we were eating, one of them said, "We believed today that you are with us." We asked him why and he said, "If you had accepted the sheep, we would have taken you to be the same as our ex-masters – the landlords and tax collectors."

We found the farmers very thoughtful and sensible. They spoke briefly and in metaphors. The conflicts between landlords and tenants were increasing daily. In most cases, the police sided with the landlords. We had seen that in Kersa, where the police commander was always creating problems for us and intimidating campaigners whenever he had the chance. He always sided with the landlords. Once, he said in Amharie to a campaigner,

wuha yetefaw gind adergihalehou!

which meant, "When I get through with you, you're going to be like a log floating in fresh water" – in other words, dead in the water.

In the hope of solving the problem between the police force and the peasants' associations, a meeting was held in Asela. Administrative and police officials came. During the discussion, a peasant said, "It is said in our tradition that when fire boils water it does so under the protection of the pot. If there was no pot, the water could easily put out the fire. Similarly, the landlords are giving us trouble because the police force is protecting them. Some of them run to you. They are our class enemies and you're their benefactors."

The government invited peasant associations' leaders to Addis Ababa, hoping to entice them into co-operating and to indoctrinate them. They stayed for a week. We met those who had gone from our area and saw that they were extremely happy about the way the government had treated them. They had stayed in fine hotels and attended a banquet where they dined on *tej* and raw meat and more. They were completely and positively changed towards the government. Their morale was boosted and they were ready to accept any order from above.

Meanwhile, at the station, there were frequent frictions between the high school campaigners. Sometimes, they quarrelled about regional differences and sometimes about ethnic backgrounds. The responsibility for diffusing the tension lay with the university students. The students from rural areas were hard workers, while those from Addis Ababa were rhetorical and irritating. Sometimes, ethnic tensions flared between the Amharas and Oromos. The latter originated mainly in Shewa Province. Actually, most of them were from land-owning families and it seemed some of the instigators were frustrated because of the land reform. We held meetings, criticised their actions and told them that both sides would be losers. In many cases they listened to us.

All kinds of liquor were sold on market days. Farmers would drink a lot then and disturb the village. Once, we were organising militias and asked for young peasants who didn't drink. The peasants laughed and told us it would be impossible to find any. *Every* man drank, though the amount differed, they said. We discussed the seriousness of the issue and decided to stop it, at least on market days. We prohibited the sale of alcohol on market days. The women nearly cried – they lived on it. We insisted and resorted to force to implement it. That worked for few days. However, we later understood that it was too harsh for the women who lived by it and so rescinded the ban.

Early one morning, I was lying on my mattress. Tadele, another campaigner called me and said that some one was waiting for me outside. When I left the room, I saw a man standing outside. He looked destitute. I went up to him and asked if there was anything I could do to help him. He told me his name was Morki and that a landlord had taken his horse by force during the previous government and had refused to give it back. I asked him many questions and he insisted that it had been taken by force and for no reason. Tadele spoke both Amharic and Afan Oromo and so I asked him to go with me to take the case to the village court.

We told the judge what the peasant had told us. The judge was willing to handle the case fairly. He knew we were campaigners sent by the Derg and that the Derg had executed 60 prominent ex-officials. During the previous government, a judge would have been less likely to treat peasants and landlords equally under the law in that part of the country. Peasants there were treated like subjects and their properties confiscated by landlords whenever they liked. The judge asked us to return on the morrow and said he would send a subpoena to the defendant that same day, so we left the court. We went to the court the next day and the defendant, Aboret, was there too. He admitted that he had taken the horse and said that he had sold field grass to the plaintiff and when the man couldn't pay his debt, he had given him the horse instead. The judge asked Morki to bring three witnesses and set a date.

Three peasants came on the appointed date and testified separately. The first testified that Aboret had gone to Morki's house and told him to get the horse ready and then took it and never returned. The judge asked, "Can somebody go to somebody else's house and order him to make his horse ready?" The witness said, "Your Honour, are you forgetting that even a man was treated like a horse at that time?" The judge was silent for a moment. All three witnesses gave the same testimony and it seemed to me that they had decided their positions before they came to the court. The judge gave his verdict: the defendant had to give the horse back. The defendant said that he had sold the horse months ago. Then the judge asked both men to bring two people each next week and to come with an estimate on the price of the horse. After a week, Morki came alone, while Aboret came with his own two people. The judge ordered the two to estimate a price. They estimated 40 Birr, which shocked us since the price of a horse would never be that low. We were very disappointed, but had nothing to say and blamed Morki for not bringing his own men. We left the court, said goodbye to Morki and went to the campaign station.

Five days later, Morki came back to the station early in the morning and had me called from my mattress. When I went to see him, he looked wretched and I felt very sorry for him. I went back and took my old shirt and gave it to him. He told me that he had seen the horse on the way. I called Tadele and the three of us headed to the place. The horse was not to be found. We went to see the current owner, found him home and explained the case to him. He shouted that someone had told him that a local peasant had been looking at his horse. "How could a local peasant look at my horse?" He was an Oromo from Shewa Province. We asked him to cool down and sign a simple statement confirming that he had the horse. He did so. He said that the horse was young and energetic. It had been three months since he bought it and he had been feeding it barley ever since. He had ridden it to funerals and when visiting friends. We thanked him for his cooperation and took the statement to the judge.

The judge called Aboret, showed him the statement and gave his final verdict: the peasant would get his horse back and Aboret was to give the money back to the current owner. Aboret agreed and a date was set for handing over the horse.

Many peasants came to court that day. We had heard that no local peasant had ever won a court case. The horse was there, full of energy and ready to take off if anyone was daring enough to ride it. The current owner's son had fallen off the horse on the way and his face was covered with blood. The owner begged Morki to sell him the horse. He offered 300 Birr, but Morki refused vehemently. The owner blamed me for his son's bloody face. I told him that I was very sorry for his son but I couldn't help him to get the horse back. He handed over the horse. It was a sensational moment for the peasants. Poor Morki was extremely happy and the situation had been the talk of the area for sometimes.

Later, early on another morning, Morki came to the station for the third time and had me called. I went to see him. He was proudly wearing the shirt I gave him. He took me aside and said, "In our culture, if a man likes another man, he will give him his second wife. If the man is married, however, he goes and visits that man's wife. So I am here to ask you to take one of my wives – if you're not married – or to visit yours if you are married." I thanked him very much but declined his offer. He felt very sorry and left. I never saw him again.

A week later, I met Aboret walking. He took me to the side of the road and gently said, "One day, I lost my mule and looked for it until dark but couldn't find it and so I went home and slept. In the middle of the night, the mule groaned in desperation for there were hyenas nearby. My horse at home heard the sound, jumped over the fence, chased the hyenas away and came back with the mule. If a peasant comes for that horse tomorrow, please don't force me to hand it over." I smiled, told him not to worry about it and left.

I was assigned to the substation at Degaga, where we had eaten the big sheep during our first visit. There were ten of us and I was the team leader. The substation was expected to have its own station soon and we were sent to do the groundwork. I was the only university student in the group. The rest were high school students and they respected and listened to me. At night, we read Marxist books and discussed the ideology. We were very much convinced by the principle "From each according to his ability, to each according to his needs." I read the books aloud and the boys listened and asked questions. The concepts were very hard and most of the time we had difficulties understanding them. During the day, we visited the leaders of peasants' associations and discussed their problems. We tried to teach the people the basics of the Afan Oromo language, but they refused to learn and asked for Amharic instead. They said that it would be helpful to learn Amharic language instead of theirs for mass communication. It took us sometimes to convince them, which we finally did through the help of the leaders of the peasants' associations. We set up a town committee, comprising villagers, teachers, forestry workers and campaigners. The committee's mandate was to manage the town's security. On Saturdays, farmers would drink and create disruptions. That bewildered the town. The committee set a rule that farmers who came from out of town had to leave by six in the evening. If they refused, they would be jailed. It worked.

Campaigners had been also deployed at the Meti substation, close to Degaga. One day, three of them were going to Kersa Station. Mesele was walking fast carrying a long stick with an iron ring at the end. Daniel, the most joyful and the youngest of all campaigners, teased Mesele for walking like a horse. Mesele kept walking fast and Daniel followed him, still teasing. This time Mesele got irritated and struck backward, hitting Daniel right on his kidney.

119

Daniel fell down. They carried him to a clinic, but he died on the way which was a tragic incident. Mesele was jailed and we felt sorry for him, too, since his deed wasn't intentional.

We went to the regional capital for the burial. A Dutchman, an expert at the forestry plant in Degaga, gave us a ride. As he was driving beside one of the commercial farms, he said, "If this farm was efficiently and effectively cultivated, it could produce in a year the same volume as the whole of Netherlands." He expressed his disappointment at finding so much misery in the midst of such vast and productive land. We couldn't answer – it was mystery to everybody. We reached the burial site. Daniel's parents were devastated. His father cried when he saw us. We couldn't control our tears. People at the burial cried bitterly. The next day, early in the morning, the father came to where we were sleeping and cried out, "I trusted you to take care of my son, but you abandoned him and betrayed me." It was a very sad moment for me. We spent two days there and returned to the campaign.

When the campaign was about two months old, about 100 new campaigners came to Degega Station. We talked to them about disarming the landlords before we returned to Kersa and we agreed on the principle. We called the leaders of the peasants' associations and shared the idea with them. The local farmers were very excited, while the Neftegnas were suspicious, but they had no choice but to accept. We agreed not mention the matter to the associations' members until the final day. The leaders sat together in a circle to make a vow. They put a piece of dried dung in the centre of the circle and put wheat seeds on top. They also put three crossed spears over the dung, then made an oath not to tell the secret to any body. As one voice they vowed, "If anyone tells the secret, let him be deprived of crops and animals. If one of the spears misses him, let not the second, and if the second misses him too, let the third miss him not." A date was set to disarm the landlords. According to the agreement, the leaders would organise their own meetings and tell their members about disarming the landlords. Then they would lead the peasants to the landlords who were suspected of having guns and would ask them to hand over their arms. If refused, they would record the names and go on to the rest.

The leader of the nearest association and three campaigners, including me, were assigned to the town. At six in the morning on the day for the disarmament, the three of us went to the designated place. There was nobody in sight including the leader. It was rather quiet that morning. We didn't see anybody and guessed the people had been told about the disarmament. We waited for an hour and neither the leader nor the peasants appeared. We waited for three more hours and nobody came. Finally, we decided to leave. Campaigners deployed to other associations did very well and met little resistance. No incidents happened and we were happy for that.

The next morning, we were told that the leaders who conducted successful firearms collections had been jailed by a police force that had come from Asela during the night. The police had been informed by the ran-away teachers during the night that local peasants had invaded the premises of the ex-landlords and killed many of them. We went straight to the temporary jail and demanded their release. In the meantime, we could hear the peasants groaning – they were beaten by the policemen. The policemen told us to leave the area, but we refused to do so until they were released. We argued that if anybody was to be jailed, it should be us, not the peasants. The police refused to listen to us and tried to scare us away by stealthily firing shots at the sky. So we said that we were afraid for our lives because of the gunshots by the landlords who refused to hand over their firearms. We decided not to leave under any circumstances.

Late in the afternoon, Colonel Zinabu, the head of the regional campaign centre, arrived in an American jeep. We were very pleased and applauded him. He went into the temporary police station and tried to negotiate with the police commander, a major, for the release of the leaders. The major refused to set them free. The colonel stayed until late that night but was not successful. Finally, he asked us to go to our camp and come back the next day. He stayed with us for the night. The next morning, we went to the police station again. The colonel sat with the major for the whole morning, trying to negotiate the release of the prisoners, but he didn't succeed. He gave up and finally left, very angry. He told us that he had decided to go to report the matter to the headquarter in Addis Ababa. We stayed at the police station the whole day, then went to our camp late in that night.

The next morning, we went to the police station again, but there was nobody there – it was totally abandoned. We heard from local peasants that the policemen had taken the leaders to Asela. We also heard that the peasants had walked, carrying the firearms on their heads, while the policemen rode on horseback. They were treated like captives on the battlefield and we were very disappointed with the government. Shortly after, we left our camp and went to the regional capital. All the campaigners from Degaga and Kersa stations left for Asela.

We camped at the compound of Ras Darge School, at the regional capital. Campaigners from other stations joined us and soon there were more than 300 of us. Colonel Zinabu visited our temporary shelters and encouraged us to stay steadfast. The peasants were now in the regional prison. We spent two nights waiting, but nothing happened. On the third day, a group of three soldiers – a major, a non-commissioned officer from the Derg, and a third from the ministry of inland administration came to town. However, nothing happened on the fourth day either. On the fifth day, that group invited the campaigners' leaders for discussions and I was one of them. We told the group that no criminal act was involved and nobody had been killed. We also told the group that the disarmament was voluntary and those refused to hand over their firearms were not adversely treated but that their names were recorded. They listened to us carefully, but never commented – not in favour of the peasants and not against them – and we left filled with uncertainty. No action was taken the sixth day. If nothing happened, we were determined to quit the campaign and go home.

On the seventh day, the peasants were released. They jumped with joy and we embraced them. It was a very memorable occasion. The group advised us to go back to our stations and substations and we did so happily. The peasants travelled by car with the group to Degaga through Nazareth, Modjo and Arsi Negelle. By the time we arrived back, the group had called a meeting and had declared that the disarmament action was right and those who refused should hand over their firearms as soon as possible and work with the associations.

Everything settled down. Then the associations' leaders fined those who had violated the oath 300 Birr each. That was quite a pinch. They also fined those who had collaborated with the policemen. The landlords had entertained the policemen with roasted meat. Those who contributed to purchasing the bull were fined 40 Birr each. Those who barbecued the meat and the women who contributed liquor were fined ten Birr each. Finally, those who refused to hand over their firearms co-operated. The associations were strengthened and people felt light-hearted. We closed the substation, handed over our responsibilities to the new campaigners and returned to our centre, Kersa Station.

Conjurers were the targets of attack by campaigners in some other areas. As a result, the conjurers' supporters killed some campaigners. That did not happen in our area because there wasn't much said about them. On the other hand, we did encounter families that were forcing their daughters to marry against their will. There were two traditions in the area. According to the first case, old men could marry very young girls, provided they paid the requisite amount of money to the girls' families. In the second case, brothers forced their sisters to marry, in exchange for the "groom's" sister. We tried persuasion and then forbade both practices. There was no resistance, but there were some complaints.

Not long after we returned to Kersa, the military government started attacking campaigners. The government accused us of reading "communist" books and exploiting peasants for our own gain. We were amazed – the Derg called its own ideology "Ethiopian socialism," whatever that was. It had nationalised land and set up peasants' associations. These were all in accordance with the beliefs and principles of socialism and communism. We thought that the government was doing one thing and saying another. We also thought that some elements within the Derg were against the land reform and against the campaigners' disarmament project. The government could have communicated its dissatisfactions to us – but instead we learned about it through the media. After the government's propaganda attack, the landlords laughed at us. This government's action led campaigners throughout the country to leave their stations. Everybody left, except for a very few in very remote places. I went home and joined my parents.

One day while I was in Addis Ababa, the radio drum began to beat. It sounded like the usual drumming that would be heard after a summary execution and I waited for the news. I was terrified. After few comments on the objectives of the revolution, the condemnation of some Derg members followed. It was stated that the condemned had acted independently, against the will of the people, and had tried to derail the revolution. What they were alleged to have done was read. Then it was announced that they had been executed. One of them, Captain Sisay, had been a contender for the leadership. The revolution was beginning to consume its own.

Three months went by. I did nothing during that time. Finally, the government issued a decree ordering campaigners to return to their stations. Those who refused would be considered to have betrayed Ethiopia. Campaigners in Addis Ababa never flinched. As the days went by, though, rumours came that some campaigners were returning. The Munessa campaigners from Addis Ababa held a meeting to decide on our future action. We were concerned about what would happen at our station if some returned early and others late – that would inflame disagreement amongst the campaigners. We decided to send representatives to the regional campaign centre and to co-ordinate a concerted return, if a return was decided on. I was one of those elected to go.

Wondime gave me some money and I left with seven others. As soon as we reached Asela, we met Colonel Zinabu and he gave us shelter but no food. The regional campaign centre had not set a date for re-mobilization and we decided to wait at our shelter until the announcement. Two weeks went by and my money was gone. Biniyam, another campaigner, decided to go back to Addis Ababa for the weekend. I wrote a note to Wondime that said, "The money that you gave me when I left home is gone. You are the only person in this world that I can go back to for more money. Please send me some money through the person that delivers this note to you." Unfortunately, Wondime had left Addis Ababa to visit a friend. Getaneh, my best friend from Lab School, was visiting my parents at the time. He had graduated from the university and was teaching at a high school in Bale Province. At the time, he had been deployed as an administrator of another campaign station. He read my note, and the next day, he was at my shelter in Asela. We embraced again and again – it had been such a long time since we had been together. He spent a night in a hotel, and the next day he gave me 50 Birr and then left for Addis. That was a lot of money and a testament of his friendship. He is a Gondare and is still one of my best friends.

We returned to Kersa after another two weeks in Asela. Almost everybody got there at the same time. The new building had been completed and was spacious and clean. The compound was big enough for us to relax and play volleyball. We held a general meeting to clear any differences that had come up at the time we left or when we returned. Some wondered why we had left in the first place if we had to return. There was some truth to that, but we knew that after the government issued a decree ordering campaigners to return to their stations we had no choice but to return. The disagreement finally subsided. Those who had to go to their substations left shortly.

This time, most of our work focussed on literacy and on orienting peasants on how to run their associations and on giving them whatever support they required. Some peasants did not believe that they had their own land. Some of the government's actions were unnecessary – like the nationalisation of flourmills and petty private properties, which was too technical for the associations to manage. As well, peasants started selling their oxen, fearing that they too would be nationalised. We thought the latter was serious since it hurt agriculture. We discussed the matter with the leaders and agreed that peasants who wanted to sell their oxen should first get permission from their associations and then produce that permission at the market if requested. We deployed ourselves at cattle markets and asked for the permits. Those who couldn't produce them were sent away. It worked.

The government organized a mass rally in Kersa. Peasants were invited and the minister of land reform and other officials had come to the area. There was a platform for speeches. The speakers included a representative from the Munessa campaigners. I was chosen to speak on behalf of the campaigners. At the time, the campaigners believed that the enemies of the Ethiopian peoples were three – imperialism, feudalism and bureaucratic capitalism. On the other hand, the minister said in his speech that the Ethiopian Peoples Revolutionary Party (EPRP) was the major enemy of the Ethiopian people. It was rumoured that he was a member of the All Ethiopian Socialist Movement (MEISON). The two parties had been set up by Ethiopian students abroad. The EPRP went head to head against the Derg and MEISON supported it for a while expecting to take power eventually. I thought that the rally had been organized to win the people to the government side fearing that the campaigners were working otherwise.

Jabir, a second-year university student at our station, was boasting of his revolutionary activities at the university. He knew we had attended classes during our third year while he had withdrawn from first year. He called Desalegne, my friend, a saboteur and they were ready to fight when some campaigners got in between them and had them go their separate ways. Jabir insulted Desalegne, who got very angry and decided to confront him. Later, Desalegne went to downtown to look for Jabir in the small bars since Jabir was notorious for his drinking. Finally, Desalegne came to know the name of the bar Jabir had gone to. He went to the bar, sat down and ordered a drink. He had a sharp stone in his pocket and a few minutes later, he jumped on Jabir and hit him in the head with the stone. Jabir was seriously hurt and his face was covered with blood. Again, campaigners got in between and stopped the fight. These kinds of incidents were common in the camp.

There was a clear difference between the urban and the rural students at the station. Some of the urban students drank a lot, talked a lot and produced little. The majority of rural students worked hard, talked a little and produced more. The rural students were drinking too but didn't end up in ditches. When the rural students got angry they were ready for a fight – they had no tolerance and wanted no discussion so senior students like me had to diffuse the tension. Most of the rural students were innocents, but a few were really demonic and would manipulate the others to fight against the urban students. The urban students were very tolerant, but they were also sarcastic and given to rhetoric. It was a challenge for us, the senior campaigners, to calm both sides.

In the middle of the second campaign year, third- and fourth-year university students were called upon to teach in the nation's high schools. I was not called and didn't know why. My friends at the department of statistics all departed, leaving me behind. Soon after they left, I was assigned to the Munessa substation. There was an old woman, Emahoy, who sold local beer in Munessa village. We frequently went to her place to drink *tella*, local beer. She was very entertaining. She was Amhara. She pretended we were her slaves and gave us different names. She called me '*Azatz*', commander. She also instructed us how to respond when called upon. Emahoy was around 80 years old and seems to have lived during slavery time in Ethiopia. It is believed that slave trade was common in Ethiopia until the mid 19th century. Slaves were sold to markets all over the world. When I was young, I had heard about slavery in Ethiopia. Gindebert, a village about 125 kilometres west of Addis Ababa was a famous slave market. Emahoy made me responsible for her "slaves" and whenever she needed something like firewood, she told me to give her "slaves" the order. She never asked us for money after we had drunk *tella,* but we knew how much we owed her and paid appropriately. The girls knew where she kept her house-bank and stored the money accordingly.

Ten of us from Munessa substation travelled to visit Lake Langano, at the foot of the hills nearby. The lake is 215 kilometres southwest of Addis Ababa and is one of the most frequently visited resort areas in Ethiopia. It has beautiful hotels and breathtaking scenery. Recreation and boating by the halves and important officials were frequent during the time of Emperor Haile Selassie I. We rented two donkeys to carry our food and nightclothes. The lake looked close from the top of the hill and we were encouraged. First, we walked down a hill that was so steep that my legs shook all the way down. I have never had any problem walking up and down the most difficult hill in the area – Koso Bankola, named after the bitter-tasting traditional medicine against tapeworms. Then we walked on flat land for about two hours, until we reached the forest in front of the lake. The forest that looked so small from the top of the hill was not so easy to cross and took us more than an hour. We arrived at an open area around the lake – it was very beautiful. As we got closer, we saw a deer nearby, eating grass, but it ran into the lake. We dragged it out and slaughtered it for food. The meat was not tasty though.

A villa by the lake belonged to a prominent ex-business man, Tedella Desta. We were told that he used to come on weekends, sometimes with Tsehafi Tizaz Aklilu Habtewold, the ex-prime minister, and that they enjoyed their time at the villa. After the revolution, however, the properties were ransacked and peasants had carried away the sofas. We moved into the villa for a few days. It had all the facilities but none were functional. The surroundings were gorgeous – beautiful green trees on one side and the lake on the other. It was very quiet, except for the alluring calls of the birds in the trees. It was the perfect place for vacationing.

In the neighbourhood, we met a young Canadian missionary who spoke perfect Amharic and we argued with him about politics and religion. He was against the ideology of the Derg – socialism and communism – but we argued otherwise. We even tried to convince him that the Bible was contradictory. After that, he avoided us – he understood that we were die-hard communists and that there was no room for conversion. That was the political fashion of the day and we were too naïve to absorb anything else. We spent a week by the lake and headed for our substation. The National Development Campaign or *Zemecha* was coming to an end. We stayed few days at the substation, visiting peasants' associations and enjoying *tella* at Emahoy's place. Finally, we decided to move on to Kersa and went to the old woman to say goodbye. She cried and we felt very sorry about leaving her.

The campaign finished after two years. It was not worth it – not because we didn't do anything but because it was not appreciated and not recognised. In all, three years of my university life had been wasted. Some students never took part in the campaign, some had connections and used them to get assigned to Addis Ababa, and some took jobs and left early. It was a disorganised program that was forced on those who had no options. It seemed to have worked for the Derg though – it got rid of students in Addis Ababa, students who would have given the Derg a very hard time. The worst part was that some students died during the campaign. It was fruitless as far as I was concerned.

* * *

The university had arranged a two-month crash program so we could graduate. By then, graduation was long overdue and I was not excited. The graduation ceremony was put off till the coming year and I wasn't interested at all. University life had become an ordeal for most students; many quit and left the country. There was too much politics involved – that helped neither the students nor the country. The emperor was responsible for some of the messes. He was worshiped by many and could have introduced political change for the better. The people would have received it gladly. He could have made himself the head of state and let the people choose their own parliamentarians and a prime minister. Instead, he considered himself eternal and didn't prepare anyone to take over after him. That was why the power landed in the hands of incompetents. Most of the soldiers that took power were incompetent at governing, loquacious and rejected by the men in their own barracks. They organized the *Zemecha* to get rid of us – they wanted us far away so they could consolidate their power.

Seven years after I began university, I completed it – it took as long as it takes to get a Ph.D. in some countries. Sixteen of us graduated in a batch, all males. At least, my parents were still alive. They were extremely happy about my graduating. Emaye kissed the ground many times, stretched her hands, stared up at the sky and thanked God again and again. Abaye looked very proud.

Graduates of statistics tried our best to find work. We organized ourselves into three groups. Group I included those with very high grade-point averages – that group could find work within the university because there were enough posts for them. The group promised not to look for jobs anywhere else. Group II comprised graduates who had planned to return to their old jobs. They too promised not to look for jobs anywhere else. Group III included those who had no job offers. I was in that group. Our group formed a committee to look for jobs. Whenever a job was identified, the committee would hold a lottery for those interested and the lucky one would be accompanied by one with a lower grade-point average. Both would register for interviews. During the interview, the one with the lower average would act unenthusiastic about the job – which would enhance the other man's prospects. The scheme worked well and the Ethiopian Roads Authority hired me as a transport economist.

CHAPTER SIX

The Ethiopian Roads Authority (ERA) was responsible for building and maintaining the national road network. I was placed in the planning branch which was under the planning and programming division. There were about 20 employees in the division at the time – economists, engineers, budget analysts, draftsmen and clerks. My duties included doing economic feasibility studies, part of the preparation for building and improving the roads. I had to travel to any place in Ethiopia where roads might be improved. ERA was initially established by the Americans and the branch was well organized for field tasks. Tents, furniture and utensils were available and a pair of field boots was issued once a year for each participant. The necessary vehicles, usually a Land Rover or a station wagon, and a Unimog Mercedes Benz would be arranged through the car pool. The station wagon was used to transport experts and the Unimog for equipment and utensils. In addition, there was a provision for hiring cooks.

My first assignment was on part of a team to study the Mota-Bahir Dar Road in the Province of Gojam, in the north-western part of the county. The project road was about 110 kilometres long and the planning branch head, Mengesha, was going as a team leader. First, the team had to arrange for letters to be delivered to the regional administrative and government development offices to request their collaboration. Furthermore, the team had to purchase food items from the nationalised processing factories. That required official letters too. The groundwork took three to five days and was usually time-taking and meant back-scratching.

Mengesha was a transport economist and he was going so that he could orient me on field studies. An engineer, Woldeselassie two drivers and a cook were also part of the team. The three of us travelled in the Land Rover, while the cook travelled in the Unimog, which also carried fuel, camping equipment, tents, utensils and bottled gas for cooking. The Unimog was very useful, for we could use its winches to drag it out and we could also use them on the station wagon when it was stuck in a ditch and or on a muddy road.

We started out by going northwest from Addis Ababa. As we travelled, we were farther and farther above sea level.[18] In the time, we would pass the Blue Nile River, 195 kilometres from Addis Ababa. The Blue Nile joins the White Nile River at Khartoum, forming the longest river in the world. We crossed Mount Entoto, the best place from which to see the panorama of Addis Ababa and Saint Mary's Church, built in 1885. We drove by Debre Libanos, 100 kilometres from Addis Ababa. Debre Libanos has the country's 13th century monastery and the Jama Gorge on the background. Thousands of people make an annual pilgrimage to Debre Libanos. We reached the 30-kilometre point on Blue Nile Gorge, descended to the bottom of it and then drove to the top. That took us about one hour.

---

[18] Ethiopia's highest peak is at Ras Dashen, about 5,000 metres above sea level and its lowest point is the Dallol Depression, more than 100 metres below sea level.

We reached Dejen Town. It lies at the top of the gorge. A 230-kilometre paved road connects Dejen and Addis Ababa. Five kilometres from Dejen, we branched off the main road and went another 36 kilometres on a gravel road to Bichena Town. The women in Gojam had shaved their heads. We were told they did so to avoid tempting men. The 103-kilometre road between Dejen and Mota was under construction. The 36 kilometres to Bichena was complete, so after Bichena, we had to drive another 67 kilometre on little more than dirt tracks, avoiding ditches and stones and brush, before we reached the beginning of the study road in Mota Town.

We often had to get out and clear our way. We couldn't make 20 kilometres per hour. At six that evening, the station wagon got stuck in the middle of nowhere. Koster, the driver, checked the engine and said it was dead. There was nothing to see except the sky above. Then Dagnew, who was driving the Unimog, came to check the car. He checked and checked. Finally, he found that we had run out of fuel. Koster was embarrassed and hated it that Dagnew had found the problem. The team had reserve fuel and so we managed to continue the trip.

We continued at the same pace, which got even more difficult in the dark. We arrived at Mota Town at eight that night. It was very dark. We couldn't put up our tents because it was so dark, so we spent the night in a pensione and put up our tents early the next morning. About nine, we went to the relevant government agencies to collect data on the type of crops growing in the area, the crop yield, and so on. By rural standard, Mota was densely populated and people there practised the traditional intensive farming. We returned to camp for lunch. The cook had prepared wonderful meal, and we enjoyed it, took a nap and went back to work.

Christmas was approaching. Although we were not with our families, we wanted to celebrate anyway, at least by slaughtering a sheep or a goat and by buying *tej,* local wine. We asked the drivers to contribute some money, but they thought we were rich men and declined. Three of us pooled some money and asked the drivers to buy a sheep or a goat. They came back with two female goats. During the slaughtering, Dagnew asked Koster whether the goats were virgins. Koster said that next time Dagnew should check the virginity. Dagnew said he thought Koster had done that. Things went out of control. Koster got offended, insulted Dagnew, stopped talking to him and refused to eat food in the camp. We pleaded with him, but he insisted. But it was a delicious lunch with good wine and I enjoyed the occasion. In the evening, we made campfire and enjoyed drinking *tej.* About ten that night, Dagnew and the four of us went to our tents to sleep while Koster had gone to town.

About 11:00, I heard Koster coming from town. He went straight to Dagnew's tent and told him to come out and fight. Dagnew responded by asking him to wait until he had his clothes on. I took my flashlight and left my tent. Koster had a knife in his hand. I called out to my colleagues and they came out too. We took the knife away from Koster, who insulted

Dagnew again. His language was really very bad. Finally, we diffused the tension and went back to bed.

The next day, as usual, we went to collect data. In the morning, we went from office to office and also visited the surrounding area. When we returned for lunch, we found Koster bleeding and groaning. We asked him what happened and he said Dagnew had beaten him. We yelled at Dagnew, but he said, "Did you see me doing that? This guy is a drunkard and fights with everybody." Although we knew what had happened, we couldn't do anything except soothe Koster. Dagnew was cunning. He knew that we had gone away and that Koster was in bed, so he sent the cook to town to buy him shaving blades. When everybody was away except the two of them, he went into Koster's tent, held him by the throat and was beating him up before Koster woke up. Koster had struggled but it was too late. Dagnew told us the story few days later.

We decided to travel along the project road. However, we found out that there was no bridge across the Abaya River, making the trip to Bahir Dar City impossible. We walked up to the edge of the gorge to look and then decided to go back up to Dejen and take the main road to Bahir Dar and then visit the remaining section of the study road. We had visited only 15 kilometres of the study road and had 95 kilometres remaining. To visit that part, we would have to travel about 500 kilometres.

The return drive to Dejen went a little better since we drove during daylight. We reached Dejen and drove another 70 kilometres along the main road, to Debre Markos Town, the provincial capital of Gojam. The area between Dejen and Markos was very green. Markos Town is very old and undeveloped and looked like a village town instead of a provincial capital. The town was filled with small bars and restaurants, which is typical of urbanisation in Ethiopia. The region was famous for *tella* and we got a chance to find out why. Beginning early that morning, we saw a lot of people inside popular *tella* bars and others sitting outside them. All that indicated the places that would have good *tella*. We went into one place and ordered *tella*. It was real beer.

We needed data from Markos and in two days collected what was available. We left for Bahir Dar City on the third day. The road was gravel, but much easier to drive on than the track road. The province was famous for its crops, but the people looked poor. We drove 265 kilometres and arrived at Bahir Dar City early in the afternoon. Bahir Dar town is next to Lake Tana, the source of the Blue Nile. The town was flat, with divided highway and trees planted all along the road. It was a fascinating place. We rented rooms in a beautiful hotel for seven Birr per night. We were mesmerised by the beauty of the city. We spent two nights there and prepared to leave for the study road.

We were going into the countryside and so needed smaller denominations of money. We went to the nearest bank. I asked a teller for smaller bills, but he refused to provide even with small amount. I asked him again, very earnestly, but he refused again. I got very angry and left. When I was on my way to the car, a priest-like panhandler followed me, constantly asking for money, but I got into the car without responding. He came up to the car and continued begging. I told him, "No thanks." He wouldn't leave. Finally, I got one Birr and stretched out my hand, as if to give it to him. He tried to snatch it from my hand; but I put it back into my pocket. He got very angry and said in Amharic,

Sebu Lemeret

which means "you are fattened for the earth" and he left. The language is colloquial and I didn't understand it on the spot. I figured it out after talking to the locals. He meant that the fat body I had would end up in my grave and I shouldn't be proud of it.

We drove southwest about 20 kilometres and branched off to the right. The road goes straight to Tis Isat, meaning Fire Smoke. The view from the thundering Tis Isat Falls is spectacular and the water rises up in a great mist after it hits the bottom. Millions of litres of water pour over the cliff and into a gorge, creating rainbows. It is one of the most beautiful places in Africa. We didn't have time to visit it. I was not keen on stopping there since I had seen it during my travels from Addis Ababa to Asmara, while I was working in Massawa. It would be the memory of a lifetime to visit it in September, after the end of the rainy season.

After we branched off and stopped our vehicles, a little boy who looked about seven years old came over to us. He said "A man had a fight with my father. When my mother got in between, the man killed her and ran away." A local man was standing nearby and said, "This boy will avenge his mother's death when he grows up." That was the tradition. It reminded me of a story I had heard earlier, when I was drinking beer in a bar one night. The woman bar owner told me about her ex-husband. When he was seven years old, he had gone to a market with his older brother and the brother had a fight with a man. After the market was over, they were on their way home when the man followed them and shot the brother. It was getting dark so, the boy picked up his brother's gun and ran for home. The killer followed him, but the little boy had disappeared from sight. Life went on and the boy was growing up. When he felt lonely, he started playing the flute, which was a sign of deep thinking and revenge coming.

He got married to the bar owner when he was 16 but never looked happy. He didn't talk too much to his wife but continued playing his flute every night. One day, he visited his uncle and asked him to point out his brother's killer. The uncle felt very happy that the boy had grown old enough to avenge his brother. He took him to the market and showed him the man. The killer didn't recognise him. Her husband studied the killer – he didn't want to miss his target. One day, the killer was ploughing his land. Her husband crawled along the ground, his gun in his hand, until he found a suitable place. Finally, he found an excellent place but saw a snake coming towards him. He crawled away. He lost his chance that day but remained determined that the deed would be done.

One night, the moonlight was so bright that the whole area could be clearly seen. Her husband left his house, his gun in his hand. He went straight to the killer's house, climbed up on the roof and brushed away the grass on top. As he looked down, he could see that the killer was in bed, with his wife sleeping in his arms. He didn't want the wife to be hurt, so he carefully dropped a blade of dry grass on the man's face. The man jumped out of his bed and grabbed his gun, but was too late. He was shot three times. The bar owner's husband assured himself that the man was dead, got off the roof and ran to the nearest forest. When some neighbours followed him, he explained why he had killed the man and said that he didn't want anyone else harmed. However, if anybody followed him, he would shoot. The people backed off.

Thenceforth, he was a fugitive. Both the relatives of the dead man and the government wanted him, dead or alive. More deaths followed and he became very dangerous. He didn't want his wife to get married to another man, so she left and travelled to a town. She opened a small bar and raised some cattle too. One night, he came to her place, shot dead two of her oxen, warned her that he would do the same to her if she got involved with any men, and went back to the forest. It took many years and many lives before he was killed. Family feuds are common in that part of the country. A man who hasn't avenged a family member won't be treated as an equal at community gatherings. Even his wife will belittle him in front of other people.

We continued our journey until we reached a small village, Adet, about 60 kilometres from Bahir Dar. We put up our tents and in a day we had collected our data. Nights were dark there, for the village had no electricity even though it was very close to one of the biggest hydropower generating plants in Ethiopia. We had light at our camp since we had bottled gas of our own. The village had some good local wine and, despite the darkness, we visited the bars at night. The wines were even better in the dark.

The next morning, we left the camp and drove to visit the rest of the study area. We went about 30 kilometres up-river. The landscape was flat and there were crops in the field. It looked to be rich agriculturally but poor in productivity. We watched two oxen struggling, shoulder to shoulder, the farmer yelling from behind. It looked very demanding physically. The lack of fertilizer, the lack of access, and backwardness in marketing have adversely affected the community. The people looked wretched, despite fertile land and the flowing rivers. Fortune and misery lived mysteriously side by side. We reached at the top of the gorge and returned to our camp early. When were back at the camp, Dagnew, the Unimog driver, offered me change for 40 Birr, in ten-cent coins. He knew about the problem I had had with the bank in Bahir Dar. He had made a deal with people living near the gorge to transport bags of honey to the village and was paid in coins.

We were told that people hoarded the coins since there was no bank around. They stored the coins in pots to keep them safe.

We finished our field trip and left early the next morning. We had breakfast and coffee in Bahir Dar City and then hit the road towards Markos. We bought grain, butter, honey and chicken on the way back since they were cheap compared to prices in Addis Ababa. We spent a night in Markos and left early the next day and arrived home after lunch. I took everything I had bought to Emaye and she was extremely happy. She stretched her hands and looked up at the blue sky in thankfulness to the Almighty.

Addis Ababa had become a nasty place politically. Many political parties had been formed, some working with the government and others against it. The most prominent pro-government party was the All Ethiopian Socialist Movement (MEISON), while the Ethiopian Peoples Revolutionary Party (EPRP) was totally against it. Other small parties that called themselves Marxist-Leninist and said that they were on the side of the oppressed peoples of Ethiopia were also active supporting the government, while the Red Star was against it. The rivalry mainly came from ideological differences between Ethiopians that had lived in Europe and North America. They all were contending for the hearts and minds of the people, by persuasion or by force. None of them left any space for people in the mainstream and all of them said they were for democracy.

Wondime had been the chairman of the election committee at the Ethiopian Airlines labour union. After the election, the government branded him a member of the EPRP since he hadn't had pro-government people elected to the executive committee of the union. The EPRP was very strong and had most young people on its side. It was ruthless too. The EPRP was alleged to have killed Professor Fikre Merid, an important man working with the government. After the election, Wondime was jailed. Emaye wept bitterly, saying, "I had two oxen to plough my field, but now one of them is gone. My life is over now." The whole family wept with her.

I had to make a field trip to Dejen, in the part of Gojam that we had been studying. I was doing origin-destination surveys of vehicles and was supervising traffic counts. A policeman was helping us to stop trucks for interviews. A massive recruitment of militia was underway in Dejen at the time. Somalia had invaded Ethiopia and the government was preparing to drive out the enemy. I met a peasant going to Dejen to join the militia and asked him where he was heading. He said to Dejen, for the militia. I told him that enough had gone already. He said, "I would rather die than go back home. My wife would undermine me whenever we had disagreements. She would tell me that I wasn't a man and would say that I would rather collect firewood and cook food with her. I will go and die like a man." Truck after truck filled with militia. The policeman said, "At one time, people around here revolted against the government. An emergency military force was sent to diffuse the situation. The military killed so many of them that at last the general stopped the killing by saying that one day the same people might help us fight back our enemies. That is now in the making." Three hundred thousand militias were trained in three months.

I returned to Addis Ababa after ten days. My brother was still in jail and Emaye was grieving and killings were going on unabated. Whenever the opposition murdered a person, the government dragged ten, 20, or even more, prisoners from jail, killed them and scattered their corpses in the streets of Addis Ababa and elsewhere in the country. When people in Addis Ababa left for work in the morning, they could not be sure of coming home safely. Both sides knew what they were doing and innocents died for nothing.

One day, I left home for work at 7:30 in the morning. I was standing at a bus stop with a community chairman from our village. He had seven children. I saw two young men coming from different directions. Suddenly, one of them shot the chairman and other one – he had acted as the killer's cover – joined the killer and both ran away. A car picked up the victim and rushed him to a hospital while people run after the young men. The two young men didn't know the village well and ran here and there in desperation. Finally, people with firearms surrounded them. One was killed and the other one committed suicide. The chairman died in hospital on the third day. Seven children lost their father and two young men lost their lives. For nothing!

Another morning, I left for work as usual. While going to the bus station, I saw the body of a young man lying by the public water tap. He was very dark-skinned, like my nephew Kassahun, and had put on the same kind of shoes. I stood motionless. I had seen my nephew in bed the previous night and couldn't believe this had happened to him. I ran back home and went straight to his bed. Someone was lying in it, fully covered with sheets and blankets. I lifted the sheets and blankets and looked. It was my nephew. Should I have been happy? How about the young man who died?

Another morning on the way to work, I saw the dead bodies of young men almost every 200 metres. When I reached the office, everybody was talking about it. We got a call from a colleague at home. Her brother had been killed. While going to visit her, I saw the bodies of seven young men lying in the street, guarded by community watchmen to prevent relatives from collecting their corpses. The bodies stayed there until sunset and then were thrown into mass graves. A woman at my office had four children. She was divorced and had kept the two youngest with her. The community watchmen, who alleged that the two were anti-revolutionary elements, imprisoned them. They were shot dead and their bodies thrown in front of their house. When the mother opened the door to go to work in the morning, she saw the bodies of her two children lying right at her doorstep. Later in the morning, some people from office went to visit her. They were beaten and thrown into jail.

It was Mayday in 1977. I had travelled to Gojam to attend a workshop. Young men had been demonstrating against the government in many parts of the country and they were rounded up and put in jail. I was in Markos for the night when community watchmen invaded hotels and homes to look for so-called anti-revolutionary elements. They woke me up in the middle of the night and pulled me out of my room. I was in my underwear. They looked at me and asked for my identification card. I showed them and they left me. Students and teachers were jailed. Nebiye, a teacher friend of mine in Addis Ababa, was jailed in Markos. He was far away from home with no one to bring him food. In Addis Ababa, those rounded up were shot dead at dawn and their bodies thrown in the street. Later, a friend of mine in Addis told me that he had seen 27 dead bodies, young men, lying in rows by a river near his house when he left for work early one morning. Every place in the country was hell, especially for young men.

My brother had a Fiat 600 car that sat idle after he went to jail. I had a driving license but had no confidence about driving. The license I had studied for meant that I didn't have sufficient practical experience. Before I went driving alone, I consulted a driving instructor and he agreed to test me in the suburbs before taking me to downtown. We had one evening together and he said that I needed more practice. I didn't want to spend more money, so I started driving at night with a friend seated by my side. The car demanded additional skill along steep hills since balancing between the gears and accelerator was very difficult. One Saturday, I went to downtown driving by myself and I stopped at a traffic light. When the light changed, I tried to move but the engine had turned off. A traffic policeman was watching me, but I couldn't move the car and a platoon had queued behind me. The policeman approached me and asked about the problem. I told him that the car had a mechanical problem. He asked me to get out, which I did, and he drove the car away from the traffic light and parked it. He asked me for my driving license and I showed it to him. He nodded his head and wished me safe trip. I had had similar incidents other times too.

Gradually, I managed to drive the car. Early in the morning, I would drop Abaye at the prison to give food to Wondime, which took him the whole morning. Abaye was about 70 years old at the time. At lunchtime, I would go back, pick up Abaye, and drop him at home, then return to work. That became my daily routine while in Addis Ababa. One morning, I drove Abaye to the prison as usual. As we were approaching it, we saw people crying in the streets. Some were standing, some sitting and others running here and there, but all were crying. Abaye and I were dead shocked and didn't speak a word between us for few minutes. Visitors were barred from getting close to the prison fence. Nobody knew why, but many guessed that prisoners had been killed. Heavily armed guards surrounded the prison, scaring people from coming close. Finally, the guards told us that we couldn't deliver food that day but could come back the next day. Emaye cried the whole night and we had no sleep at all.

I left early the next morning to try to find out Wondime's fate. The queue was more than 100 metres long and it took me more than three hours to reach the gate. The guards checked our identification cards and that took another half an hour. Finally, I managed to get into the compound. I had his name registered and waited. My heart was pounding until I knew the final.

Some were returned for their loves were not there. I saw Wondime coming and was relieved. He told me that on Saturday night, the guards picked a certain number of prisoners to take and kill and that the rest of the prisoners tried to stop them. One prisoner had disguised himself and couldn't be identified. It took half the night to find him. Finally, they got him and took the ones they wanted and killed them. One of them had been a colleague of Wondime at Ethiopian Airlines. The man was a professional auditor. The prison administration had asked him to audit the jail café, which he did, and his report indicated that there was some corruption. They advised him to change his report, but he refused. Wondime suspected that the incident led to his death.

Abaye got too weak to deliver food to Wondime and Kassahun my nephew started taking it by bus. Every day, he would wake up early, buy milk at a farm and take the milk and some food to Wondime. Early one morning while he was going for milk, he was picked up by security men and thrown into jail. Abaye threw himself down in a faint, while Emaye seemed numbed. It was quite an ordeal. While Kassahun was in prison, they asked him for his code number in an opposition party. He had no idea what they were talking about and gave them our house number instead. Then they understood that he was a layman and released him after a week.

Every now and then I saw graders and bulldozers going towards the eastern part of Addis Ababa, about ten kilometres away from the centre of the city. I heard that mass graves were being dug. In the middle of the night, political prisoners were picked up from the jails and taken away and gunned down. This happened in western part of the city as well.

One day in November 1977, I arrived at the office early. It was a cold morning. I parked my car in the compound and stood in the sun to warm up. Amare, the chief cadre at the ERA, parked his car not very far from mine. He got out of his car, came to me and asked to drop by his office sometime during the day. I went to my office, signed in and went straight to his office. He invited me to sit down and I did. He asked me about work and I responded positively. He then asked me to register as a party member. I frankly told him that there were many parties in the country at the moment and that I had no I idea which was which and so needed some time before taking a position. It was true that there were leaflets, papers and documents distributed by different groups and it was difficult to figure out what was going on. He asked me how much time I needed and I said a year or two. Amare smiled, said that his office would be open to me any time and wished me a nice day. In two weeks, Amare was jailed and I was momentarily relieved. However, he was released after few days.

Indris was my officemate. He was very gentle and very generous and his pay never lasted for the whole month. He would give money to whoever asked him and ended up broke by the end of the month. He never said no to anybody. He came from Welo Province and would give a reference to anybody travelling from there to Addis Ababa. His house was always crowded with guests and his colleagues joked that even the space under his bed was always booked. He borrowed money to give to the stream of people coming from his area. Sometimes, colleagues turned away his visitors and hid him behind the file cabinets. It was sad that those that he hosted got jobs, established families and built houses while Indris had none of that. He was one of the kindest and most generous people I've ever met.

Terefe was a young man at the ERA who visited Indris two or three times a week, but I barely knew him. They discussed things in secret and I never paid attention to them. Sometimes during the day, Indris would give me underground papers to read, which I guessed Terefe had given him. I usually read them and returned them to him. One day, Terefe approached me and asked me to join the EPRP. I was not interested and I told him I would think about it. In the meantime, I told Indris and he said that there was nothing wrong in joining the party. I was disturbed since Wondime was in jail and my parents had no one to support them. After few days, Terefe came back to me and said he would introduce me to someone and then we would be by ourselves. I told him I was not prepared for party activity and left. He never came back to me. Later in the year, Terefe shifted to the government side and had many EPRP members jailed, including Indris.

It was Ethiopian Christmas, January 7, 1978. It was a Saturday afternoon and I had queued for petrol at Kebena Shell station – petrol was rationed at the time. I was about 200 metres from the station. Tassew, a friend of mine from a leather factory in Modjo, was coming by bus to my place, for a visit. When he saw my car, he got off the bus and joined me. I got fuel in an hour and was going home when I saw three friends that were teaching at Addis Ababa University – Tegene, Teklu and Tegegn. I stopped my car and we talked and finally agreed to meet at the Fassilades Bar, close by. Next, I met Kebede, a friend who was working at the ministry of foreign affairs, and asked him to join us at the bar and he agreed.

The six of us entered the bar. Two men were inside already. Some of us got stools and sat by the balcony, others stood and Tassew sat by himself further away. We drank beer, talked to each other, teased each other and laughed but didn't enter into any political discussion – that would have been dangerous at the time. After an hour, a man wearing a round hat and sunglasses came in. He sat by the main door and ordered cold beer. In less than five minutes, a tall man with a scarf round his head came in and sat at a table close to the balcony and ordered a Coke. We didn't pay much attention to either of them but talked and joked amongst ourselves. A few minutes after the second man entered, Tegegn sat down on a chair by the table opposite the coke-drinker. Teklu stood by Tegegn and the two continued talking.

At about five that evening, we decided to leave. While we were on our way to pay our bill, the man by the door stood up, pulled his gun out and ordered us not to move. The man with a scarf pulled a rifle out too and aimed it at us. They told the bar owner to close the back door and then to keep still. We knew that they were government cadres since this was happening everywhere. First, they called Tegegn and asked him for his identification card. He had just come back from the United Kingdom, where he'd been doing his postgraduate studies and he did not have his ID yet. He showed his passport instead. His first name, Feseha, was similar to an Eritrean name – the Eritreans lived in the north and were fighting for independence at the time. They asked him how much money he was contributing to the Eritrean Peoples Liberation Front. He didn't understand what they were talking about since he comes from western Ethiopia. They told him to stand facing the wall and searched his pockets for firearms. One of the two cadres searched while the other one checked his picture against several other pictures. They took his wallet, pulled out some pictures and asked him who the people were and where they lived. It was quite an interrogation. Then they told him to sit on a sofa.

Next, they called Teklu and checked his ID, searched him for weapons, looked in his wallet for pictures and addresses, and asked him to sit beside Tegegn. Then they called Tegene, who had an album in his pocket with many pictures and addresses. They asked him about every photograph and every address. They also compared the pictures with the ones they had with them. In the meantime, the man with the scarf was coming and going. It took the cadre more than an hour to check Tegene. Finally, they asked him to stand by the balcony. I was called fourth. I have a broad chest and a muscular body. One of them told me to look at his gun and then said it was ready to fire. I nodded my head in submission. They searched and checked me and then asked to stand by the balcony. At one point, one of them called the other one by name. One of the two people who were in the bar before us told them not to use names since it would be dangerous, but they ignored him. Next, Kebede was called and they did likewise with him and asked him to stand by the other wall. They didn't call Tassew, maybe considering him a proletarian since he worked at the tannery.

I had stood by the balcony deep in thought. Wondime had been in jail for almost a year. My parents were too old to support themselves. I was thinking about their fate if something happened to me. One of the cadres looked at me and asked me what I was thinking about. I said nothing. The same man who advised them not to call names said; "Those who think deep at this time are anti-revolutionaries." They did not respond to his comments but asked me where I lived and the name of the cadre in my community and I told them the details they required. They told me to sit down. The same man who branded me for anti-revolutionary offered me a seat. I declined.

They invited us for questions. I asked them saying, "If you read our minds, we might be supporters of the revolution. Why are you terrorising supporters of the revolution with the firearms you hold to protect the revolution?" One of them said, "No, we are not here to terrorise anybody ." This time, that same troubled man among the two before us raised his hand for a question and asked if he would be allowed to drink his beer. They ignored him. After few minutes, the same man asked if he would be permitted to pick up the ballpoint pen that had dropped from his pocket. This time, they were annoyed and called him for a search. He jumped up and down until told to stop. He was then asked to sit down; he had totally panicked. It seemed to me that he had experienced similar ordeals before.

Next, they asked us what we were contributing to the ongoing revolution. Teklu started by saying, "After my graduation in 1972…" The cadre stopped him, saying, "Shit! I am not here to listen to your life history!" The cadre looked at me. I said, "I took part in the national development campaign." He said, "Shit! A lot of anti-revolutionaries took part!" Next, Kebede said, "When I was in third year at the university, all our year-mates boycotted classes against the government – except for nine of us." The cadre didn't comment, maybe thinking that was true. We thought our friend had done a good job.

Finally, the man with the scarf said to his fellow cadre, "These people have done what we told them to do. If we have to take anybody, we better do that and go." The other cadre said, "We will take the first two" – meaning Tegegn and Teklu. I asked why and one of the cadres said, "What do you know about them?" I said, "They are my friends – at least I know them somewhat." Kebede also pleaded. They thought for a while. Finally, they told us to repeat slogans after them: "Down with EPRP! Down with feudalism! Down with imperialism! Down with bureaucratic capitalism! Down with anti-revolutionaries!" We shouted enough to please them. They left the bar and drove away in their Peugeot 504. We didn't say anything, paid our bills and went our separate ways. The outcome could have been very different. If the two men who were in the bar before us had been members of the opposition party, they could have pulled their guns out and we could have been caught in the middle. At the time, both sides were engaging in shootings. The country was on fire.

Two days later, on January 9, 1978, I had a long day at my office and left late in the afternoon. It was Monday. I went to park my car in my friend's, Aregay's garage, as I usually did. His wife Asnakech was pregnant and I was driving her to work in the morning. She was at home. I sat down and talked to her for 15 minutes, I left the house and started going towards my place. Four cars were parked along the main road. By the road, I saw Solomon, a young man from my village. He had been jailed with Wondime, for being a supporter of EPRP, and was later released. I greeted him and he did likewise and left. Immediately, a Peugeot 504 came and parked on the opposite side of the road. Someone half-opened the door. I was suspicious and so watched for few minutes. Just after Solomon passed the parked cars, a man with a gun in his hand got out of the Peugeot and headed towards Solomon. Solomon ran as he was being shot. I later heard that they emptied their guns at him and left him dead, his eyes shot out. His mother was single. She went crazy and the villagers cried the whole night. Crying was the music of the day.

At the time, I knew four young men in my village, including Solomon, who had successfully completed the Ethiopian School Leaving Certificate Examination with distinction and who were ready to enrol in Addis Ababa University. They were all branded as anti-revolutionaries and killed. However, the government cannot be blamed for everything. The so-called anti-revolutionaries also killed the fathers and mothers of many young children – they said that they were pro-government elements. Some of the so-called anti-revolutionaries, especially those who led the young, shifted to the government side and had their own friends jailed and killed.

My office at the ERA was on the sixth floor, facing the main highway at the Sengatera traffic light. After the light, one street runs northwest to Merkato, the central market; the second one runs west to Mexico Square; the third runs east to Unity Square; and the fourth runs south to the Lagar Customs Office. It was about four in the afternoon. I saw a grey Peugeot 404 coming from the east. It turned towards Merkato. A young-looking man was leaning against an electric pole. He was on the street that runs to Merkato, right after the light. When the car reached the pole, someone from the Peugeot fired at the young man and then the car sped off. The young man was dead. That was common at the time. In this instance, it could have been that a man had shifted to the government side. He might have phoned a friend in the opposition and asked him to meet him at the light. The young man wouldn't have known that his compatriot had betrayed him. Then the betrayer would take a hatchet man to the appointment and have his friend assassinated. Most of those killed were between the ages of 18 and 30. Ethiopia lost its brightest and best.

* * *

My next assignment was to study the Mizan Tefer-Tepi Road, 48 kilometres long and in the south-western part of the county, in Kefa Province – the birth place of Abaye. The road was one of two recommended by the World Bank. The other road – Shishinda-Tepi – was 74 kilometres long, had been studied and was found feasible. The Bank insisted on the study of the former for comparison – it wanted to finance the one that would be the most beneficial to the country. This time, I was the leader of a team made up of Atfre, an engineer, Sida, a recently recruited economist, and Abahana, the Unimog driver and a cook. The station wagon that the head office provided was old and was meant to transport us up to the provincial maintenance district at Jima City. Atfre was supposed to drive the station wagon up to Jima, where we were supposed to then get a better car and a driver.

We had to go through the usual bureaucratic red tape to get ready for the trip. Preparations would sometimes take three days, sometimes five days and sometimes more than a week. A trip that was supposed to start on a specific day could be postponed to another day and then postponed again. Sometimes, we had to be determined to leave Addis Ababa even if all the requirements had not been fulfilled.

We left Addis Ababa late in the afternoon and spent the first night in Ghion Town, 114 kilometres from the city. We started out early the next day. The road crosses the Gibe River, one of the longest rivers in the country. After Gibe, we climbed a cliff and drove to Jima City, 350 kilometres west of Addis Ababa. The distance by the road between the Gibe River and Jima was less than 200 kilometres but was filled with zigzags and took us more than four hours. We arrived at Jima City around lunchtime. Jima is one of the biggest cities in Ethiopia and serves as a commercial centre for the surrounding coffee-growing lands. It is said that when Italy invaded Ethiopia in 1933 it had planned to make Jima City into Rome II. Jima is on a rolling plain. There were four big hotels in the city, but three had been nationalised by the government. Two had belonged to Egeno, a Gurage businessman who came to the region as a shoe-shiner. He had worked his way up, had managed a large coffee plantation and owned the two big hotels. The plantation and one of the hotels were nationalised and he was jailed. So much for his hard work. After nationalisation, the hotels deteriorated drastically.

We camped across from the district road maintenance office and went to collect data. It took us two days to finish in Jima. The station wagon that we were promised never came. But we were told that we could collect the car at the Dimbira construction site, 150 kilometres away. We drove southwest on a dusty rolling gravel road, in the same old station wagon and with our engineer serving as the driver. The landscape was green and full of traditional crops, but the people looked poor, which was a paradox for such a fertile area. About 50 kilometres from Jima, we reached at Gojeb River. It joins the Gibe and the two make the Omo River, which flows to Lake Rudolf or LakeTurkana, a lake between Ethiopia and Kenya that has two respective names.

Crossing Gojeb River, we saw fields covered with pineapple plants and root crops. The land was green and beautiful. However, the people looked still poor and desperate. Nationalising the land had helped the tenants psychologically, but they were still farming traditionally. People there eat root crops instead of the grain that is so common in central and northern Ethiopia and they looked bigger. We reached Bonga Town, the capital of Kefa Awraja and Abaye's birthplace. Bonga is famous for its *tej*, local wine, but we didn't try it because it was early morning. The road between Bonga and Mizan Teferi was under construction and we drove for another 50 kilometres to reach the Dimbira construction camp. The road cut through virgin forests and tall grasses. We didn't see many houses, just dense forest. It was one of the greenest parts of Ethiopia.

The Dimbira camp was well established. It had an American project manager and an Ethiopian deputy manager. The manager provided us with accommodation and food. I met Beshir, the deputy manager, the next day and he took me to his office and showed me the engineering reports for the road project. He was keen to learn about the economic aspect of roads in general and talked a lot about it. I was very impressed with his interest. Most engineers in the ERA were not keen on that subject at all. I had heard that there was a time that the senior engineers were against the ERA buying economics books. They were interested in building a beautiful road from one point to the next and were oblivious to the purpose of the road. However, Beshir challenged me to explain how economists could justify one road and be against another. I found him to be a liberal engineer.

I had heard that Beshir was very die-hard about his principles and never bowed to his bosses. Once he had gone to Jima with his colleagues for a weekend. They enjoyed themselves in Jima but were overdue at the camp. They arrived in camp on a Tuesday afternoon and he asked his colleagues to stand in line, then he called the finance man and told him to fine his colleagues and Beshir himself three days pay each. No complaint. After the revolution, the labourers at the camp had rebelled against the upper echelons of the ERA and had demanded that Beshir and other senior staff leave the site, threatening their lives. All the other staff left, but Beshir refused, insisting that only the general manager could remove him from his post. The labourers radioed their demands to all the project sites in the country and they did that for similar actions elsewhere. However, Beshir never flinched. Things went out of control and there was a total work stoppage. The military administrator for the province arrived and listened to the labourer's complaints about their bosses and he listened to Beshir too. Finally, he ordered the labour leaders to broadcast a reversal of their decision. They did and it was embarrassing for them. Then, the military administrator fired the instigators, sent the rest back to work and returned to Jima. Politics subsided at the site thenceforth.

Such incidents were not uncommon. At the beginning of the revolution, Dr. Wondimu, an urban engineer in Addis Ababa, was working in his office in the city when a mob of labourers jumped on him and beat him to death. He had nothing to do with the revolution, was the product of a very poor family and had climbed the ladder of life through his own hard work. The government sent troops to catch the killers. At first, no one would give the names of the core leaders but when the troops had rounded up all the labourers and threatened to shoot them, they identified the core leaders, who were executed on the spot.

There was no station wagon at the Dimbira construction site. In addition, the Unimog's starter failed and we had no replacement part. We called the head office for the part and they promised to send it soon. We stayed there for five days, but no part arrived. Abahana said it would be impossible for him to drive the Unimog without the starter. He wouldn't be able to keep its engine running along the remaining section and the road was very treacherous. The rainy season had already started and the track was full of mud. If the engine stopped, we'd be stuck for a very long time. The garage foreman promised to give us a mechanic-driver who could keep the Unimog's engine running. We told the head office to send the part by plane to our next destination, Mizan Teferi, and got ready for the journey.

Abaye, my dad had given me some hints about the surroundings. Now I regretted not having the details. I spoke with a site guard and he told me about a man who had been talking about a missing relative with similar story and then he took me to his place. We talked for hours, but I was not convinced that his missing person was Abaye – the man's story was a recent one. I thanked him and left.

After lunch, we started our journey down a very rough road and in the same old station wagon. It was muddy, but our new driver managed to keep the engine running all the way. The 65-kilometre trip took us seven hours and we arrived at Mizan Teferi town after eight that evening. The town was dark and we didn't know where to park our cars. Abahana called the community guards, opened the canvas of the Unimog and showed them the small cylinders of bottled gas that we had for camp lights. He told them, "This is dynamite, used for road construction. If anybody touches it, it will explode and destroy the whole town. We will leave the car here and you are responsible for whatever happens." The guards got scared and promised to add more guards. They watched all night.

We rented rooms in a hotel and spent the night. The next morning, we found our cars and the loads intact. The town was very backward. People wore very old clothes and the children were half-naked. Stores and shops were almost empty. On the other hand, a kilogramme of oranges sold for fifteen cents and a 300-banana bunch sold for one Birr. We were served bananas for breakfast, lunch and supper. Coffee grew all around. It was a paradox – rich resources and extreme deprivation.

We put up our tents on a field two kilometres out of town and began collecting data during the day. Our cook made us a very good supper. *Tej* was abundant and cheap. After supper, we were drinking *tej* by camp-light. We laughed about what Abahana said to the community watchmen the previous night. He told us another story: "Once, I was going to north-western Ethiopia, driving a Unimog with surveying equipment. It got dark on the way and I decided to spend the night in Bure Town, Gojam Province. While I was looking for a room, I met Megerssa – the brother of Gobenna, who was the personnel administrator at the ERA. Megerssa was working as a clerk at the road maintenance section in Bure Town. I knew he wasn't getting along well with his brother since Megerssa had been there for a very long time without getting a transfer to Addis Ababa. I said to him, 'Your brother has finally remembered you.' He said, 'What?' I continued, 'You have been transferred to the head office and I am here to transport your personal belongings to Addis Ababa.' He was very excited and invited me for supper and all kinds of drinks. After eating and drinking to my satisfaction, I said, 'Please make everything ready by early morning' and left for my bed. I got up at five in the morning and left for northern Ethiopia before Megerssa woke up. I didn't return the same way and I didn't see him for another year. He didn't talk to me for a very long time".

He also told us another story: "I have a very close friend in Addis Ababa. Once, I had left the office after lunch and was going home. I stopped at his place and met his wife. I told her that her husband had been jailed and asked her to prepare his supper so that I could take it to him. She killed a chicken and made very delicious meal – it smelled wonderful. She put the food in a big bowel, covered it with a clean piece of cloth and gave it to me. I took it home and had excellent supper with my family."

The study road was 48 kilometres long. The locals told us that only 15 kilometres – up to Sheko Village – could be reached by vehicle. We decided to leave the Unimog and the cook behind. We packed our sleeping bags, food and water, and started our trip with the old station wagon. We drove along the first 15 kilometres on a very rugged road – it took us two hours. We reached a very small and very poor village. The people looked wretched and helpless. However, the landscape was green and very beautiful. We gathered our data. The people told us that we couldn't drive any further because we would run into rugged hills that were very difficult to cross. We hired two people to guide us and to carry our belongings. Now there were six of us. It was raining. We walked through forests so dense that we could not see the sky. All we could see was the elephant and buffalo waste beneath our feet. Coffee grew wild and lay scattered on the ground. There were few settlements and the local men walked almost naked. It was hard to imagine that the country ever had a government that cared for its people. It seemed the people were unaware of any government and the government oblivious of them.

The guides told us that some criminals from northern Ethiopia had run away from justice and settled in the area. Men who were caught up in family feuds would do that and stay hidden like monks for the rest of their lives. Sometimes, their victims' relatives would come after them, vowing revenge. We had to find a place to spend the night and a peasant family offered us a place in a single-room house. The husband was Amhara from central Ethiopia and was married to a local woman. They served us meal with a big *injera* made of millet and sauce. It was very kind of them. All eight of us slept in the same room, some of us snoring and some wide-eyed all night.

The rain had stopped during the night and the next day looked fresh. Our host and his friend took us to the Beko River, which was flooded from the rain. The river had no bridge, so local people crossed by means of a bridge woven of plant stems. It was broken when we arrived. Our host and his friend had a plan to get us across the river. They took two very long dry tree limbs and some rope, laid them across the river and fixed them so that the "bridge" looked like a right triangle. We were at the 90° point and our destination was at one of the 45° points. We crossed the river by holding on to the rope above us and inched ourselves sideways along the tree limbs. Sida, the junior economist said, "I could have never done if it hadn't been for you." He was right, and I appreciated his comment since the head office was more concerned about the safety of its vehicles than the safety of its employees. At the time, neither employees nor vehicles were insured. Of course, if anything had happened to us, the head office would have considered us crazy.

We thanked the two people and continued our journey. The riverbank on the opposite side was very steep and we had to crawl up it. We were sweating. Once we reached the top, the terrain was flat and there were coffee plantations all around. Shade trees were planted in rows to protect the coffee bushes. One of our guides told us that the plantations were privately owned but had been nationalised. We walked fast and reached Tepi Town, the end of the study road, at about noon. The town was heavily populated by rural Ethiopian standards and there were coffee markets bustling with traders who had come from distant places. Most of the people in town were from northern Ethiopia. I was surprised to find that Amharic dominated the town and that local languages were barely spoken there.

People from a tribe that lived in the forest came into town on Saturdays to sell pottery. Their prices were fixed and they had never liked mixing with people from the town. If a buyer wanted to haggle, the seller would break the pottery into pieces and go home. As the town expanded further, the forest people tried to distance themselves more and more. Other craftsmen who made leather skin, the Menja, also lived in the area. Socially, they were looked down. They were not allowed to enter other peoples' houses and were never given drinks from others' glasses. They had to sit outside during weddings and other social gatherings. The glasses they used would be thrown away or broken into pieces.

We gathered data. The area within a 10- to 15-kilometre radius of the town was covered with coffee bushes. Subsistence crops like maize and root crops grew between the coffee bushes. It was hard to believe such poverty prevailed in a country with so many resources. Coffee was transported to city markets and shipped internationally and some of it went to local consumption. The taxes collected there were used elsewhere. All the big traders lived outside the area and – except for the collection of coffee – were not interested in the region's development. The people were totally forgotten.

There was air transport between Tepi and Mizan Teferi, so on the fifth day we flew to our camp. The airport at Mizan is five kilometres from the town and we had to walk, carrying our belongings, and arrived at our tents about lunchtime. However, the trip was not over yet. We had to pick up the station wagon that we left at Sheko Village, 15 kilometres away. Thus early the next morning, Atfire and I walked to the village. That took us three hours. The car was waiting for us. We ate our lunch, had some *tej* and drove back to our camp.

The study road crossed the Kefa and Illubabor administrative regions. We had to visit Jima, the capital of Kefa Province again to corroborate our data, and we had to drive to Metu, the capital of Illubabor Province, to collect the remaining data. Metu is 475 kilometres from Mizan Teferi. We travelled to Jima, spent the night and headed for Metu the next day. The road between Jima and Metu was paved with asphalt and gravel and ran through an area green with forests and coffee bushes. It also crossed the Sor and Geba Rivers, tributaries of the Blue Nile. The landscape and the scent in the air were mesmerising. Along the way, we watched a forest being burned for slash-and-burn agriculture. Such practices would lead to drought and starvation. We reached Metu in half a day.

Metu was breezy and surrounded by green areas and different kinds of trees. It had been recently established, with administrative offices being moved from Gore Town, 24 kilometres west. The revolution was blowing its horn there too, and so-called anti-revolutionaries, mainly the young, were being jailed. We stayed there two days and returned to Jima and then to Addis Ababa. It took us three months to complete the report. There were no computers at the time – even calculators were scarce and those available were slow. With the help of computers, the report could have been finished in a month and half. The study road was found to be more economically feasible than Shishinda-Tepi Road. The ERA submitted the report to the World Bank.

In the meantime, the political situation grew even worse. Now employees were being "asked" to "voluntarily" reveal themselves as anti-revolutionary elements or as members of opposition parties. The government had embraced a party it later rejected and that party's members were then deemed anti-revolutionary and jailed. The cadres of today were the prisoners of tomorrow. As well, many were seeking short-term gains at their fellows' expense. Thus, to reveal suspected anti-revolutionaries, the cadres of the day organized gatherings of the employees of different government agencies. In addition, they had a list of names. They hinted that those who were on the list but didn't reveal themselves would be dealt with more seriously. The cadres wanted to prove their loyalty to their masters.

A date was set for the ERA's staff to meet with the cadres. Panic prevailed for days before that happened. The bosses, the intelligentsia and the young were the targets. The day finally came. Our lunch break had been cut to an hour and many at the office couldn't manage to go home and eat, nor could they afford to eat out. Many people must have had empty stomachs that afternoon. Every ERA employee in Addis Ababa and the vicinity was supposed to be there. Field trips were suspended. Those who didn't show up that day would be seen as anti-revolutionaries, so even the sick had dragged themselves to the office. Amare, the chief cadre at the ERA, and his entourage were there and looked happy that the time for revenge had come. In addition, a notorious woman cadre, Tensae from a nearby community was the "captain" for the day. She had been a ticket person on a city bus.

First, to warm us up, we heard some propaganda about the revolution. Then we were given instructions on how to act when we revealed ourselves as anti-revolutionaries. Next, the cadres called for volunteers to reveal themselves. Initially, few people – I believed this was arranged in advance – talked about their roles as anti-revolutionaries. What they described was superficial. Then the cadres called for more revelations, but nothing significant happened. Finally, they started reading out names. We were sweating and our hearts were pounding. Some smoked cigarette after cigarette and some sat motionless. The names had nothing to do with the revolution and were just on the list because of personal grudges. They read out the names of the personnel manager and his assistant. They read out the name of the assistant to the general manager. Most of the people on the list were managers and deputy managers – their names had been provided by the employees in their offices. Tensae insulted us and ordered us to Stand! or Sit! as she pleased. It was demoralising for everybody except the loyalists. Fortunately, my name wasn't called.

Those whose names were read out were registered. Cadres that had worked and lived for years with the victims asked them for their names – it was as if they had never seen them before. Those called were taken away and beaten until bloodied. Some of them couldn't walk because of the tortures inflicted on their feet. They stayed in prison for about three months. Two were killed. One, Debebe was killed because he blocked a position for Amare, the ERA's chief cadre. The position required a degree that Amare didn't have. I knew Debebe very well. He was branded as a member of an opposition party. However, I had heard him many times condemning killings of poor community leaders by the same opposition party he was branded of being a member. As informed, the second victim, Kifle was killed for his opposition to the purchase of medical equipment for the ERA's clinic. The health officer was a cadre at the time and the victim was alleged to be a member of the Eritrean Peoples Liberation Front. He was a very decent man and had many children at home.

Now that the Mizan Teferi-Tepi Road had been to be more feasible than the Shishinda-Tepi Road, an engineer and an economist came from the World Bank to appraise it. I travelled with them to the site and visited Bebeka plantation, 30 kilometres west of Mizan. Some coffee bushes were so heavy with beans that they nearly touched the ground. Oranges and bananas were abundant. The engineer and the economist tasted the oranges and one of them said, "I haven't tasted such sweet and juicy oranges anywhere." We were told that before the revolution a foreigner had owned the farm and that fruit had been sent by cargo plane to Nairobi for marketing. It had been a very profitable business. After the revolution however, management was poor and fruit rotted on the trees.

The news that the Mizan-Tepi Road had been found to be more feasible reached the elite in Shishinda-Tepi. They had contacts in cities and towns and in government offices. The people of Mizan-Tepi were not educated and not even adequately clothed. There was nobody to help them. Lobbyists from Shishinda-Tepi came to Addis Ababa to pressure the government. They argued for the Shishinda-Tepi Road, we defended the report's findings. Then the president of the day, Mengistu Hailemariam visited Tepi Town. We heard that the elites called a demonstration against the Mizan-Tepi Road. The president gave in to the demand. The Shishinda-Tepi Road was built at a cost of 32 million Birr. .

The next year, the president visited the Bebeka plantation where he was briefed that the whole area between the plantation and Tepi was suitable for growing coffee. He ordered the construction of the Mizan-Tepi Road and paid for it with money from the Cuban government. The Mizan-Tepi Road became well travelled and the Shishinda-Tepi Road became a white elephant. What a waste of national resources in a poor country like Ethiopia!

Wondime was still in jail and Emaye cried day and night. Whenever I was in Addis Ababa, I visited him every Sunday. Most of the time, the queue at the prison was long – more than 100 metres – and it took more than one hour in the queue before we had our five-minute visit. Whenever the radio broadcast the sound of the revolutionary drum, Emaye would stand close by until the announcement ended. Then she would ask me, "Are they going to release prisoners?" However, political prisoners were going in, not coming out of jail.

One Sunday, I went to visit Wondime as usual. Before I saw him, I talked to another prisoner from our village and he had told me that I needed to caution my brother about talking to other prisoners. Some prisoners from opposition parties had changed sides and were supporting the government. When I saw Wondime, he looked very tense. I asked him what had happened to him and he told me that he had been segregated from all prisoners and placed in a separate room. That was a sign that he was to be eliminated and I got panic-stricken. He also told me that the man I had talked to was one of those who now sided with the government. The man's family was very close to us and we thought of him as our brother. The times were very bad: fathers stood against their children and children against their fathers, brothers against brothers, and friends against friends. Life was terrible and humanity lamentable in that part of the world. I said goodbye to Wondime and left.

Aregay was our helpful friend, and he had a very reliable friend who knew a key person in the Derg who at one time had been responsible for the jail. In addition, his friend knew the current chief of the jail. I went straight to Aregay and told him about Wondime's situation. He promised to do his best and went to his friend the same day. His friend managed to contact the chief and both went to meet with him the next day. Wondime was summoned to the meeting. The chief told them that he had gathered a lot of information against Wondime – some prisoners had come to him voluntarily. It often happened that prisoners, hoping for their own release, accused close friends. The chief advised Wondime to be careful – he wouldn't give him another chance. He was released from solitary confinement and rejoined the other prisoners.

Just before I left for the office one morning, Emaye asked me for money. It had been three weeks since I had given her money for the whole month. She was a very generous hostess. I said, "Emaye, look at your friends that have no children. They are sitting beside the church, begging. However, you are not properly managing the money I am giving you." She got very angry and yelled at me and said "Don't compare me with them. They are there because of their misfortunes and I have you because of my fortune. If you have any money, please give me some. If you don't, please tell me so. Under any circumstances, please don't compare me with those at the church." I kept quiet and never raised the issue again.

I had left home early to meet my friend Getaneh. After spending some time with him, I headed home. Kassahun, my nephew, ran to me and stood gasping. I asked him what happened. He said, "My uncle has been released from prison!" I couldn't believe him. Many political prisoners like him had been killed, but I walked home fast. My sister knelt to kiss my feet. I refused and ran over to Wondime to embrace him. We embraced for a very long time and wept. With a full heart, I thanked the Almighty. Emaye kissed the ground over and over again. Abaye was stunned. Neighbours had come to congratulate Wondime and us. Emaye slowly walked over to me. She'd been crying for almost two years and was losing her eyesight. She held my two hands and kissed my forehead three times.

My brother was lucky. People who had done nothing vanished– they had never been involved in political activities, but the time and the place betrayed them. Bezu, a friend at Addis Ababa University, was teaching in one of the southern provinces. He had come to Addis Ababa to visit a friend. He was in bed at his friend's place while the friend was out for the night. Political cadres came that night to get his friend, and when they couldn't find him, they took Bezu, killed him, and left his body by a nearby bridge. Near Arat Kilo, cadres entered a house and killed a young man in bed. Then they found out that he was not the one they were looking for, said "sorry" and left. Near Piazza, cadres came to take a young man to prison, his mother resisted, they killed both and left. There were many incidents of that kind. Wondime thought of himself as a man who had risen from dead and called his first son Alazar – Lazarus.

* * *

One day in October 1978, my boss Mengesha called me to his office to go over potential road projects. He also told me that the next study would be the 300-kilometre long Ghinir-Mechara Road in south-eastern Ethiopia. I

177

would be responsible for conducting the study. He told me that the project area was risky, due to Somali invasion, and that caution would be required. I accepted the assignment and left his office to prepare for the field trip. A few days before the field trip, a close friend of mine, Hailu, asked me to meet him. When we met, he told me that he had decided to marry his fiancée and had chosen me as his best man. I told him I was honoured and happy to do it. I went to a tailor and arranged for a black-and- white suit. I would have to finish my fieldwork as soon as I could and return for the wedding.

We started our journey late in that day and rested for the night in Asela Town, 175 kilometres south of Addis Ababa. Then we realised that one of the team members had left his sleeping bag behind. Because we often left in haste, things like that happened many times. Fortunately, however, my friend Desalegne was working in town at the Chilalo Agricultural Development Unit, so I collected a blanket from his place. The next day, we resumed our journey, crossing private and state farms in Arsi Province, then climbing and descending the hills and mountains of the Bale Province. At 225 kilometres from Asela, we passed the famous Bale Mountains National Park on the right. The park covered about 2,300 square kilometres of land, endowed with baboons, grey duikers, klipspringers, mountain nyalas and reedbucks. The large open lands were beautiful. Finally, late in the afternoon, we reached Robe Town, about 425 kilometres from Addis Ababa. The ERA had a maintenance camp in Robe Town and we raised our tents there. The camp was highly protected because the military had fuel tank inside.

We visited the town early next day but stayed in camp the whole afternoon. The militiaman guarding the gate seemed to be homesick – he sang nostalgic songs all afternoon. We had our supper at the camp and were sitting around talking. Then we heard a voice say, "Stop!" We kept silent. Then we heard a shot fired – as though at the sky, followed by another shot, sounding as though it had been fired low. We thought it hit something. When we heard moaning, we guessed a person had been shot. The camp manager came and told us that the militia had shot someone and asked us to help him report it to the police station. The militiaman, the camp manager and I went to the police station, where the camp manager reported the incident to the police chief. The police chief said that the militiaman had to be disarmed before the wounded man could be taken to the clinic. The militiaman turned his gun on the chief and said, "I am not carrying this gun in vain. I haven't left my family behind for nothing. I will shoot you if I have to." He was furious. The chief was panic-stricken and agreed to go to the camp.

When we got to the car the militia refused to get in. He said, "I can't sit in the same car with a reactionary. Let him go and collect his kind." Fortunately, the victim wasn't dead. He was drunk and going home and when he saw the gate wide open, he thought it was the road going to his place and so he just kept on going, even after he was told to stop. He was lucky to have survived. We picked him up and took him to the nearest clinic. The next morning, the incident was reported to the colonel stationed at the provincial capital, Goba, 15 kilometres to the west of Robe. The colonel came to the camp the next day and congratulated the militiaman. He said,

"You should have killed him."

We went to Goba the third day, to visit the relevant offices and to talk to the provincial administrator. He was a colonel in the army and a Derg member. He was an enthusiastic and very co-operative person, very interested in the study road, encouraged us and promised to support our work. We continued on our way to the study area and travelled 60 kilometres southeast to Goro Village, followed that route for about 20 kilometres, turned northeast, crossed the Sofomore natural tunnel, and then on to Ghinir. Now we were at the beginning of the study road. On the way, we saw Weyib River enter the Sofomore tunnel and vanish.

Like many small rural villages, Ghinir had local bars. It was tense due to the Somali invasion and for safety we set up our tents in a military camp. We briefed the military leader about our mission and discussed on further travel along the study road. He told us that the area was a war zone and promised to provide the necessary military support. We agreed to start the trip the next day, then went downtown. There were *tej* bars and we went into one to check out the place. There were few people in the bar and the woman who owned it was the loquacious type – somebody who would talk about many things in a few minutes. She told us about a famous rebel named Hussein Bule who lived in the forest and who had given serious trouble to the military by attacking Ghinir many times. She said, "One day two militia had gone to cut grass. Suddenly, a lioness jumped on one militia, with her mouth wide open to bite him. He put his arm right down her throat and the other militia shot and killed the lioness. They loaded the carcass onto a jeep and came to town. They were so pleased that at first we thought they had captured Hussein Bule, but he is still at large and dangerous." We got scared.

Two trucks of soldiers were ready to escort us to the study site. We had been told that we could only travel up to Sheik Hussein, a village 125 kilometres away. We couldn't go further because the Wabeshebelle River had no bridge. We started our journey slowly and travelled very cautiously. On the way, we saw military trucks that had been exploded and burned into ashes by enemy mines. As we drove further, the area looked drier and was covered with shrubs and thickets. At one spot, the driver couldn't get the station wagon across a very sandy stretch of track. It was very slippery. As the driver struggled to get us across, the axle broke. There was no way to repair the car until we found a replacement axle. We decided to leave the car and so climbed into the Unimog, with the tents and cylinders.

We reached Sheik Hussein at four that afternoon. The village was named for the Sheik Hussein Mosque, which was named for a holy man who had lived many years ago. We were welcomed and invited to visit the mosque. We took off our shoes and went inside. Sometimes the ceiling was so low that we had to craw. People told us that it was impossible to take a picture of the mosque – many had tried and failed. It was painted bright white, so it could be the reflection that made photographing it impossible. We had no camera and so couldn't try. I had seen Muslims in Addis Ababa collecting money for the annual pilgrimage to the Sheik Hussein Mosque. They would sit along the side of the streets of Merkato, the central market, and beat drums. On the ground in front of them would be a piece of cloth. Muslims and Christians alike would drop coins or paper money on the cloth. Sometimes they would go door to door and ask for money and sometimes they would panhandle. Muslims from throughout Ethiopia would make the pilgrimage –the Sheik Hussein Mosque is the Mecca of Ethiopia.

Ethiopian Christians and Muslims live in brotherhood. When Muslims hold weddings, they prepare separate food for their Christian guests. Christians do likewise. When Christians build churches, Muslims donate money, and when Muslims build schools, Christians donate money. Intermarriage between Muslims and Christians is common in Ethiopia. Both foreign and domestic elements have tried to create animosity between the two, but to no avail. I believe Ethiopia is one of the few countries in the world where Christians and Muslims live in brotherhood and sisterhood. It is blessed in that respect.

Not far from the mosque, the Wabeshebelle River flows, meandering into deep gorges. The land around the mosque was very dry and there wasn't a lot to see. We thanked the people of the area for their hospitality and started back to Ghinir Town. We went about 30 kilometres and rested for the night in the forest. We required neither tent nor sleeping bag, just a mattress on a canvas bed. There was no moon, but stars were shining above us. To the south of us was a hill and to the north the Wabeshebelle River Valley. It was very quiet and deserted; I got scared and couldn't sleep. The next morning, we were told that there had been a skirmish between Somali forces and Ethiopian militias the previous night. We hadn't heard anything. Two militiamen were killed and their bodies had to be transported to Ghinir with us. The bodies were loaded onto the military trucks and few militiamen transferred to the Unimog. It was a tight fit, but we had no choice since the station wagon had broken down.

For safety, we travelled very slowly. We said goodbye to our station wagon, at least temporarily, and headed for Ghinir. Sixty kilometres before Ghinir, we took a break at Jara Village and drank some *tej*. Abdissa, the junior economist, had been challenging my instructions. He had been at the ERA long before me and thought that accepting my instructions would make him inferior. I was junior in seniority and felt a failure if my instructions were challenged even in the slightest degree. We couldn't get along. The *tej* was very strong. I had two glasses of it and felt very drunk. I guessed that Abdissa felt likewise. He brought a man with him and asked that he be given a ride to Ghinir. I told him that was impossible. He asked me why and I told him I was the boss. He turned to the man and said, "The Emperor has refused to let you on. I am sorry I can't help you." I didn't answer, but others laughed. Later on, I thought that both of us had overreacted.

We reached Ghinir in the afternoon. We spent a night and headed for Goba. I called the head office to see about the part we needed and was told that since there was a flight between Addis Ababa and Goba, the part would be in Goba very soon. The part arrived on the fifth day. The provincial administrator arranged for a mechanic and a helicopter and our driver flew to the site with the mechanic. They came back the same day – it was the wrong part. I called the head office again. We waited for ten days, but nothing was happening. Finally, the head office told us to go to Asela, where another station wagon and a driver would be waiting for us. After Asela, we would continue our trip and complete the remaining part of the study road on the other side of the Wabeshebelle River. We had to leave our driver behind and drive to Asela in the Unimog. By this time, I was late for the wedding. I missed the chance to be my friend's best man. He had given me the top spot, but it wasn't meant for me. I called home and told Wondime that I couldn't be there for the wedding and asked him to tell Hailu that I was deeply sorry for that. I kept my black-and-white suit though.

After ten days in Goba, we headed down a dusty gravel road. The first 185 kilometres were hilly and mountainous while the remaining 125 kilometres were rolling and flat. The road was surfaced with red gravel. By the time we reached Asela, we looked like red clay ourselves. I took a hotel room for the night – I wanted a good bath to wash off the dust. In Asela, another station wagon was ready for us and we left for Harerghe, the largest province in Ethiopia. Originally, Harerghe and Bale were one province and called Harerghe. The original Harerghe covered one-third of the country. After it was split, Harerghe was still the largest province, followed by Bale. Both are the least populated provinces. Somalia usually invades Ethiopia through the two provinces, either as the "liberators" of the Ogaden Region in Harerghe or as supporters of the Oromo fighters in Bale. This has been going on since Somalia's independence in 1960.

We had our breakfast in Nazareth Town, 75 kilometres northeast of Asela and 100 kilometres southeast of Addis Ababa. The road was paved and flat so the driving was good. After Nazareth, the 125 kilometres road to Awash was also paved and flat and the driving was even easier. After Awash, we turned right off the main road to the port of Asab. The road was gravel, but wide and flat until Asebe Teferi town, 85 kilometres from Awash. Most of the people along the route were Afar or Issa. Both tribes extend to Djibouti, with the Afar traditionally occupying the Danakil Depression and the Issa extending south into Somalia. Both are nomadic and graze their goats and sheep on the sparse vegetation. We rested for a night at Asebe Teferi. The town was established many years ago, but facilities were very poor. It wasn't bad for one night though.

After Asebe Teferi we crossed mountains and hills until we reached Kulubi, the home of the famous Church of Saint Gabriel. Saint Gabriel is famous for the annual Christian pilgrimage to it. People that hope for health, children and wealth travel there twice a year, in December and July. After their prayers were answered, some walk naked round the church, some bring rats, rabbits, and so on, with them. They think that if they don't make such vows, their prayers won't be answered. Others bring expensive things – golden umbrellas, bulls, and so on. It is the richest church in Ethiopia. We passed Kulubi and arrived at Diredawa City during lunchtime. Diredawa was one of the few heavily populated cities in Ethiopia. It was famous for its cement and cotton factories and is the commercial capital of Harerghe Province and was founded at the beginning of the 20th century when the railroad from Djibouti reached the area. The city's growth had resulted largely from trade brought by the railroad.

When I was in the Lab School, students from Eritrea and Diredawa had bitter arguments over two famous soccer players. The two brothers, Luciano and Italo were born and brought up in Eritrea, but they had moved to Diredawa to play soccer for the cotton factory. The students from Diredawa boasted that the brothers were the best players in the country. The students from Eritrea would say, "They are our players, we built them up," and the students from Diredawa would respond, "We bought them because we have the money." The two sides argued a lot about it, and the rest of us had to listen – we were all in the same dormitory.

Diredawa had many buildings and shops and was famous for contraband goods from Somalia and Djibouti. It was sandy, surrounded with treeless chains of mountains and no rivers that flowed year round or lakes that were always full. It seemed deprived of nature. Diredawa could have been a very beautiful city if there had been something growing on those majestic hills. Commercially, merchandise was plenty and I managed to buy some clothes for my parents. As soon as we reached Diredawa, we went straight to the district road maintenance office to arrange to set up our camp. We met the district manager, an engineer named Bizuneh. He was tall and muscular, with a broad chest and strong arms, and was a major in the Ethiopian Air Force. I asked him for a place to put up our tents, but he refused, arguing that the refugees during the Somali invasion had stayed in the compound and left litter all over the places. I asked where we could set up camp – the compound would be best since it was close. I also said that we had stayed in military camps in the past. He exploded and said, "There is a military camp across, you can go there and camp! I have said you can't camp here!" I kept silent – he looked physically tough and I even thought he might jump on me. The room was quiet for another five minutes. When he was sure he was in complete control, he said, "Okay, you can camp."

I had heard that Bizuneh was a bold person. At the beginning of the revolution, he was head of road maintenance at the head office. It was the fashion of the day throughout Ethiopia for workers to force out their bosses. At the head office, workers posted the names of senior managers, including Bizuneh, at the gate, warning them not to enter their offices. All but Bizuneh went home. He broke the iron chain at the gate with his car and went to his office. Nobody dared stop him then or later.

After we had put up our tents in the compound, I mentioned the incident to the guard at the maintenance district. He said I was very lucky. I asked him why and he said, "Last time the garage was under maintenance and the floor was paved with cement and was wet. A Cuban soldier drove over the wet cement. Bizuneh dragged him out of his car and threw him out of the compound." I thought I was really lucky.

Harar City, the provincial capital, was 50 kilometres away and we travelled there to talk to the administrator. Harar was beautiful. It's known as the Walled City, after a wall built in the 16th century to protect the Adere society against invading warriors. The Adere have a more oriental culture, are followers of Islam and are believed to have lived in the area known as Jegol for many centuries. There were many mosques and the city looked breezy and fresh. Although there are fewer than 100,000 Adere in Ethiopia – a nation of 70 million people – they are key players in the economic and social development of the country. We visited the provincial administrator, a colonel who cordially received us in his office and was very pleased about our mission. He called the Awraja administrator in Mechara and asked him to give us all the help he could, then wished us good luck and escorted us out of his office. We returned to Diredawa.

From Diredawa we travelled along the same road until Asebe Teferi, and then shied to the west 15 kilometres before reaching the town. Then we travelled another 98 kilometres, crossing the towns of Bedessa and Gelemso, until finally reaching Mechara, the other end of the study road. We stretched our tents at Micheta, a village five kilometres away. We visited Mechara Town, famous for its coffee and *chat*. People chew *chat* leaves to increase energy and stimulate pleasure. We visited the Awraja administrator, who also received us cordially and had arranged for a military escort to travel with us. We thanked him for his co-operation and left his office to collect data.

We were going to have to depend on the military to guide us – the place wasn't safe and we knew nothing about the situation. We started out immediately after lunch, with a truck of soldiers following us. Heavy rainfall had muddied the dusty track and we wished the trip had been postponed until next day. However, the military leader said, "Once you start marching, there is no retreat – you must go forward." Driving was very difficult, especially for the military truck, which got stuck every few kilometres and we would have to use the Unimog to drag it out. Fortunately, the rain stopped. The landscape was flat and the lands uncultivated and without settlements. We were told that Ras Birru, an ex-landlord, had owned almost a million hectares of that area and had not farmed it. His children had controlled huge tracts of land in Arsi Province, had evicted small farmers, but had put the land under maximum cultivation. We travelled for about 100 kilometres and stopped for the night at a place called Direabona. It was the site of a police station that had been burned to ashes by Somali forces. The area was deserted and we saw no signs of life. We spent the night without shelter.

The distance between Direabona and Wabeshebelle River was about 50 kilometres and there were not even tracks to drive along. We had to walk to the riverbank. It would have been nasty if it had rained overnight. We started our journey early the next morning, carrying food and water with us. We walked very fast and sweated a lot. Soon our clothes were soaked and by noon we had gone as far as we could, about 35 kilometres. Forest blocked the view of the river, but with the help of binoculars, we could see the distant gorges. We started back after an hour's stop for lunch at a very small village. We were by then dehydrated. The people boiled coffee leaves for us, saying that it would quench our thirst. The people who lived there seemed totally forgotten – there was no health centre, school or clean water – but they were properly clothed and looked healthy. It seemed that contraband goods reached them from Somalia and Djibouti. We had our lunch, drank some cold water and sipped the drink made from boiled coffee leaves. We walked fast but were exhausted. Abdissa tripped on a stone at the edge of an escarpment and was about to tumble down when he grabbed the branch of a tree and managed to save himself. It would have been very disastrous to all of us. We reached our camp at 6:30 that evening. We left the next day for Mechara and had no problem getting back. We collected some missing data in Mechara and headed for Addis Ababa.

* * *

I had to go to Metu for a seminar organized by the provincial administration to discuss agriculture, health, education and transport. A senior engineer and I were assigned to report on the ERA's activities in the province. We drove to Jima City and then to Metu. The provincial administrator was an army colonel and a member of the Derg. He looked pompous, not humble like the administrators for Bale and Harerghe. The seminar hall was decorated with palm leaves, flags and posters. It looked like a political meeting, not a seminar to discuss economic development.

The seminar started on Monday, chaired by the colonel. He controlled the floor, was arrogant and bombastic, used English words that had no relevance to the subject. The seminar was in Amharic and the majority of the participants were peasants who had never heard a single English word. Knowledge of English was seen as a sign of intellectual superiority, so English words were blasted about for no purpose – other than showing off. Even the head of state did that. I remember that during the national development campaign one student used to say, "I am going to frustrate myself" when he meant he was going to relax.

At the seminar, one agricultural representative was accused of being responsible for the poor honey harvest. He was accused of leaving the hives empty. An expert on bees defended him by saying, "Bees are not soldiers. One can't tell them to enter and leave at his or her convenience. When there are no green plants and flowers outside, you'll find bees in their hives. But if there are flowers and plants available, you won't find them there." The colonel got furious and said, "Shut up and sit down! You're talking tales!" The expert sat down and the hall became tense. After that, some presenters couldn't even read their papers properly – they were scared to death.

After the seminar, we went to Gambela, a remote village by the Sudanese border. At Gore Town, 25 kilometres past Metu and towards Gambela, the gravel road dipped steadily until Bure, a small village 45 kilometres away. Then, it dropped steeply on the way to Gambela, 100 kilometres away. The flat, fertile land was adjacent to the Baro River. The river swept away soil and carried it to Sudan and Egypt. The people looked destitute. It was perplexing to see such misery and deprivation in the area of abundant and fertile land and plentiful water. To reach the town, we had to cross the river by canoe, which was a bit scary. The engineer told me, "I once came to Gambela in a group. There were government officials and intellectuals from the university. We got in the canoe, but before we started out, one of the officials stood up and lectured the rower, through an interpreter. He noted what our jobs were and the number of children we had. Then he told the rower that he had to be very careful since so many dear lives were in his hands."

Gambela was very hot and full of mosquitoes. The hotels were shabby. There was one good hotel, the Ghion, but it was too expensive for me and I took shelter in a ramshackle hotel room full of mosquitoes. The engineer boarded at the Ghion – he was senior and well established. Surprisingly, he caught malaria while I stayed safe. I thought it might have been because of the age difference – he was in his 50s while I was in my early 30s. Some rural road construction was going on and he was interested in that. It was extremely hot and dry while we were there. The area looked ideal for irrigation – it had the Baro River and a flat plain and the land adjacent was fertile.

* * *

At the time, members of the Derg were fighting amongst themselves for leadership, and with oppositions which wanted power and separation. All the while, the northerners were fighting for independence. The Eritrean Liberation Front was fighting for the independence of Eritrea and the Tigrean Peoples Liberation Front for the independence of the Province of Tigray. The former had good reason – Eritrea had been colonised by the

Italians and annexed by Haile Selassie government. But the latter fight was confusing because Tigray was the source of Ethiopian civilization and denying that seemed contradiction of Tigray's history. Southerners had joined the state relatively recently. What were they if Tigreans were not Ethiopians?

Due to the war in the north, the government had strengthened its development activities in the other regions. Thus the next study road was Chida-Sodo, where a 160 kilometres stretch was planned which would connect the provinces of Kefa and Sidamo. I was responsible for the study and I was excited about visiting the area because the road under consideration would cross Emaye's birthplace.

We drove to Jima first and then to Chida Village. The study road started about 85 kilometres southeast of Jima. A gravel road connected Jima and Chida Village. Chida was tiny, sparsely populated and without government offices. It had great agricultural potential. We set up our tents by the market. There was no settlement nearby. Market day was Saturday and the next market day would be tomorrow. Early the next day, a few peasants started coming to the market. As the day progressed however, the numbers grew, and by late afternoon, it was full of people. Most people came for raw meat. Cows were slaughtered at the market, but people didn't take the meat home – they ate raw right at the market. I learned that about 30 cows were slaughtered there every Saturday. It's an old tradition. People also brought crops to sell and drank local vodka, *'areke'*. Prices were extremely cheap, about a fifth of the price at Addis Ababa's markets. People lived from hand to mouth, despite the abundant land.

We visited local bars. The *tej* was excellent, cheap and made of pure honey. Raw meat was available too. We ate some and felt very healthy. Then, we travelled along the track that followed a valley. The track zigzagged and was filled with stones, making the journey difficult. We couldn't go more than 10 kilometres per hour. The next village was Waka Town, where Emaye was born. It was 75 kilometres from Chida. At the foot of the highlands, 13 kilometres before Waka, there was a grass-surfaced airport. Waka itself was in the highlands and we had to drive up the hills slowly for the terrain was steep and rugged. Our food spilled all over the Unimog and the cooking oil containers leaked and spoiled it.

Tsegaye, the station wagon driver, got mad about the spoiled food and yelled at Cherinet, who was driving the Unimog. I said to Tsegaye, "Cherinet didn't spoil the food intentionally – it's partly his food too. Why are you so mad?" Tsegaye was the youngest driver I had met up to then. He drove fast and was rude, while Cherinet was gentle, kind and a very competent driver. Both came from the same part of Welo Province. Later, Woldeselassie, the engineer, and I took Tsegaye aside and scolded him. As a result, he stopped talking to all of us. It took us 11 hours to cover the 75-kilometre section and we were exhausted and frustrated. We put up our tents on the outskirts of town and then went to see the area.

We talked to the Awraja administrator, a civilian who was very enthusiastic about the road. He cordially received us in his office. The road was overdue, he said, because the area was densely settled and actively farmed. He also told us that Waka was established many years ago but had no access to Jima or to Sodo. He invited us for super at his place. We ate raw meat and drank *tej* that we enjoyed very much. We discussed the project for hours and left his house late in the evening.

Waka lies on a ridge with valleys on both sides. It was beautiful late in the afternoon, with the sun in the west. The hills and valleys were so green. I thought Emaye must miss it dearly. She had never had an opportunity to come back and visit. When she left, she didn't know where she was going and she landed in a place where she knew nobody. There she met the man she married. He was from nowhere too. She had nothing but love to give to her children. But her son had managed to get a university education and had come to her birthplace as part of his work. She had never dreamt that might happen. I thought it was a big success for her and for me.

People were very anxious that we understand the importance of the road and followed us wherever we went. We talked to the leaders of the farmers' associations and hoped that we had the power to decide to build the road and begged us to see that it got built. That Saturday we visited a big market, ten kilometres away. It too sold raw meat and coffee was so cheap that I bought 5 kilos of it for Emaye. I bought her root crops too. It was a rich area but had no road to external markets. Farmers sweated for marginal prices.

We went to a local bar to eat lunch and were brought *injera* and a local cheese splashed with melted butter. It was delicious. We met an old man in the bar who complained about his uric acid. Woldeselassie advised him to stop eating raw meat if he wanted to feel better. The old man said that he preferred dying to quitting raw meat. He said, "I have enjoyed it all my life. Why should I stop eating for the little life I may have left?"

The Omo River is about 45 kilometres from Waka. It was on our way and had a mobile bridge but not suitable for cars. We drove a little while, planning to see the bridge. We visited the site and we had to visit the remaining portion of the road from the other side of the river. To do that we had to drive over 550 kilometres. The administrator promised to meet us on the other side and we set a date to meet.

We started the return trip. It had rained the previous night and the road had become muddy and treacherous. The station wagon got stuck easily and the Unimog had to keep dragging it out of the mud. Tsegaye still was not talking to us. As we were moving slowly along, Tsegaye tried to avoid a muddy place and ended up between a tree and a rock at the top of a cliff. If not for the rock, the car would have rolled off the cliff and all the three of us would have been smashed to death. Because of the cliff, Woldeselassie and I couldn't get out of the car on our side, so we slid out through Tsegaye's door instead. We reached Chida Village and put up our tents in the middle of a field. Next, we went for lunch to a small restaurant. Lunch meant raw meat there and we drank *tej* for digestion. It was very refreshing. Later, we made a campfire and sat around it and talked about the day until 11:00 that night. There were thunderstorms that night and the strong winds shook our tents for hours. We were really scared and kept calling out to each other to check to see if everyone was all right. After the storms were over, nightmares kept me awake. We headed for the next section of the study road early the next morning.

We crossed Gibe River and drove 35 kilometres towards Addis Ababa, then branched off the main road to the right and took the road to Endeber. Endeber is the centre of the Gurage – one of the most industrious tribes in the country. The Gurage include intellectuals, soldiers, businessmen and shoe-shiners. They number about two million and have an enviable culture. Every year at Meskal, the holiday in celebration of the finding of the True Cross, they return to their traditional lands with gifts for their relatives. They are Christians as well as Muslims. They spend about a week there, receive blessings from their elders and return to their homes. The Gurage are also famous for their economic and social development of their traditional lands. They form committees to raise financing from within the tribe and to solicit money from Gurage in the Diaspora. Those who don't co-operate are ostracised. They have built community roads and collect tolls to build schools and clinics and to purchase electric generators. They are an example to all Ethiopians.

We passed Endeber and travelled south for another 80 kilometres until we reached Hosanna, a town known as Wachemo by those who native to it. The people are the most literate in the country and were educated through the Protestant churches and at government schools. It is also one of the most densely populated areas in the country. Most people work as labourers in sugar manufacturing. Bekele, a friend at university, came from the area and had told me a lot about it. We rested for the night at Hosanna. It's a very clean town, with good hotels at reasonable prices. The food was good too.

Sodo, the capital of Wolaita Awraja, is 96 kilometres southeast of Hosanna. The people had bitterly resisted Emperor Menelik II's expansionist drive. He was the architect of modern-day Ethiopia and the man who defeated the Italian invaders in 1896 at the battle of Adua. The gravel road between Hosanna and Sodo was very rough, but the scenery was very beautiful. While in Sodo, we visited the Wolaita Agricultural Development Unit (WADU) and other relevant agencies. Like the people of southern Ethiopia, the people of Wolaita prepare food from *enset*, also known as "false banana." It is very laborious to grow *enset* and extract the starchy edible part. Many types of foods are prepared from *enset* and the people depend on it highly, especially during droughts. The crop requires weeding and must be fertilised with manure. Cultivating it demands a lot of heavy labour for not that much nutritional value. Growing high-quality *enset* means constant weeding or mulching and also depends on the maturity of the plant. The root is their main source of food and, unlike the banana, the plant has no edible fruit.

We stayed in Sodo for two days, then left for the field visit. We had covered the first 120-kilometre stretch and now had the remaining 40 kilometres. First, we drove to Bele, a village about 40 kilometres west of Sodo. The area is poor and overpopulated. During the previous government, the area was known for its commercial cotton plantations and for soybeans. After land was nationalised, it was ignored. It looked suitable for commercial farming but was being under-utilised. There were no government offices but there were some schools and clinics. We met a teacher who told us that the area had become economically depressed after the revolution.

We drove to the bridge and met the Kulo Konta Awraja administrator there. The bridge was a short one and we crossed it two or three times. One of the cadres proudly told the administrator about the anti-revolutionary students that he and his colleagues had thrown into the river from the top of the bridge. It was not hard to imagine that many young people must have been killed in similar circumstances around the country. We went back to town with the administrator and headed for lunch at the at the teacher's place. The administrator was very keen on getting the road built and stressed its importance again and again. I too wished it would get built soon. It would help not only to move goods between Jima and Sodo but to make it easier for people to interact. The Dawro people in Kefa Province and the Wolaita people in Sidamo Province speak the same language and have similar cultures. The road was long overdue.

We left Bele and stopped in Sodo for breakfast. Sodo was famous for fresh butter, so I bought some for Emaye. I had bought *teff* for *injera* at the market in Chida, coffee and root crops in Waka and now butter in Sodo. Emaye would be very happy. Before we took off for Addis Ababa, we spent a night in Shashemane Town to relax. I came to know that, Ali Musa, the rogue soldier there had killed hundreds of students and business people. Even hearing his name shocked people. I was told that he had killed once a number of people and buried their bodies in a mass grave. People saw the soil on top moving – some of his victims had been buried alive. Another story told of a man who had travelled from Addis to Shashemane. He didn't know Musa but had heard about his atrocities. The man was looking for a room for a night and went to a hotel where Musa was staying at the time. He asked the receptionist for a room, but insisted that it not be near the rogue soldier's room. Musa overheard his name and told the man, "If you spent the night here, you're a dead man." The man left the town within an hour.

We left Shashemane and drove northeast along the Rift Valley. Lake Langano and Lake Ziway were on our right and Lake Shala and Lake Abiyata on our left. The road was paved, the terrain was good and the driving excellent. After we'd driven 177 kilometres from Shashemane, we turned left and headed north. We passed Modjo Town and then Debre Zeit Town and were back in Addis Ababa.

Emaye was sitting at the doorstep. I called her from a distance. Her sight had deteriorated during Wondime's imprisonment but she knew my voice and said, "Alemye! You are back!" She kissed the ground three times, stood up, stretched her hands to the sky and said, "Saint George of the Lydia! Thank you!" She meant God. I went inside the house to greet Abaye and he was happy too. He thanked Saint George of Baha and he too meant God. Baha was not far from where he was born and had Saint George's Church. I handed over the butter, coffee and grain to Emaye and she kissed the ground again and again, thanking God.

The political tension in the country had subsided. However, uneasiness has prevailed because of harassment from community cadres. They called meetings on Sundays, to keep the people from going to church. Orthodox Christians wouldn't give up their worship easily and boycotted the meetings. Even the so-called Marxist-Leninist politicians who they said believed in materialism went to church.

* * *

Welo Province is known as the source of Amharic music, one of the most popular music in the country. When I was very young, *azmaris* from Welo stayed at our house. *Azmaris* are travelling minstrels and an important part of Ethiopia's everyday life, even today. They perform at weddings and public meetings held in *tej* bars. People in Welo are admired for their good-features. It was said that in olden times, Welo was also famous for its abundant crops and its cattle. After the harvest, farmers used to make piles of the crops. Then they would fire bullets at the piles. If a bullet went through, the harvest was considered too poor to use and the piles were burned to ashes. However, Welo has been associated with drought lately. The drought of 1973-1974 killed about 750,000 Ethiopians, most of them in Welo. The area was hard to reach that made food distribution very difficult. The international community and the government were determined to build roads, especially rural roads, and quite a few did get built. The government had also committed itself to building feeder roads. To that end, a 250-kilometre road linking Woreilu, Tenta and Bet Hor was envisaged. I was assigned to carry out the feasibility study

Our first destination was Desie, the capital of the province and 400 kilometres north of Addis Ababa. The road to Desie was paved and was the oldest road in the country. As I rode by my elementary and high schools, old memories came to mind. When I looked at the elementary school, Emaye came to my mind, begging the director to let me enrol and then bowing to him. The high school reminded me the stipend I received and how I shared it with Emaye. I cherished her. She never gave up on life.

We crossed hills and mountains and looked out at the cattle and monkeys in northern Shewa Province. We ate our lunch at the Chirameda Restaurant, famous for its roast chicken. It's about 205 kilometres from Addis Ababa. The chickens were very large, which made some people refuse to eat it – they suspected that the chickens were really vultures. We arrived at Desie in early afternoon, reserved rooms in a hotel and began to look around the town. The Tosa Mountain on the northern side looked too heavy for the town and the town itself looked squeezed in, with limited possibility of expansion. It was crowded, had lots of young people and plenty of bars, nightclubs and hotels.

The Unimog did not arrive. We hadn't worried about that on the way since the road was good, but it was not there the next day either. We were worried and so called the head office. They told us that there had been an accident. Finally, the Unimog arrived late in the afternoon. The accident had happened near the Legedadi militia training camp, 25 kilometres out of Addis Ababa. While the Unimog was passing the camp, militiamen were disembarking from a truck. One was struck crossing the road and died. The accident was a serious matter, since the militia were at the time the most valuable people in the country. They were fighting rebels and secessionists in the north and more enemies in the east. Indeed, there were militia all over the country. As a result, the driver had to face military officers. We usually carried a letter that explained what we were doing and that sought co-operation from government agencies. That helped him a lot. He signed that he would appear when summoned and they let him go free. We had already started collecting data in Desie. We continued our journey the next day and then headed to Woreilu, the beginning of the study road. The distance between Desie and Wereilu was 90 kilometres, over rugged and barren terrain. The domestic animals were thin and struggled to walk. The land had been over-grazed and was uncultivated. Prolonged neglect of afforestation and poor soil conservation had seriously damaged the land.

We reached Woreilu Village where we saw monkeys and chimpanzees that moved boldly and proudly and seemed afraid of nothing. Woldeselassie, the engineer, and I tried to chase some of them away but they turned towards us instead. They never even flinched, so we thought it would be wise to get away from them. There was a rural road construction camp in Wereilu. We set up our tents and went to visit the construction engineer. He told us how devastated the area was, how helpless the people were and how skinny the animals were. He said that the people should be resettled to more fertile lands. We needed to confirm or refute his arguments. Nonetheless, construction of rural roads was intensive there, in the hope of improving food distribution.

We visited the relevant offices and the surrounding area and it seemed that no agricultural surplus could be expected. Resettlement did seem viable. Then we headed north to Tenta Town. The road was very rough and also the food I ate the previous day had upset my stomach, so we had to stop many times along the way. Fortunately, we had a first-aid kit with us and I managed to treat myself. That trip was the worst I had had so far. Tenta Village about 70 kilometres from Woreilu had very few trees. The land was dry, with underweight cattle struggling to eat. It was very disheartening.

We stayed at a granary – it was big but almost empty. We visited the market and all the merchandise that came from towns and cities. There were few crops for sale. Cattle were sold at very cheap prices and we bought a nice sheep for 20 Birr. In Addis Ababa, that sheep could have brought the owner

150 Birr. Most people looked destitute, although the people of Welo were described as very diligent and happy. When I was very young, I had seen them travelling by donkey, horse and mule to western Ethiopia during the coffee harvest. They would harvest coffee for months, then sell their draft animals, and return home with some cash. Some settled where they worked and became prosperous. It was terrible to see them in such a precarious situation. We collected our data and headed to Wegel Tena. On the way and from a distance, we saw Magdala Village to the west. Magdala is where Emperor Theodores II committed suicide to escape capture by the British army in 1868.

We crossed the Teleyayen River. It was wide but dry at the time. We knew about its power, however. In Amharic "Teleyayen" refers to the impossibility of communication between friends and relatives living on opposite sides of the river when it floods during the rainy season. When we crossed it there were rocks in the middle. Next we headed further north, past barren rocky hills with no life and offering no possibility of a livelihood. We climbed rugged hills and mountains and arrived at a plain that led us to Wegel Tena. We camped in a grain store there too and it too was almost empty. Outside, people were starving. It was appalling. Famished people were going from place to place in search of food and finding none. Their clothes were completely worn out, their bodies were unbelievably thin and their faces looked lifeless. The man who worked as the administration secretary was wearing pants that were worn out in the seat and patched with pieces of different coloured cloth. He was supposed to being paid, but I presumed that was not enough to buy him decent clothes. People were starving here while fertile lands were lying idle in the western and southern parts of the country.

Bet Hor village is 40 kilometres from Wegel Tena, the end of the study road. We headed towards Bet Hor and camped again in an empty granary. We visited the remaining section of the study road. There was little settlement and it seemed deserted. Five years had passed since that last major drought, but it seemed not to be over there. We headed back to Desie by a different route. We took a shortcut and reached Kutaber, a village notorious for the killings of peasants. I heard it was the same rogue soldier, Ali Musa that massacred civilians and buried some of them alive in Shashemane Town. In this case, peasants had revolted against the government and were travelling towards Desie when soldiers under his command gunned down thousands of them. I couldn't buy anything for Emaye this time – the place had nothing to buy, not even for the people who lived there.

* * *

At the time, Ethiopia had fewer than 25,000 kilometres of road within its 1.1 million square kilometres of area. It had fewer than 100,000 vehicles, making road density about 20 metres per square kilometre of area and vehicle density about four per kilometre of road. In contrast, in the United States, there are more than six million kilometres of roads within its ten million square kilometres and more than 200 million vehicles, making the road density more than 600 metres per square kilometre of area and vehicle density more than 30 per kilometre. Not only that, trucks in the US travel more than 100,000 kilometres per year. In Ethiopia, it is about 50,000 kilometres. Similarly, cars in the US travel more 20,000 kilometres per year. In Ethiopia it is less than 10,000 kilometres per year. This shows how underdeveloped transport is in Ethiopia. Due to limited transportation, regional integration is poor and the people at the periphery are totally forgotten.

Wellega, in western Ethiopia, is one of the richest provinces. It has abundant coffee crops and lots of minerals. However, most of the province is out of the reach of the central government. As a result, the Assosa-Guba road, with a length of 140 kilometres, was being proposed. It would connect the Provinces of Welega and Gojam across the Blue Nile. I was assigned to conduct the study of the section near the Sudanese border.

Shiferaw, the Unimog driver, was new to the group and he refused to buy food with us. He insisted he could survive by himself. We thought that was strange, but we agreed. The rest of us packed our field materials and headed west. The first 25 kilometres were narrow and zigzagged. That stretch ended at Holeta, a village used as a training base for non-commissioned military officers. Most of the Derg had been commissioned there, including President Mengistu. Despite its proximity to Addis Ababa, the village was undeveloped. We continued our journey and passed Addis Alem, the town that had been the headquarters of Emperor Menelik II before he moved to Addis Ababa. Emperor Menelik was both an important and a very controversial figure in the Ethiopian history. He had defeated the Italian force at the Battle of Adua in 1896, setting an example for other colonised African countries. Menelik was also the architect of modern Ethiopia – he unified the western, southern and eastern part of the country. But in the process he also subjugated the local people, took their lands, and imposed Amhara domination.

We continued our journey, passing Ambo, a town known for its mineral water, and then Gedo, a village with a junction to Finchaa, itself a village known for generating the most hydroelectric power in the country and also for a huge sugar plantation in the lowlands. We drove still further and arrived at Bako, the border town between Shewa and Wollega Provinces. It was a well-populated town but did not have electricity despite its proximity to the Finchaa Dam. The night was very dark. There were small bars and hotels scattered throughout the town, so we visited a *tej* bar, which was very crowded. We sat on seats made of mud and stone and covered with carpets of palm leaves. It was noisy, with lots of loud jokes and louder laughter. We enjoyed the wine, listened to the jokes and added our laughter. We stayed there until nine that evening then went to our hotel. It was a poorly managed place. The night was long and dark and the bed uncomfortable. As always, we had left in a hurry and had left some things behind.

The next day, we headed to Nekempte, the capital of Wollega Province. Wollega is famous for its coffee, gold and other natural resources. However, the city was undeveloped, and had very few good hotels by Ethiopian standards. We pitched our tents and went to collect data. People didn't like visitors from Addis Ababa at the moment. And they didn't like visitors that spoke Amharic, the official language of the country. In Wollega, people spoke Afan Oromo, the language of the largest tribe in the country. They thought themselves highly suppressed by the central government although they were among the most privileged of that tribe. Most of their lands had not been confiscated by Menelik II or by Haile Selassie. Some of their aristocrats had married into the royal family. Others among the Oromo's had suffered more, but the Oromos of Wellega spoke out about it the most. I thought that was the work of the politicians.

The administrator of the province was a soldier and member of the Derg. As informed, he had been in the national police force band. I never met him but heard he was incompetent. At the time, the police force was very corrupt. I had also heard he was particularly notorious for dodging his debts, avoiding paying even the smallest shops in Addis Ababa. We walked around the town to get a feel for the area. It was poorly designed and had unpaved roads. It was very unfortunate for a province with so many resources. The people had the right to complain to the central government about economic development but they had no language rights. All the same, every tribe has its exploiters and exploited and it doesn't make sense to condemn anybody based on ethnicity. Some hotels refused to rent rooms to guests of some ethnic groups. That was irrational and poor business ethics. On the other hand, I found many people very kind and helpful.

Our next destination was Ghimbi, 113 kilometres west of Nekempte, and known for being the region's commercial coffee centre. The area in between was very delightful. It was full of virgin forests, the sounds of flowing rivers and beautiful landscapes. The famous Didesa River lies between the two towns. It is one of the nation's large rivers and carries our soil away to neighbouring Sudan and Egypt. We have lost more from our rivers than we've gained from them.

Ghimbi Town was on a hill, but didn't look attractive – it was very rugged. However, the hotels and bars were very clean and prices were reasonable. Ghimbi reminded me of a colleague. Kenaa worked with me at the excise tax department in Asab. I met him on the road once when I was at the university and he was a political cadre. He was a native of Ghimbi area. During the revolution, elites from the area were in the highest echelon of the political hierarchy and they were proud of that. Kenaa said, "Currently, cadres travel to the Soviet Union and to Eastern Europe for political indoctrination. In the future, Ghimbi will replace them all." It didn't work out that way. Many were killed, chased out of the country or ended up in jail by the very government they had set up. They thought they could easily manipulate the soldiers because of their better academic training. However, the military was adept at politics and ingenious at intricate criminal conspiracies. At the beginning, the Derg favoured them because that helped the Derg eliminate the opposition. Later, they became the targets. Once President Mengistu said, "Those who wanted us for lunch found that we had them for breakfast."

We headed for Asosa Town. After ten kilometres, the road to Dembidolo branched off to the left. Dembidolo was well known for its natural and intellectual resources. The Protestant religion is dominant in Wellega in general and in Dembidolo in particular. Missionaries from the West had built many modern schools and the people had benefited from that. They were very proud of their academic successes and they deserved to be. Many medical doctors, engineers, pharmacists, and so on, had been born in the area. The town of Nejo lies 70 kilometres from Ghimbi, on a plain. The surroundings were beautiful and the hotels and bars well managed. It was a market day and many peasants had come from distant places. Chopped meat was being roasted in a large pan in the middle of the market and people would taste it, using fork-like sticks, before they bought. They could go on tasting the meat for quite a while. The sellers were lucky – in Addis Ababa they would have gone home empty-handed.

We left Nejo and headed for Asosa. A good rural road had been constructed and was serving well but traffic was light at the time. We drove through Mendi, a village 70 kilometres from Nejo. We had no time to stop but looked at it through clouds of dust. Mendi reminded me of a girl who had been with us during the national development campaign. She'd been in her second year at Addis Ababa University and was energetic and enthusiastic. She was one of the most dedicated girls in the campaign and had contributed to raising the consciousness of women since she spoke Afan Oromo, the language of the region. The road was flat from Mendi onwards. We crossed

211

the Bambesi River, about 50 kilometres from Mendi. It flowed through an uncultivated savannah. It was amazing to see that vast arable land lying idle in a deplorably poverty-stricken country. Who is to blame? Of course nature is not!

We travelled 47 kilometres further from the Bambesi River and arrived at Asosa, a village, 680 kilometres west of Addis Ababa. The land is flat and there is little agriculture there, though the potential is huge. The people looked wretched. However, liquor bars were busy at night, the common sign of urbanisation in Ethiopia.

We set up our camp in an open space in the town and visited government and other relevant offices. We visited bars at night to learn more about the area. There weren't many people in the bars though. Local people rather preferred *areke*, a traditional vodka-like alcohol sold in ramshackle houses. I saw some people staggering from it. We visited the market but didn't see many crops and there was no merchandise. The remoteness of the place and the marginalisation of the people were obvious.

Next we went to the Dabus River, 40 kilometres away. It flows to Sudan and the land around has vast potential. However, agriculture was poor. Sudan and Egypt make use of the soil that the river sweeps away. Ethiopia has come to mean drought and starvation. It is *the* illustration of natural calamity. The aid collected in the name of starving Ethiopians has been of most benefit to aid agencies and institutions – aid creates jobs. I had heard that expatriates coming to work for NGOs were not interested in being assigned to non-resort areas. They wanted to work close to the Rift Valley Lakes or near other resorts. If famine ever disappears from Ethiopia, many, many international workers will lose their jobs. They have been there for 30 years now, but there is still no sustainable development. Donors in foreign countries are generous, but the aid melts away and only negligible amounts reach those in need. The middlemen benefit the most. Nobody has been seriously concerned with solving the real problems and it will remain that way for a very long time to come – the donors donating, the supposed recipients starving and the middlemen benefiting.

We drove west for 46 kilometres along the main road to Kurmuk Town on the Sudanese border and then branched off to the right. We saw settlement filled with people from drought-stricken areas in Wello, northern Ethiopia. They had begun to grow crops and towns were springing up. It seemed like the right kind of scheme for the country. It makes no sense to cling to over-cultivated lands.

Menge is a very small village 20 kilometres further along. Merchants buy gold from the area, gold sieved from a nearby river. Most of the merchants were from Sudan. Groundnuts were in abundance and we bought a bucketful for four Birr. As we travelled further to Gizen, a village at the Sudanese border, the area looked abandoned. Gizen was very remote and backward and sold nothing but alcohol. Sudanese soldiers crossed the border to drink alcohol and Ethiopians went to Sudan for medical and other social services.

We crossed the border and visited the shops and markets on the other side. They were much better shops and had lots of fabrics. It must have been very demoralising for the people on the Ethiopian side.

We left the camp behind and drove to the Blue Nile River. There we saw a small group of nomadic people called the Parpararo. The men were almost naked. There were no crops in the fields and no domestic animals. I didn't know how they survived. It seemed that neither the glorious Haile Selassie government nor the revolutionary Derg had ever reached them. There was no more to be seen and we turned back since the river was not crossable to visit the other side.

Next we visited Kurmuk, a village 96 kilometres west of Asosa. It's another border village. There are two Kurmuks, one on the Ethiopian side and the other in Sudan. It was a prosperous place by rural Ethiopian standards and we were told that the other side was even better developed. We were not allowed to cross – it was feared that we might be fleeing the country. We were told the rule was a recent one, imposed after an Ethiopian scientist tricked the border police into letting him cross over. He was there for a field trip and had camped in the town. That first morning, he started jogging. That day, he jogged towards the Sudanese Kurmuk but returned. The next day, he jogged a little further, and the next day a little further. He kept extending his route until he crossed the border. Then he defected to Sudan. Defections were common during the military government. We returned to Asosa and headed for Addis Ababa. I hadn't bought anything for Emaye this time. Coffee was cheap but we were not allowed to buy even the smallest amount.

Our mission was not over yet. We hadn't visited the section on the other side of the Blue Nile because there was no bridge. We spent few days in Addis Ababa, replenishing our groceries. Shiferaw, the Unimog driver, said he wanted to contribute for food this time. He did not say why and we didn't ask him.

Emaye and Abaye were getting older and weaker. Both had stopped going to church and were spending most of their times at home. Every day at six in the evening, Emaye slowly and carefully left the house. She was half blind now. Once she was out front, she would stand straight, stretch her hands towards the sky and look up. She prayed and prayed for hours, thanking God for all the good things he had done to her through her children and begged for longer lives for her husband and herself and for more opportunities for her children. Abaye was getting sick and his sight was not good either. Sometimes, he shivered and grew faint. Wondime and I had taken him to clinics and hospitals but he was not feeling better. Unfortunately, we didn't have enough money to get him good medical care.

Anyone could see the economic difference those in our village who had children and those who didn't. Those with working children got help and felt better and lived longer while those without ended up as beggars and some even died early. When I went to church, I saw several of them sitting and begging. They were like my parents and when they saw me they acted likewise. When I had money, I dropped coins in their hands. When I didn't, I would walk the other way. Some of them would come to the house and ask Emaye for food. She never turned anyone away, even when there was very little. She always shared what she had. Whenever people were very hungry, they went to Emaye. It was very sad.

We travelled to Gojam to complete the study road. We arrived at Markos Town the first day and settled at the Rural Roads Camp. Our station wagon had developed mechanical problem on the way and we wanted have it checked at the district maintenance shop nearby. They checked and told us that the car had a major mechanical problem and that we would have to get a part from Addis Ababa. We would have to wait in Markos until that happened. Easter was approaching and I had planned to buy grain, butter and chicken for Emaye on my way back. One week had already passed and the part hadn't arrived. Another week was soon half over and the part still hadn't arrived.

Fasika – or Easter – is a very important holiday in Ethiopia. Orthodox Tewahedo Christians fast for 55 days – they abstain from meat, eggs, butter and dairy products. As the holiday approaches, people get prepared by buying sheep and chicken to slaughter. Priests and other firm believers stop eating and drinking anything from Thursday to Sunday. On Friday, people go to church to pray. During my boyhood, people would confess the sins they had committed. The priests would tell them to stand up and bow a certain number of times – the number depended on the seriousness of the sin. On Saturday evening, people would go to church to pray and stay there until two in the morning, until the priests had declared that Christ had risen from his grave. Then, people went home and broke their fasts. They usually didn't go home until three or four in the morning.

After Easter, people took bread and wine or other alcohol to their children's godfathers and eyefathers. An eyefather was the man who had covered the boy's eyes while he was being circumcised. Godfathers and eyefathers would reciprocate by buying clothes or giving some money to their godsons and eyesons. My eyefather had a record player, the only one in our village. He would play records for me when we went to visit him after Easter. I thought the music was Italian, but what I was really interested in was watching the record play. I boasted to Wondime that his eyefather didn't have a record player.

I thought that Easter in Markos would be very lonely. However, when we found out that we wouldn't be home by then, we started preparing to celebrate with whatever we could manage. We bought chicken, butter, *injera* and coffee. Our cook prepared a delicious meal. On Easter morning, Seife, the engineer, and I went to buy *tella*, local beer. As we walked from door to door to look for *tella*, people invited us for food. We got invitation after invitation. Finally, an elderly woman asked us to come in. She was alone and told us about the hospitality of the people of Gojam. She said,

"After harvest, farmers give to the paupers before taking anything home. They feel the harvest won't be blessed unless they share with the poor."

We had a very good Easter at our temporary place. In keeping with Ethiopian tradition, we had scattered green grasses in the room as a symbol of a good harvest. We ate i*njera* and bread, with chicken and mutton sauces, and some roasted meat. We had bought very good *tella*. After our meal, we drank coffee and enjoyed the scent of a smoking piece of myrrh. I hoped that Emaye and Abaye were having a good Easter too.

The part for the station wagon arrived the week after Easter. We had the car fixed as soon as we could and left for the study area. We drove along a gravel road across rolling terrain for about 160 kilometres. The area was well suited for agriculture – Gojam Province had fed the whole nation during grain shortage in 1979-1980. We branched off the main road and drove towards the west at Kosober Village, heading for Chagne Town, 57 kilometres away. A good gravel road connected Kosober and Chagne and we reached our destination early in the day. Kosober is the centre of Agew Awraja. Near the end of the 10th century, Yodit, then the Agew leader, ended the thousand–year Axumite Empire and attempted to eradicate Christianity. In Ethiopian traditional tales, she is known as one of the great destroyers of churches. Her dynasty prevailed for about 130 years between the 10th and 12th centuries. Today, the Agew are adherents of the Ethiopian Orthodox Tewahedo Church and number about 750,000. The Agew are the only people in Ethiopia that plough with horses.

Chagne was filled with bars. One person told me that it had been two years since the Ethiopian Roads Authority (ERA) had established its camp in the area and all the children less than two years of ages belonged to ERA staff. I thought he was joking. However, it was common for ERA employees to settle wherever they went. Some of them would have two or three wives in different places, which would remain unknown until such men died and all their wives would apply for pensions. The people of Chagne came from diverse ethnic backgrounds and many people had come from outside the area. The most significant economic activity seemed to be road construction.

We left for the study area towards west. The altitude slowly dropped as we drove towards Mambuk, a village 50 kilometres from Chagne. The Beles River flows from Mambuk and joins the Blue Nile and then flows towards Sudan and Egypt. There was virgin land and it looked like it had good agricultural potential. The road stopped at Mambuk village and the way ahead was track. We drove for another 120 kilometres and reached Guba Village, the other end of the study road. It looked abandoned and was thickly covered with stands of bamboo. We were told that it had been settled at one time but was deserted due to lack of water. We left the main track and tried to use the Unimog to drive through the bamboo, but it was impossible even to imagine that we could reach the Blue Nile – the bamboo was growing that densely. After five kilometres, we turned back – we had another 95 kilometres to go and it looked like we would not be able to manage the terrain and that there would be few, if any, settlements. Even the return drive was difficult. It took us twice the time to reach the point we had started from.

Instead, we went to Bambudi, a village on the Sudanese border and about 100 kilometres away. We drove along a track, over hills and across rugged terrain. Settlements were sparse and there were vast agricultural areas. We had been told that the land was ideal for cash crops such as cotton, soybeans and groundnuts. However, people survived by hunting and subsistence farming. They also ate rodents that looked like large rats. To hunt the rodents, they would set fires around their burrows, forcing the animals out. Then they killed and roasted them.

The trip to Bambudi village was very tiring. We set up our camp on the outskirts of the village and visited the place in the evening. Bars were plentiful, as usual. We went into a local bar and watched some teachers from the highlands perform. They performed in pairs. One would recite a long poem while the other accompanied him on a traditional instrument. It was very entertaining because most of the pieces celebrated the town's fame for its housemaids who married teachers. The town had no potable water, so people got their water from dirty ponds. As the day passed the pond water would get warmer and warmer, increasing the prospect of bacterial contamination. Fortunately, we had a water purifying container and metal bottles to store water. We soaked sisal rope in water and wrapped the bottles with it. That kept our water cool.

The Blue Nile runs beside Bambudi. The river is wide there but looks motionless. It is amazing that Ethiopians could starve when the country has such land and water. There is no one to blame but the elites and the authorities. We crossed the Blue Nile and entered Sudan, where the border guards welcomed us and offered us cold water, a tradition in the area. They were extremely wholehearted in their hospitality. However, the Sudanese side looked even more backward than Bambudi – we saw no settlement, just barren land. The Sudanese border guards crossed into Ethiopia to eat and drink *areke,* local vodka.

We drove around Bambudi, visited the surrounding areas and talked to people in communities where hunting was the mainstay. They didn't look destitute. Wild game was apparently available, but we didn't see any. We left Bambudi and drove to Chagne. It had rained for a few days and the land was now very green. Just ten days had passed, but it was amazing to see how fertile the soil was. We arrived back in Chagne and visited some more places. That night we dropped into the bars to say goodbye to friends. Our next trip would be to Bahir Dar, to visit industries that might use the raw materials produced in the study area.

Bahir Dar is a city that always seems new, even to frequent visitors. The air is very refreshing and it has beautiful scenery, especially Lake Tana in the northern part of the city. I was informed by church people in Bahir Dar that there are more than 35 islands in Lake Tana scattered about the surface of the lake. Out of those, more than 15 shelter churches and monasteries of immense historical and cultural interest which are decorated with beautiful paintings and housing innumerable treasures. I didn't have the opportunity to visit any of the islands. Thousands of tourists from around the world visit the islands every year.

The trip had been tiring, so we enjoyed touring the city by night and taking a look at the places like the Tana Hotel. We visited the market to see what crops were being sold. The people at the market looked very poor, which was surprising since Gojam was known for its bountiful crops. The land was flat and always green, but the people looked poor. It may have been because no one wanted to invest in the area after the military government began to nationalise properties.

We drove back to Addis Ababa, stopping now and then so I could buy foodstuffs for Emaye. Gojam was an ideal place for that. I bought *teff* for *injera*, butter, chicken and onion – it was very cheap. We stopped in Markos for a night and, as before, rested at the rural roads camp. I went to a bar with Shiferaw, the Unimog driver. We had never had a chance to talk. We found a bar that was quiet and decent, ordered beer and started talking. The first thing I asked him was why he had refused to buy groceries with the group during the first part of the study. He seemed very gentle and mature. He told me that he had been conscripted into the military as a boy scout and later as an infantryman. He had served with Mengistu Hailemariam, the head of state for a very long time in the eastern part of the country. He told me that Tsegaye, the station wagon driver on Chida-Sodo road, had given him bad impression of me. I had scolded him when he had a fight with the Unimog driver because some cooking oil spilled during rough ride along the escarpment. Shiferaw said he changed his mind about me after watching me during the first half of this trip. He had 11 children and was very responsible. We got closer after that and he told me stories.

"Once, one of my daughters was seriously ill and I was spending the night with her at the Princess Tsehay Hospital in Addis Ababa. I stayed all night with her and left in the morning. Her mother stayed with her during the day. One night, I was so tired that I was dead asleep. I woke up after four hours, at four in the morning. My daughter was not in bed. I was numb for few minutes. Then I ran to the nurse's office and the nurse was taking nap. I woke her up and asked her about my daughter. She was very annoyed at me for disturbing her, so I got antagonistic in return and demanded to know where my daughter was. She said my daughter had died and that her body had been taken to the morgue. I pulled out my gun and told her to put my daughter back in bed. She refused, but I shoved her with the gun and scared her to death. She took me to the doctor's office. He was napping too. She didn't want to wake him up, so I woke him up instead. She told him the story and he yelled at me, calling crazy. I pointed my gun at him. He told the nurse to bring the body back and she did.

"I stood close by her bed, staring at her face. I stared for two hours, without moving. I saw her face gradually getting redder and redder. I ran to the doctor's office and woke him up, saying that she was alive. The doctor said I was crazy and asked me to get out of his office. I pulled my gun out again and pointed it at him. He walked to her room, cursing me all the while, and I followed him. He looked at her face, then stood stock-still. After a while he said, `Incredible! She *is* alive!' And she was." I asked Shiferaw if she was still alive. He said, "Of course. I will take you home one day and you will meet her and her mother."

"Another time, my second daughter got sick – one of her legs went numb. I went from hospital to hospital, from doctor to doctor, even to conjurers but to no avail – I lost hope. One day, someone said I should go to Mechara Town, in Harerghe Province, and visit a conjurer there. It is tough to be a parent. I borrowed some money from ERA's employee co-operative and my daughter and I took a bus to Mechara. We had nobody to stay with or to talk to about the conjurer. I asked people where he lived and they showed me right away.

"About seven men were seating in rows and chewing *chat* and spitting on a patient. They were chanting words I didn't understand. We sat down and waited until they finished. Then I described my daughter's condition. They took my daughter to another room and asked me to return the next day and I went to a hotel. I went back the next day and they were spitting on my daughter. I kept quiet, watched for a while, then left the room and returned to my hotel. I stayed for a week. I visited her, sometimes spending the night. Then, after a week and in the middle of the night, they gave me a cloth bundle and told me to go and bury it in the middle of the graveyard at the church nearby. I didn't know the place, it was the middle of the night, it was very dark outside, and I was really terrified. I thought of refusing, but remembered that her mother was devastated by our daughter's illness. I asked for directions and left the house.

"I walked very slowly, the slightest movement scared me – it was more frightening than anything I faced on the battlefield. After half an hour, I reached by the church and began searching for the graveyard. I walked in the middle of the graveyard and stood there for a few minutes. Nothing moved. I buried the rag bundle between tombs and walked fast for the house. When I went in the house, my daughter jumped out of the other room, grabbed my leg and said, "Ababa!" I was dumbstruck. I couldn't believe it. I paid them and left for home the next day." That night Shiferaw and I became friends and we remained friends until he died few years ago. I have been to his place many times and have met both daughters. His wife has told me the same stories.

We left for Addis Ababa early next morning. At the time, the government was encouraging citizens to own their own homes. Land was being distributed and mortgages were available at low rates. Those who were willing to use building societies were offered mortgages at four percent, while those who wanted to go it alone were charged seven percent. First, I was registered with a society, but I changed my mind since progress was very slow. As well, I had seen many building societies fail and people lose long-time friends because of selfishness. It wasn't only the financial losses caused by delays that bothered me. I didn't like the bickering between members. It would be awkward to have a bickering person as a neighbour.

I applied to the Municipality of Addis Ababa for a piece of land. Aregay, my engineer friend worked for the municipality and had told me how and when to apply. I was issued about 400 square metres of land. At the back, it adjoined another plot and Aregay told me to apply for another 100 square metres. I did. I did not have time to collect the ownership title. Then I went to the mortgage bank and asked for a loan. I was granted a loan of 18,000 Birr.

Shortly after, I started building the house. It was very small, 54 square metres and I had spent only one-third of the money by the time the framework was completed. I thought the money I had borrowed was a lot and that I would save some of it for furniture. I invited a friend who had recently finished building his house to come and visit me. When I told him what I had left, he laughed and said, "I could build two like this for what you've already spent. But I couldn't finish it with double the amount you have left." He was right. The money ran out while the finishing was half done.

The revolution was still underway and the government had introduced political discussion, '*Wiyiyit*' forums at all government offices and agencies. Two days a week, Mondays and Fridays, there were political discussions in offices and on construction sites. For an hour, government workers stopped all work that wasn't absolutely necessary and met in groups. However, only cadres that chaired the meetings and some party members wanted to participate. Some people slept and others didn't listen. It was terribly boring. Taxi vans were called *Wiyiyit* after the discussion forum. *Wiyiyit* passengers usually were strangers and so didn't talk to one another. I attended the meetings whenever I was not on field trips. Sometimes, I avoided them by saying that I had urgent work and my boss backed me up. At one meeting, I sat down beside Shewaye. I had seen her before and we had said hello, but we hadn't talked. She was very quite and gentle by nature and was even quieter at the *Wiyiyit*. Finally, I broke the ice and said, "How is work?" We started talking and she told me that the end of the budget year was coming and that she would be working on ERA's property inventory for three months and would be getting overtime pay. I knew that she wasn't married, so I said, "Will you invite me for tea when you get your first pay?" She said she would, "with pleasure." I was happy about that.

At the end of her first month working on the inventory, I saw her at the political meeting and she said, "I got my first pay. Are you ready for tea?" I said, "I am even happier than you are." We arranged to meet at the Ambassador Hotel at three in the afternoon on the coming Saturday. She was on time. I arrived early. We entered the hotel and ordered tea – I didn't want to order beer the first time. I asked her if she was married. She didn't answer but began to cry. I asked her why she was crying. She didn't answer, so I kept quiet. Something was wrong, but I didn't know what. We talked about something else and spent the afternoon together. She paid for the tea and we left the hotel after agreeing to meet in two weeks.

The following Monday, I told the story to a close friend at the ERA. He told me that Shewaye had a son by a man at the ERA. The man had initially promised to marry her but later changed his mind. That wasn't uncommon and I appreciated her problem. I had encountered similar experience before. Kidan, a girl in my village went to Dejazmach Wondirad Elementary School with me and after finishing high school she became a teacher. She wasn't married and I had seen her going out with some men. While Wondime was in jail, I ran in to her and we began to talk. She was learning driving and asked me to help her. We met often and I showed her how to drive Wondime's car. After driving practice, we would go to a bar, order tea and talk about many things. Then I'd drop her off at her place. We got together twice a week, but didn't talk about serious matters like marriage. Gradually, however, I began to want to know if she intended to get married. One evening after driving practice, we went to the bar and began to talk. Eventually marriage came up. I asked her if she had a fiancé and she said she didn't. Then I asked her if she was ready for marriage and she said she was. I kept quiet, happy at heart. I was getting ready to go on field trip to Mizan Teferi and told her I would meet her as soon as I got back. She agreed and I dropped her at her place and went home. I decided to propose to her as soon as I returned from the field trip. I had told Wondime about it and he had agreed. The field trip lasted a month. When I got back, Wondime told me that Kidan was married. I couldn't believe it, but it was true. Unfortunately, though, she got divorced a year later. By then she had a baby daughter. I saw her one more time. She was shy, but I encouraged her to talk and we discussed mundane matters and went home. I haven't seen her since. I have seen many innocent women victimised by men who are predators.

Two weeks after we had tea, Shewaye and I met at the same time and place. This time, we talked about marriage and then I asked her if she would marry me. She told me about her son and I said that it was okay, that I was willing to have him as a son. Finally, she said she would have to think about it and we decided to meet again. When we met the third time, she came with her niece, a university student. I thought that she brought the niece to get her opinion of me. I could have brought my nephew, but I am an independent person and never blame anybody for my failures so I hadn't brought anybody. We had a general conversation about the matter and then parted.

We met another time at the same place. She was interested in marrying me. I told her that I had started building a house and that I could show her the land and the house the next week. I also told her that I couldn't afford to buy her jewellery and clothing for the wedding. Shewaye is very honest and aboveboard and said that she would handle her own clothing and that she had a golden ring and could add some more to that and have rings made for both of us. She also said she would buy an L-shaped sofa for the house. I was honoured by her generosity. We agreed that we couldn't afford to invite more than very close family members and friends. Instead, we decided to give a leaflet declaring our marriage to our other friends. We didn't want to go into debt since we had seen many marriages that ended up in divorce before the wedding debt was paid.

Wondime and his close friend Peter contributed money for the wedding. Metish, Peter's sister, took charge of preparing the food for the wedding. I met her when I was visiting Wondime in jail – her brother also worked at Ethiopian Airlines and he too was jailed. While I was in Addis, I visited Wondime every Sunday and would see her there. She was one of the most caring and kind human being I ever met. She got sick with the sick and hungry with the hungry.

June 28, 1980, was our wedding day. It was Saturday. Six of my friends went with me for the signing at the municipal hall in Addis Ababa Municipality. Shewaye came with her group. We finished the ceremony in an hour and went to her place for lunch. Her mother, sisters, brothers and in-laws were there. After lunch, we went with friends to a park where we spent a few hours having drinks and taking pictures. Finally, we headed to my place. My parents were at my place; we kissed them and greeted my relatives. It was a good day. The next day, we invited her relatives and neighbours to visit and had another good day.

My wife Shewaye is more than a wife to me. She is very responsible and has never complained about what we can't afford. Instead, she makes the most of what we have. We never had to borrow money or ask for an advance on our pay. When we couldn't afford to buy chicken, sheep and other meat for holidays, it didn't matter. We didn't have enough utensils at home. Our house was not fenced and our windows were not curtained. People walking by our house at night saw the two of us eating our supper. Our house was unprotected and thieves troubled us at night, but we were tenacious and kept working on our house. I went to Arusha, Tanzania, for six weeks for a seminar on transportation management course. At the time, Shewaye was pregnant with my first child. I managed to save some money and we finished our bathroom. We started a wonderful life.

* * *

The Konso of Gamo Gofa Province are highly skilled and hard-working people. They are famous for their complex system of stone terraces, built to prevent soil erosion during the rainy season. Their hilly lands are not suitable for using livestock to plough, so they use hoes and pickaxes. They also use sticks for digging holes. The Konso soil and water conservation methods are exceptional by Ethiopian standards and are centuries old. Their terracing and soil conservation system grew out of their harsh environment and their need to survive despite having no outside support.

The Konso village lies 595 kilometres south-west of Addis Ababa where three roads cross. One of those goes to Yabello Town and then to Kenyan border. However, that road was not an all-weather road, so the government decided to do a study to see if it could be developed to connect the Gamo Gofa and Sidamo Provinces. It was thought that a better road would help strengthen trade between Kenya and Ethiopia. I was assigned to be the team leader for the economic feasibility study. We prepared our field materials and equipment and headed for Arbaminch City, the provincial capital of Gamo Gofa and 505 kilometres south-west of Addis Ababa. The city was divided into two, with part of it in the highlands and part in the lowlands. We set up our tents in highlands near the Bekele Mola Hotel. Bekele Mola, the owner of the hotel, was well known for being a hotel entrepreneur along the Rift Valley lakes and had hotels from Addis Ababa to Moyale on the Kenyan border. He had won an award from Haile Selassie I Foundation for his entrepreneurship.

The hotel at Arbaminch had an ideal location – on top of a hill looking towards Lake Abaya on the east and Lake Chamo on the west, with a hill in between. Tall trees grew along the escarpment and there were many fountains. The name Arbaminch means Forty Springs. At night, the starlit skies above and the lakes below make for very beautiful surroundings. Lake Abaya is larger than Lake Chamo, and as the wind blows from east to west and the waves sweep across the lakes, it looks like Abaya struggling to take-over Chamo, with only the hill keeping them apart. It was a very beautiful place.

The local market in Arbaminch is open at night. It had fish in abundance. We bought one that weighed ten kilograms and Shiferaw, the Unimog driver, made delicious soup and the cook fried some fish for supper. All we lacked was some alcohol for digestion. That reminded me of the story I heard about Dagnew, the Unimog driver on Mota-Bahir Dar road. He had travelled with World Bank experts to an Ethiopian lake that had plenty of fish. The experts had whiskey with them. They caught fish and fried them with cooking oil that Dagnew supplied. They didn't share their whiskey with Dagnew although he had expected to be offered some. He kept quiet for two days. On the third day, they went fishing again and again asked Dagnew for cooking oil. He had little English, but he said, "No whisky, no oil!" Thenceforth, whisky was traded for cooking oil.

We enjoyed supper with soup and fried fish and talked about life. Seife, the engineer, said that a peasant in Addis Ababa had nearly stolen his 12-year-old son. His son was leaving home early one day for school and had been standing in front his house, waiting for his friend. A peasant selling firewood was walking his donkeys to the nearest market. When he saw the boy, he ordered him to walk ahead with the donkeys and the boy did. They had gone for about a kilometre when the boy saw a village soldier returning from a night duty and ran to him for protection. The peasant escaped, leaving the donkeys behind.

Seife's story reminded me of a story about two foreign teenagers who had been kidnapped by peasants in Addis Ababa and taken to rural farms to work as cowherds. The parents looked for them all over the country, they ran newspaper ads and radio announcements, but were not successful and finally left for their country. Many years later, the boys – now grown men – were found selling grain in a market. They spoke Afan Oromo and dressed like typical Ethiopian peasants. The only reason they were noticed was their white skin.

The Dorze live west of Lake Abaya and Lake Chamo, on a mountain near Arbaminch City. They are a small group, numbering fewer than 30,000 people, and speak one of the Omotic languages. The Dorze are famous for their weaving. A large number of them have moved to Addis Ababa and settled in the northern part of the city in an area known as Dorze Sefer. They live and work together as a community. Others see weaving as a low-class occupation, but the Dorze are admired because of their skilled craftsmanship in making the traditional costume, the Dorze *tibeb*. They have their own traditional songs for celebratory and for mourning rituals.

At the time, Arbaminch City was not well developed. It had a cotton plantation and great potential for agriculture but its potential remained untapped because of lack of interest and poor technology. It was amazing to see such vast lands lying fallow in a country where people starved. We travelled to Konso, a village 90 kilometres further west. The road had a good gravel surface and we arrived at Konso early in the morning. The village was very small, hot and dry. People were struggling for survival. The Woito River was close by but was not used for agriculture because people lacked the appropriate technology.

We spent two days in Konso, collecting data, and resumed our trip on the third day. The study road ran southeast towards Yabello and the first 30 kilometres were along a valley. We had to drive slowly until we reached the Segen River. After crossing the river, we by-passed Teltele, a village famous for its cattle market, and turned east onto a good gravel road that ran through a savannah. After we'd driven about 30 kilometres on that road, a leopard leapt into the road and fell under the Unimog, which hit it but didn't kill it. It limped away into the bush. We weren't daring enough to park and see the end of the episode. Instead, we drove fast and arrived at Yabello Town at noontime.

In Yabello, we stayed at public house that was still under construction. The six of us set up our canvas cots in the same room. We thought the cook was using too much food, especially too much meat. Seife volunteered to manage the food. He had large cuts of meat brought in and then hung it from a hook on a pole in the middle of the room. Every morning, Seife called the cook in and negotiated with him about the amount required for the day. Seife would then put a mark on the remaining meat and leave it hanging.

Yabello lies on a dry plain 400 kilometres from Moyale, a town on the border with Kenya. Mega Town is 100 kilometres from Yabello and towards Moyale. The land is not suitable for crops but it is good for raising livestock and I knew that Yabello and the area around it was famous for its cattle. We visited a cattle research centre and then travelled to Mega. There was lots of merchandise available in Mega, especially utensils, which were presumably contraband brought in from Kenya.

We finished the study and went to Awasa. On the way, we travelled through the forests of Hageremariam and the coffee centres of Yirgachefe, Dilla and Yirgalem. The distance between Yabello and Awasa was 200 kilometres but felt much shorter because of the beautiful surroundings. Sidamo Province produced the highest volume of coffee in the country. In Ethiopia, coffee is traditionally drunk ceremonially as well as for refreshment. Before Abaye left home in the morning, he used to say, "Saint George of Baha, please provide me at least with a cup of coffee." A cup of coffee is dearer than a meal in traditional Ethiopia and the country consumes more coffee than it exports. My sister began drinking coffee when she was four years old. As a grown woman, she drank eight cups of black coffee every day. My sister would give up anything for a cup of coffee.

We reached Awasa Town before noon and camped at the foot of a hill on the outskirts. Awasa is one of the most beautiful places in Ethiopia. Lake Awasa lies in the Rift Valley to the west. The landscape is especially beautiful in the afternoon. The land is among the most fertile lands of the county and is along the major highway running to the Kenya border. Awasa is also close to Shashemane, which leads west to Arbaminch and beyond. In all, it occupies a strategic location, especially for economic development.

In the evening, Shiferaw and I went to a bar. He's the driver who told about his daughters' miraculous recoveries. We ordered beer and he told me another story: "During the time of the massacre in Addis Ababa, a man named Ayele knew that his brother had been brutally assassinated by Kibru,

a community cadre. Ayele knew Kibru, but Kibru didn't know him. Ayele was a driver in a private company and Kibru was working in a government office and frequently had to go to Awasa. Ayele had been keeping track of Kibru for some time. Ayele looked for a job in Kibru's office. He waited for more than two years and finally managed it. One day, Ayele was assigned to drive Kibru to Awasa. They spent two days here. On the third day, Kibru asked Ayele to drive him out of town. As they were travelling, Ayele turned off the road and into an open field and stopped the car. He got out, pulled his gun out and told Kibru to get out too. Then Ayele told Kibru about his brother – his name and the date and time and the place of his death. Kibru bowed and begged for his life. Ayele had waited for years for that moment. He killed him then went to the Awasa Police Station and gave himself up."
I thought that Ayele might have been from northern Ethiopia where family feuds were very common.

We visited the necessary offices and Lake Awasa, including its surroundings. I had seen the lake when I was in the Lab School but the town had changed a lot since then. Many modern houses had been built and there were clean bars and hotels. Awasa had had a beautiful hotel, built by Bekele Mola, and it had been used to house the military. When it was returned to him it was in deplorable condition. We finished our work and headed for Addis Ababa. I didn't buy anything to take home because the government didn't allow it. There were checkpoints all the way to Addis Ababa and even the smallest amounts of grain, charcoal, coffee and flour were confiscated. I arrived home after lunch. Shewaye, my wife was pregnant and had gained weight.

It was nine o'clock at night, Friday, April 10, 1981. According to our calculations, Shewaye had been pregnant for exactly nine months. When she thought that her labour had begun, we rushed to the Princess Zewditu Hospital, a missionary hospital that had been nationalised by the government. After checking her, the doctor said that the baby was not due yet. He said that even if it had been time, the hospital had no room. Next, we went to the Black Lion Hospital. The doctor there checked her and advised her to stay. I left her in the hospital and went home. I returned to the hospital early next morning and my wife had delivered a baby boy, weighing 3.35 kg. I was extremely happy for her and the child and took them home the next day. We named him Surafel, after one of the guards at the gate to Heaven.

It was now a year since our marriage and three months since our son was born. I felt relaxed and wanted to get the revised title for our land. I went to the municipality's engineering office and checked and was told that the title had been sent to the archive for registration. I went to the archive and the man there told me that it wasn't possible. I asked him why and he said that my application had been made before I built my house and was now invalid. A new application was required. I went back to the engineering office for help, but people there seemed frightened of the man at the archives, so I thought that he might be a political cadre.

Gebre, an engineer in my office, had been the municipality's chief engineer, so I went to him for advice. Gebre called a senior engineer at the municipality and talked to him about my case. He told me to go and see the senior engineer the next day. I did. After we talked, he wrote a note, which he gave me to take to the man at the archive. The man refused to read it. At the time, a miserable looking woman there seemed to be having the same problem I had. She said to me, "Why don't you fly, instead of walking on foot like me?" I didn't understand and so didn't respond. Later on, I figured out that she was telling me that I should offer the man a bribe. I didn't know how to arrange a bribe and I forgot about it. I tried to get the problem fixed but without success.

Finally, I went back to Gebre and beseeched to help me. He was a very considerate person and I had often seen him doing something good for someone. Gebre had a special love for children and was happy on my having a son. Gebre called a boss-cadre at the municipality and explained my problem to him. Then he told me to go to that man's office the next day.

The next morning, I was the first person at the building – I was there even before the boss-cadre himself. He came in about 15 minutes later. I followed him to his office and told him the whole story. He had the man at the archive come to his office and asked him why he had not issued me my title. The man stated his position. The boss-cadre said, "Who are you to being doing that? You are an archive-man and your job is to process documents. If I hear any more complaints, you'll be in deep trouble. Get this fixed as soon as possible!" The man from the archive was speechless and left the office quietly. I bowed to the boss-cadre, followed the man from the archive back to his office, got my title and left. Six months later, I read that the archive-man had been sentenced to 17 years in prison because of fraud. That was the benefit of piloting.

* * *

We were deep in the south-western Ethiopia again, but this time, studying the 300-kilometre-long Felegeneway-Jinka-Nemreputh Road that ran to the Kenyan border. It crossed many different kinds of landscapes and ethnic groups. The 160-kilometre-long Sodo-Felegeneway Road connected to the study road and ran through lands that were thick with giraffes, zebras, deer, antelopes and more.

Kucha or Selam Ber Village lay on Sodo-Felegeneway Road. Emaye had told that her father had been born in Kucha. The village was known for its fresh butter. There was an iron bar blocking the road there, a checkpoint to inspect for contraband coffee, charcoal and grain. Shiferaw was behind us, didn't see the iron bar, ran in to it and damaged it. He had to have the five meter long bar fixed at a maintenance shop in Felegeneway.

We camped in a very beautiful place on the outskirts of Felegeneway Town. Fruit trees, fields of vegetables, and green areas surrounded it. Papaya, pineapple, banana and lemon were sold very cheap. The Ethiopian Orthodox Tewahedo Church had a priest but no deacon – no one to assist at all – which was very unusual. I remember a situation like that when I was in Waji Genbo during the national development campaign. The priest there had to rely on some campaigners to help him carry the *Tabot* during the Epiphany. The *Tabot* is a holy carving with inscriptions from the Ten Commandments and represents the Ark of the Covenant, which the Israelites used to carry the Ten Commandments on their journey to the Promised Land.

The Epiphany – or *Timkit* – commemorates the baptism of Jesus Christ. It is celebrated for three days between January 18th and January 20th. On the afternoon of January 18th, priests, accompanied by the faithful, carry the *Tabots,* which are covered by ornamented cloths to a central point. They place the *Tabots* in tents near consecrated pools or streams. Along the way, the faithful blow trumpets and ring bells as the priests burn incense. Early the next day, the priests and the faithful commemorate the baptism in the pool or stream. After the ceremony, processions return the *Tabots* to their churches. Only the Saint Michael's *Tabot* stays behind until January 20th. When I was a young boy, Abaye and I would accompany the Saint Michael's *Tabot* to Janmeda - the largest field in Addis Ababa and the central point for the ceremony. We were baptised by sprinkling from the pool.

The priest's compound in Felegeneway was filled with plants and looked very beautiful. The priest supplied us with fruits and vegetables and we made fruit salad every morning, mixing papaya, bananas, watermelon and lemons. The prices were very cheap – there were few markets nearby and most fruit spoiled in the garden. We made bonfires at night, and sat around and talked until late. We also visited the town at night. It had no electricity although it had a sizeable population.

One night, we heard shooting in the neighbourhood. We kept silent and waited. We didn't dare leave our tents because our camp was in the forest and there were no police around. After an hour, people began to come out of their houses. They were crying and weeping. We left our tents and were told that a man had been killed. We couldn't do anything to help in the middle of the night, so went back to our tents and spent the night listening to people weeping. When we left our tents the next morning, we saw men running in small circles and jumping and throwing themselves to the ground. The women were standing apart, crying.

Abaye had told me how people in his birthplace mourned. When a family member died, men would come out naked from the hip up. They would be carrying sharp spears. They would cry and pierce their backs with the spears. In Emaye's birthplace, people would tie bunches of thorns, soak them in cold water, and brush the thorns across their faces until they were covered with blood.

We were told that there was neither a road nor a track from Felegeneway to Jinka. Mount Senegal lay in between. We decided to travel to the foot of the mountain, visit the area, then go through Sodo and Arbaminch to Jinka – It would be a 480-kilometre trip. When we reached the mountain we could see that the area had vast potential for agriculture – it was grassy and covered with trees. We climbed part way up to see more. Felegeneway Town was at the foot of Mount Senegal and Bulki Village lay to the northeast, at the top of another hill. The air was fresh and the scenery very beautiful. It was very quiet. We breathed the fresh air again and again for few minutes. Nature provided us the best part of it.

We drove back to Sodo and then southwest to Arbaminch and on to Jinka Town. On the way, we passed Konso Village and the Woito River. After crossing the Woito, we turned right towards Keyafer Village and then to Jinka Town. We camped in the compound of the agricultural office in Jinka. The guard pretended to be from the city. Although the place seemed very peaceful, he promised complete security. I asked him if he had ever travelled in a station wagon and he said that he had even ridden sitting on the rack. He thought that was more advanced than sitting inside. Most probably, he had sat on the rack. In rural Ethiopia a van typically carries 25 to 30 people. At the time, Ethiopia had the highest rate of traffic accidents in the world.

Jinka was very beautiful. A grass airfield stretched right across the eastern part of the village. The land sloped gently from north to south and was surrounded by coffee bushes and green plants. Coffee was cheap, so this time the drivers were determined to carry as much coffee as possible and to dodge the checkpoints somehow. They bought a lot of coffee. I bought the least, ten kilograms of it. We rode towards Mount Senegal on horseback – there was no way to drive to it. The peak is flat and not very populated. The area isn't dry, but it's not agriculturally rich either.

Next, we decided to go to the area between Keyafer and Dimeka which had no road at the time. We thought it wouldn't be farther than 50 kilometres. We decided to return by way of a much longer all-weather rural road. We left the Unimog and the cook behind and took the station wagon. First, we drove 46 kilometres back towards Keyafer, then we turned right along a track and travelled through forests that had no significant settlements. However, the area looked very fertile and suitable for settlement – it was flat and had rich soil. We came to Dimeka, a village of about 20 houses, and saw very few people. We didn't stay long for it was getting late and we had to get back. We drove about 20 kilometres towards Turmi in the west and then turned east towards Keyafer. The area looked extremely dry and we couldn't understand why on earth anybody would have built the road here instead of through Keyafer-Dimeka. Later, we heard that the provincial administrator, a soldier, had insisted. It reminded me of what a friend had told me: "You know that your subjects have accepted your orders when you force them follow them against their will. That is how you prove your authority." The administrator was the same rogue soldier that massacred lots of people in Shashemane Town and at Kutaber Village.

From Turmi, we drove down a hill and went towards Keyafer and reached the Chew Bahir, a desert land. The area was flat and very sandy. Chew Bahir means Salt Lake in Amharic, Ethiopia's official language. We were told that if someone ended up in the middle of Chew Bahir, there would be no way out. Once a foreigner found himself stuck there in his car. He couldn't get out and the car melted into the sand. Nobody knew what had happened to him and no one was daring enough to attempt going inside. Along the road, there were many deer and antelope, freely ranging, often into the middle of the road. There were no settlements and no traffic whatsoever –it looked like the road had been built for the deer and the antelope. Heading east, we left the Chew Bahir and turned left towards Keyafer. We left the road that went towards Konso on the right. As we started ascending the highlands, the station wagon's fuel tube got blocked. By now it was after six in the evening and it was getting dark. Going downhill was not a problem, but driving uphill was difficult. So, we drove backward uphill and at times we had to push the car. We arrived in Jinka Town after midnight.

We had the car fixed the next day and went to visit the nearby Mago Park. The road between Jinka and the park was under construction and the landscape was very green. On the way to the park, we crossed about 20 kilometres of hills and forests. We drove around the park for a while but didn't see anything. We were told that our timing was off – we should have come later in the day, not before noon, since the animals would not come out to eat till about midday. After eating and drinking water, they would rest in the shade and that was the appropriate time to see them. Our trip was wasted.

We took the rural road to Dimeka and camped there for few days. The people of the area were from the Hamer ethnic group and were nomads. Some missionaries had built a building there, but local people had destroyed it during the revolution, apparently for no reason. The missionaries in Dimeka had provided drugs and clean water. They had taken care of people during childbirth and had handled emergency cases. However, ignorance and thoughtlessness had led people to destroy things. As well, people in the area would leave their children in the forest if the children's upper teeth grew in before their lower teeth did – otherwise misfortune might befall the family. The missionaries used to secretly rescue such children and take care of them.

As informed, guests were highly respected in the area and donkeys would be slaughtered if a highly valued guest arrived. There were cattle in abundance, but these were kept as marks of status and honour. Both men and women wore no clothing from the waist up. Milk, cheese and local wine were abundant and very cheap. The local cheese was extremely delicious. The people boiled coffee "skins" and drink the liquid. A sack of dry coffee "skins" or "Keshir" could be traded for a cow. The people had no interest in us and didn't care why we were there. They were very proud – probably because of the many cattle they had, or by nature. They were very dark-skinned. The men were slender, tall and handsome, and the women were beautiful with nice bosoms. They made me remember something that my geography teacher, Roseless – at Haile Selassie I Secondary School said while describing the word "knoll": "A knoll is like the bosom of beautiful girl."

The village's political cadre invited us to see a wedding. We couldn't drive there, so we walked two hours to reach the place. All the villagers had gathered and the young women were drinking local liquor distilled from sorghum and millet. They gave us some to taste and it was very strong. The young men of the village had been in the nearby forest for three days, preparing strong sticks, which they would use to beat the young women. After the women got drunk, they went close to the forest and called to the young men and teased them to come and beat them. The young men rushed out and beat the young women until their backs were bloody, but the young women teased the young men and said they had not done it well. The men kept beating them. We could see the bloody welts from the distance. As people watched, they shouted for more and tougher beatings. It was very disturbing to me and if I had had the power I would have stopped it right there.

Eventually, the young men went back to the forest and the women back to their drinks. After about an hour, the men came out of the forest again and went to a house for food and drink. Women came out of the house and shouted for more beatings and were beaten again. The belief was that women who weren't beaten that day would not be beloved by the bridegrooms. The issue would come up whenever there was any misunderstanding.

Next, the men headed for an open field. There were 11 oxen, standing in rows. Their backs were covered with fresh animal excrement, making them slippery. The bridegroom stood naked on one side of the oxen. He jumped on top of the first ox in the row, then ran across the backs of the rest, then jumped to the ground on the other side. Then he jumped back on the last ox, ran to the other end, and jumped down. Villagers congratulated him for crossing without failing off. Now he would go and live in the forest until he met the woman he wanted for his bride. He would always have food with him, and when he found the woman he wanted, he would take hold of her and put the food in her mouth. She would know what he meant and would sit down with him and tell him her name, something about her family, where she lived, and other personal information. Then he would go home and tell his parents that he had found the right woman. The two families would arrange the marriage without any more ceremony.

We stayed late into the night. The men were naked from the waist up and had painted their bodies with white stripes, making them look like zebras. They danced, jumping very high. Their bodies looked they had been crafted by artisans.

The new husband would now begin to face a series of challenges. His wife would ask him for goat meat from another tribe and he will have to go and raid that tribe. She will ask him for milk from Kenya and he will have to make a cattle raid into Kenya. He could die doing that, but it was part of his responsibility as a husband. Some other tribes in Ethiopia and Kenya have the same custom. Being a husband in those tribes was very risky and I didn't envy the men.

We reached our camp after midnight. The moonlight was beautiful and we could very faintly hear the singing from the wedding. It was a very peaceful place. We stayed one more day in Dimeka and then we began our journey to the Omo River and then on to the Kenyan border. We stopped in Turmi to buy a wooden tool, *Mukecha*, for use to grind plant stems and grains for *tella,* the local beer. Turmi was famous for that grinder and my wife had told me not to come back without it. I got one that was very heavy: it won't wear out, it can't be easily carried away, and it can be handed down from generation to generation.

We drove to Omo River and camped on top of the bank. We couldn't cross the river – there was no bridge. There were police vehicles on the other side, presumably carried there by boat. We asked the police for a ride to the border and they drove us there. The landscape was totally barren and there were no significant settlements. However, it was ideal for irrigation. There was a police outpost 20 kilometres from the river crossing. As we travelled, I saw a traffic policeman from Addis Ababa who had become notorious for snatching money. He fined drivers for no reason. I had heard that he had been transferred to a remote area as punishment. It was a punishing place to be and as we passed him I wished him good luck. We drove to the border with Kenya. The lake there has two names. On the Ethiopian side it is known as Lake Rudolph; on the Kenya side it is Lake Turkana. The lower valley of the Omo River is renowned for the many fossils discovered there, especially *Homo gracilis.*

It was the only clearly marked border crossing I had seen. Nothing demarcated Ethiopia and Somalia, and as a result, the Somalis had started many wars against Ethiopia. Somalia claims the eastern part of Ethiopia, the northern part of Kenya and the whole of Djibouti – an area greater than Somalia currently holds. It seems quite an ambition but difficult to achieve.

We returned to our camp and headed to a rural road construction camp near Turmi for the night. We decided to leave early for Sodo the next day because the area between Turmi and Konso is very hot. The drivers had suggested that we try to reach the Alemgena checkpoint, 19 kilometres west of Addis Ababa, by late the next day. We would need to do that to pass through with our coffee. Woldesenbet, the station wagon driver, had hidden his coffee in the car, between the front and the back doors. He had unscrewed some nuts at the top and poured the coffee beans inside. He had more than 100 kilograms hidden. Shiferaw had even more coffee inside his tent, wrapped very tightly. Shibabaw, the engineer had 20 kilograms, Teferra, the cook, had seven, and I had ten. I had mine in the car – the worst that could happen was that it would be confiscated.

At that time, it was a crime to bring large quantities of coffee to Addis Ababa clandestinely. Those who had tried and had been caught were photographed, their pictures broadcast on television, and jailed. The drivers knew that and I had told them that it was a risky undertaking. However, they were determined to go through it – coffee bought for four Birr in Jinka would sell for 16 Birr in Addis Ababa.

We left Turmi at four that morning, while it was still very dark. We drove up a hill and then down towards the Chew Bahir. After few minutes on the flat road, we saw a leopard in the middle of the road. It looked very black and was staring straight at our lights. The leopard's eyes seemed to bulge and its body seemed to grow larger. We got scared and asked Woldesenbet to cut the lights, which he did. After five minutes, Woldesenbet turned on the lights and the leopard had disappeared into the bush. We drove away fast.

We crossed the Woito River, left Konso on the right, and headed for Arbaminch and then for Sodo for the night. We wouldn't have to leave early next day because we had more than a day to cover the 300 kilometres to Alemgena, the checkpoint. We left Sodo late the next morning and drove to Hosanna Town, 96 kilometres away. We had coffee there, and relaxed for few hours and left Hosanna that afternoon. We reached Butajira, 99 kilometres away, at six that evening.

Butajira was home to the industrious Sodo-Gurage people. Many successful businessmen and intellectuals came from Butajira. They had formed a committee that worked with the government to build a 115-kilometre gravel road from Butajira to Alemgena. Sileshi, a man in our office, came from the area and had told me that he had to visit his parents every year during *Meskal*, the day of the finding of the True Cross. During the visit, his father would bless him. The people were followers of the Orthodox Tewahedo Christian Church. When he visited, Sileshi would take clothes and shoes for his parents and his father would thank him for what he had done and bless him for the coming year. Sileshi told me that it would be terrible to pass a year without his father's blessings. They have the highest respect for their parents and their elders.

We reached the Alemgena checkpoint at ten that night. The two drivers had agreed that Shiferaw, the Unimog driver, would be in the lead. But as we approached the checkpoint, Woldesenbet, the station wagon driver, accelerated and overtook Shiferaw. At that point, Kassa, a man from the head office who happened to be there, shouted that he needed a ride to Addis. Woldesenbet stopped to pick him up and a customs officer came running straight to us, suspicious about our late arrival. He knocked on the station wagon's doors and the coffee beans rattled. We cursed them for betraying us. The customs officer brought sacks and collected more than 100 kilograms from the station wagon and about 150 kilograms from the Unimog. Kassa knew the customs officer very well, so he begged him to let us go and also that he let the drivers keep some – their pay was low. He agreed and let each driver keep 20 kilograms. The rest of us got nothing. Even the cook lost his coffee – and he too had a meagre income. What a waste of time and a loss of money! I arrived home after midnight.

CHAPTER SEVEN

The World Bank had been insisting on the establishment of a monitoring and evaluation system within the Ethiopian Roads Authority (ERA). However, the ERA had been reluctant to act. I thought that ERA officials saw it as a way of auditing its work and that it might haunt them by making them more accountable. Discussions had been going on for some time and had begun even before the ERA recruited me. Finally, the Bank held back a loan of about US $ 70 million. The ERA had no choice but to concede. The Bank and the ERA agreed to hire a consulting firm to carry out a study and to propose a system.

Delcan International of Canada was rated high and was invited to begin negotiations on a contract to do the work. One day, my boss, Mengesha, brought a tall, well-built and good-looking man to my office. His name was Dave Duggan and he was Delcan's vice-president. He was a very quiet person and we didn't talk much. We began the negations the next day and, as requested, he submitted his cost breakdown. ERA officials asked him to cut back on the costs, but he was firm in his position. They asked him to think about it and come back the next day. He came back the next day with the same proposal. ERA officials concluded that he was not there to negotiate. Eventually, they temporarily called off the negotiation.

After he left, ERA officials met and concluded that he had come not to negotiate but to impose his will. Some weren't happy at all with his attitude and asked me to prepare a letter ending the negotiations. Then a senior engineer came up with a suggestion. He said, "This man could be expecting our estimates. After examining our costs, he might suggest that we take the average as the final costs. So let us carefully come up with our costs – especially the expert costs – and give the estimate to him when he comes back. If he still insists on his estimate, we will give him a letter of termination and go to the next best bidder." The other officials agreed and I was assigned to write the letter. Mr. Duggan arrived on time on the appointed date and ERA officials were on time too. The ERA costs were handed over to him. He took sometime to go through them and did some calculations. Finally, he said, "Let's take the average." Bingo! Everybody was happy. I was very impressed by Mr. Duggan's approach and by the ingenuity of the ERA engineer.

Six expatriate consultants were proposed for the study. The project director, Conrad, was a Canadian who had emigrated from Poland and was the oldest on the team – he was in his 60s. The team leader, Terry, was a 24-year-old American and was the youngest. He had a two-year contract. The transport economist, Gregg was also a Canadian and also on a two-year contract – he was in his mid 30s. The agricultural economist, Max, was a Canadian who emigrated to Canada from Peru – he was in his early 40s. The survey designer, Allan, was a Canadian who had gone to Canada from Australia and was in his 50s. And the systems specialist, Lee, was a Canadian who had emigrated from China and was in his mid 30s.

Conrad, Terry and Gregg arrived first. Initially, we took Terry for a Canadian and Gregg for an American. Terry was gentle, well-dressed and quiet, while Gregg seemed like a hippie and looked to have slept with his shirt on. Gregg boasted of being a true Canadian, while the others were immigrants and he didn't like Americans. Gregg told me that he was from British Columbia and that he supported the New Democratic Party in Canada. He was very blunt and seemed to be sympathetic to Africans. Conrad was older, highly educated, experienced and talked like a philosopher. I had a hard time understanding him. He once said, "I always see things negatively. Finally, if that happens, it's no surprise because that eventuality was expected. But if things turned out positively, it's quite an accomplishment and very enjoyable." I had been thinking the opposite and he confused me. Terry looked a joyful person and behaved likewise.

Max and Allan arrived few days later. Both were tall and were gentlemen. Max looked watchful and judicious but simple, while Allan seemed knowledgeable, forward-looking and confident. They complemented each other. We had learnt from the Ethiopian Central Statistical Department that Allan was a world-class professional with many publications and we were delighted to have him on the study. Max was halfway through his Ph.D. on agricultural economics and would often say, "'I'll see it,' said the blind man."

Mengesha, the manager of the planning and programming division was the project co-ordinator and I was the principal counterpart. We had to arrange

255

separate housing for Terry and Gregg. The former had a fiancée and the latter a wife and a four-year-old daughter. Terry seemed like a family man and Gregg like a party-man with no responsibilities. It was difficult to find places since houses and apartments belonged to the government. No one could get through the bureaucracy without having cash in hand. The consultants found that strange. Terry settled in the old city centre – it had a quieter environment, while Gregg chose the downtown – there were many bars around.

Lee arrived last and we were amazed to find that a Chinese could be Canadian. We had thought that all Canadian professionals were white. One of our secretaries said, "He's not Canadian, he is Chinese." He was very gentle, smart and serious about his job. The consultants held meetings about the kinds of data that would be required and about the design of the survey. I travelled ahead and recruited enumerators. I also travelled with the consultants. Max was very kind and interesting but also sarcastic. I liked him most for his simplicity and easy-going behaviour. Once, we went to Arsi Province for a survey. As we were riding along in a Land Cruiser, he was talking into a tape recorder, recording his observations. We found that strange – it was new to us. Teressa, the local engineer looked at him confusedly and said, "With whom are you talking?" Max responded, "With whom I am talking? With myself."

Max wanted to get a real feel for the peasants and how they earned a livelihood. We once visited a peasant's house in Arsi Province and the man invited us for lunch, which was porridge. We sat around a wooden bowel filled with porridge and ate with a single wooden spoon, which we passed from one to the next. Max looked a bit uncomfortable but ate like the rest of us. Finally, the man brought glasses of fresh milk. Max declined. The man humbly stood up and said, "This place is famous for its cattle. It would be very unkind for us to send a guest home before he drank milk." Max took a glass and drank it. I was concerned about his health, but nothing happened to him.

Another time, I travelled with Max and Gregg to Gojam and Bahir Dar City. When Max saw the fertile land of Gojam, he looked at me and said, "What is wrong with you? Give it to me – I can fix it in two years." When he saw Bahir Dar City, he was speechless – mesmerised by its beauty of its surroundings. Lake Tana lay north of the town and there the Blue Nile began it its trip towards Sudan and Egypt. The landscape was astounding.

Max and Gregg reserved two rooms at the government-owned Ghion Hotel, while I went to look for a cheaper one. The hotel charged foreigners double the rate for locals, but the local rate was still too expensive for me. Unfortunately, the hotels in town were totally full. Max and Gregg agreed to pay for me to stay at their hotel. One of them asked the receptionist if there was a room available and was told yes. Nevertheless, when the receptionist looked at me, he changed his mind and said there were none. It was not good to be a local person.

Gregg was not comfortable about eating any place but big hotels. On the other hand, Max preferred local places. He wanted to know more about the people and the food. Once I took him to a local restaurant in Bahir Dar. The city was hot and there were a lot of flies in the place, but Max just chased the flies away and ate. He never had any problems with the food. Another time we were in a remote place in the general area of Bahir Dar and we went into a very small restaurant. Max ordered scrambled eggs for breakfast. While we were eating, I asked him, "How is it?" He said, "Better than the Hilton."

In a small town, Bichena in Gojam, the three of us reserved rooms for two nights. We were there to observe a survey having to do with a market. The ceiling in Max's room had a hole in it and I offered him mine. I suspected that there were rats in his room. He refused and spent two nights there without complaint. But Gregg complained about everything all the time except in the bars in Addis Ababa. On the way back to Addis Ababa, the driver and I wanted to take grain to our families. There were serious shortages of grain in Addis Ababa at the time. We had no choice but to load it behind us in the car. Max didn't care and Gregg complained all the way back to Addis Ababa. We knew it was very uncomfortable for them, but it really was a matter of survival for our families.

Gregg and I went to Arsi Province to conduct five days of traffic surveys. The survey site was seven kilometres past Asela Town. We stopped vehicles and asked the drivers where they began the trip and where they were going.

One day, we were going by car for lunch. From a distance, I saw a young girl about 11 years old crossing the road. She had wrapped her head, including her ears, with a piece of cloth and appeared not to be hearing anything. I thought that Shiferaw, our driver, had his thoughts elsewhere and that he wouldn't see the girl at all. As we approached her, I called his name and told him to be careful, but it was too late. Instead, he sped up, trying to pass her before she crossed the road. The girl looked back and then walked faster. Shiferaw tried to stop the car but went off the road and hit the girl. It didn't look serious to me. I jumped out of the car and when I saw that her forehead was bleeding, I wrapped her head with the cloth, put her in the car and we headed to the hospital.

Fortunately, the accident was not fatal, but the doctor said she had to stay in the hospital for few days. Gregg got very scared and decided to quit the survey and return to Addis Ababa. We told him it wasn't serious, but he was determined and left that afternoon. He felt very uncomfortable out of Addis Ababa. The girl went home healthy and her family was very grateful at the beginning, but later they decided to sue Shiferaw. We thought that they did it because of the influence of people around them – it was very common. The case took some time and Shiferaw had to go to Asela on court dates. It was expensive in time and money.

During the surveys, we had some problems with the peasants. The questionnaire was general, but some questions offended the peasants. At one market place, men didn't normally carry chickens – it would have

259

been disgraceful for a man to do that. In ignorance, we asked a peasant if he had carried any chickens. He looked us over, right from our feet to the tops of our heads, and said, "Do you have better questions?" We got scared since he had a gun and looked very combative. Max and Allan were there and advised us to be careful. Every man in the area was armed and didn't care what anybody thought, including the government. During the Derg Revolution, there was no literacy campaign there.

People there were loyal to the emperor and refused to participate in any government activity. When we were there, some people in the area told us not to try to do the survey in the afternoon since the men would be violent after drinking in the market. Normally, they went home shooting and would kill over minor disagreements. Whenever the government sent troops after them, they went to the forests and did more harm. Disputes over killings usually led to family feuds.

Three months after the study began, the consultants prepared an interim report. The ERA general manager, Ato Keleta, called a meeting - Ato in Amharic is the same as Mr. in English. The consultants presented the report very well and defended their positions convincingly. Management was very satisfied with their work and thanked them. In the middle of the discussion, Ato Keleta raised a point. He noted that some ERA staff would need to be trained to make sure the system ran as it should. Management agreed and a committee was formed to select trainees. Delcan was responsible for arranging for training in Canada. I was chosen to be one of the trainees.

We would go in two groups. At the time, the study was halfway through. Mengesha was worried about including me in the first group for I was the principal counterpart and my absence might adversely affect the study. On the other hand, he knew I was anxious for the training and that nobody could be sure of anything because of the political uncertainty in the country. One day, he called me to his office and said, "The follow-up for the study will be too much for me if I include you in the first group. However, if I hold you back until the second group, anything could happen and your chance could be spoiled. That would be beyond regret for me. So I have decided to include you in the first group and to take the consequences." I thanked him and left his office.

After Max knew that I was going to Canada for postgraduate study, he invited me to lunch and told me that he had a small transport consulting firm in Ottawa, Canada. It was a one-man firm and he had found it very difficult to run the firm in addition to managing his animal farm. He needed someone to manage the firm and asked me if I had intended to stay in Canada after I finished my studies. He also said he would arrange for me to immigrate and for housing in Ottawa. I thanked him for considering me, promised to think about it and tell him later. Despite his generous offer, I wasn't keen on accepting it. As long as we had that military government, getting my family out of Ethiopia would be impossible.

Shewaye, my wife, was pregnant with our second child. We had been expecting the child's birth for 15 days. Still no child. A month went by. Still no child. We got worried. Shewaye had had monthly check-ups since the sixth month of her pregnancy and the doctor had been telling her that the child was fine. However, the child refused to be born, perhaps suspecting the bitterness of life in that part of the world. Finally, the doctor decided that Shewaye should go to the hospital and he would induce labour.

Shewaye entered Black Lion Hospital on Friday. I visited her early on Monday. Nothing had happened during the weekend, so I went to my office. I left the office at five that evening, borrowing a consultant's car to go to the hospital. I drove into the compound, checked with the nurses and they told me that she was in labour. I sat in the car alone, contemplating the bad and the good that might happen. So many women die during delivery in Addis Ababa. I remembered a woman who had delivered a baby in the same hospital. After delivery, she saw the child sleeping naked in a bed and so took off her clothes and covered the child with them. The woman died of a draft through the window while the child survived. Another time and another place, doctors operated on a mother who had high blood pressure and she died instantly. Things like that happened many times and worried me too much. I went to the nurses at quarter after eight and they told me that Shewaye had delivered a 4.1 kilogram baby girl. I was very happy. I was also happy for the combination – now I had one son and one daughter. We named her Mistre, a short form of Mistre Selassie, which means The Mystery of the Trinity.

The consultants had been concerned about my wife's problem too. I gave them the news the second day and Max asked me what the child's sex was. I told him she was a girl and he said, "Some people are lucky." I knew he had two daughters. When Allan came from Canada the second time, he brought lots of clothes for our daughter and Terry sold us a two-cylinder stove at a very cheap price. It was not easy to get that kind of stove at the time. Similarly, Gregg sold us a refrigerator at a very low price. They were very concerned people.

Emaye wanted to have my daughter circumcised. I refused out right. She insisted, saying that circumcision was part of womanhood and if not done, our daughter would have problems during childbirth and wouldn't be accepted socially. I refused to listen. Every time we had a conversation, she would raise the issue. I stopped responding. That is the only time Emaye and I have completely disagreed. After pestering me, she knew I wouldn't budge and stopped talking about it any more.

Because of Gregg's behaviour, Delcan asked the ERA to replace him. Mengesha and I knew he was blunt and couldn't get along with the rest of the consultants. He was also acting strange, even with his family. However, his wife was so kind and compassionate and his daughter so young and beautiful that we didn't want their lives to be disturbed. He had been doing his job very well and was competent. Finally, we insisted that he should stay and Delcan agreed.

Abaye was getting sick. He had been staying home for a very long time now. Whenever I went to visit them, he would appeal to me not to bury his body close to the river that ran by Saint Michael's Church since he didn't want for his remains to be washed away. He would pray, "Please, Saint George of Baha, call me on a sunny day while my eldest son is around. If I die on a rainy day, people will curse me and call me a sinner for getting them wet and muddy." Back then – even now – ordinary Ethiopians didn't have cars. Having a car was – and still is – unimaginable by many. Car ownership is one in more than 500 people. Rain meant being wet and getting muddy and people blamed the deceased for the rainy day and considered the person a sinner. Abaye didn't want that to happen after his death.

Desta, a neighbour, had come from Emaye's homeplace many years ago. She looked younger than Emaye and sometimes lived close by for sense of security. Sometimes, she moved, though, to be with different husbands. She had no children and was dependent on us. She was unpredictable, so I was not comfortable with her. Once, when I was a child, she lived alone in a forest some distance from our place and asked Emaye's permission to take me for the night. Emaye agreed. I was not at all happy, but said I would go, to please Emaye. Desta led the way to her place and I followed her at distance, grunting inside. After travelling for some time, we came close to her house. I changed my mind and ran back home. Emaye didn't say anything. Later, Desta got married and moved close to our place. Lately, she had been very sick. She couldn't afford medication and was waiting for her death. In our village, that was what happened to people without working children. Finally, she passed away. Abaye couldn't go the burial and so spent the day sitting in front of our house, greeting people who had come.

Early in the morning on the third day, I left for Desta's place. According to the Ethiopian custom, neighbours visit the dead person's home on the third day, to mourn and to cry again. On the 12th day, relatives take some food and drink for the poor to church and the priests would pray for the soul of the dead. On the 40th or 80th day, a big feast is prepared for neighbours to eat, to remember the dead. Then, the soul is remembered every year for seven years, though small offering of food and drinks at the church. On the seventh year, official remembrance will be over after a big luncheon. As I was going to Desta's place that morning, I found that Abaye had been sick the whole night. He was gasping when I arrived. I asked him to let me take him to a hospital, but he refused outright. He lay on his back staring at the ceiling. I was staring at him as his gasps sharpened and he passed away. He was 75 years old. Emaye cried bitterly for she lost her lifetime friend. They had lived together for almost fifty years. I was very attached to Abaye.

I remembered the bonfires. Every Orthodox Tewahedo Christian house has bonfires three times a year – on *Buhe* – Ethiopian Halloween, Orthodox New Year[19] and *Maskal*.[20] An elongated bundle of splintered wood is prepared for every male in the house. On the eve of the holiday, about eight o'clock, the bundles are set alight and carried out of the house as a sign of better days

[19] September 11th or 12th.
[20] Marking the finding of the True Cross.

to come. When I lived with my parents in Addis Ababa, I never missed a bonfire. Abaye would wait for me. Even if I was late, I would come.

I went to Saint Michael's Church to arrange for burial. I had remembered that Abaye had constantly beseeched me that he be given a good resting-place for his remains. I went to the graveyard with Ashenafi, a man who built tombs. It was very crowded. Ashenafi looked for a place for more than an hour and finally showed me two spots and asked me to pick one. I had no experience in figuring out which spots had had previous burials, so I picked one at random and asked him to dig. Then I went home to be close to the body. I returned to the graveyard about ten that morning. Ashenafi told me that no one had been buried there and I was happy that I could fulfil Abaye's wishes. In Ethiopia, burial where no one else has been buried means that the dead is without sin. The day was sunny and bright – that was good because nobody would curse him for the weather.

On the 40th day, we arranged a luncheon for neighbours and colleagues. We had the luncheon in a tent in front of the house and while people were eating, we could see heavy clouds coming towards us. We thought that heavy rain was on the way and worried that it might spoil the day. The clouds slowly approached the hill on the northern side of the tent. I remembered Abaye's plea to the Almighty for a sunny day. Amazingly, the cloud changed direction and moved towards the west. The day was perfect and we were pleased for the dead and for ourselves.

After I saw that Abaye's wishes were fulfilled, I seriously started thinking about my postgraduate study. I came to know that I would eventually go to the University of New Brunswick's Fredericton campus. I had never heard of the university or the town. I had heard about McGill University in Canada but nothing else. I had also heard about Montreal and Prime Minister Trudeau. I had come to know more about Canada and had read that the prime minister had been a popular man at parties before he was married. I had also heard a lot about Prime Minister Trudeau on the British Broadcasting Corporation (BBC) when I was working after I finished high school. I had liked his foreign policy, especially towards Cuba – students at Haile Selassie I University liked Fidel Castro and Che Guevara. Berhanu, Teressa and I were given the green light to study in Canada for eight months. We started working on getting our visas and submitted a letter from ERA to the Canadian Embassy in Addis Ababa. Doctors were designated for our medical exams and the results were sent to the Canadian High Commission in Nairobi, Kenya. My friends got their visas within a month, but mine was delayed and I was asked again and again for more information about my medical history. Gregg proposed that I be replaced, but my boss insisted that we be patient. It took another two weeks, but I got my visa early in September 1983. My colleagues had left in August.

I designated Shewaye to collect my salary – the government was paying salaries to trainees abroad. We would get full pay for the first six months and half-pay for the next six months. Shewaye knew how much we gave to Emaye and her mom every month. I went to Emaye to tell her goodbye.

She never felt comfortable about my going away. However, she knew she didn't have any choice, kissed me on my forehead and wished me good luck, stretched her two hands out and looked up at the sky and said, "Saint George of the Lydia, I have given him to you. Please follow him."

My son was two and a half years old and my daughter was seven months old. It was the time a father needed to be there and the most entertaining time to be around them. I kissed my children and left home. Relatives and close friends had come to the airport to wish me goodbye. I embraced my wife and the rest of them and went into the terminal. Wondime walked with me to the end and wished me good luck.

CHAPTER EIGHT

I flew on Ethiopian Airlines. It was not my first time to fly – I had flown locally and internationally. The plane left Bole International Airport in Addis Ababa early in the afternoon on September 4, 1983, heading for London, England. I felt sure that I had left my country when the pilot announced that we were in the Sudanese airspace. Sometimes, planes would be called back to the airport after take off because someone had told the government that an anti-revolutionary person was leaving the country. Wondime had been dragged off a plane to the United States.

The entertainment was excellent. The hostesses were dressed in the national costume and looked very beautiful. They smiled and offered us drinks. We had lunch on the way and the plane landed in Rome for 45 minutes. The plane left on time and travelled to London. It was late evening when we reached London and we could see the lights of the city below and traffic moving in all directions. We arrived at London's Heathrow Airport at ten that night. When I got off the plane, I saw an employee of Ethiopian Airlines holding up a sign with some names written on it. My name was there. She asked us to follow her, gave us information about hotels where we could spend the night and told us what time to be at the airport the next day.

I went by taxi to my hotel. The hotel was very beautiful and I had good dinner and then went straight to bed for it was late. When I woke up the next day, it was raining heavily. Breakfast was included, so I had a hearty breakfast and then left for the airport. The airport was very big and very busy. I had never imagined that it would be that big. There were many restaurants and bars within the airport and it was a strange experience for me. I left London on an Air Canada flight to Montreal early that afternoon. It was a very good airline and the hostesses were pleasant and wore the maple leaf on their chests that made them even more pleasant. When the hostess served lunch, she asked me what I wanted to drink. I asked for beer and she brought me beer in a can.

I had never seen beer in cans and didn't know how to open it. I looked around, but nobody else was having a can of beer. Finally, I decided to try to open it and when I did, the beer splashed all over me and on the man sitting beside me. He was not disgruntled at all – he just mopped his face and his clothes and sat quietly. That would get me into trouble back home. I was surprised and embarrassed. The beer was good, but what I had was only half a beer and I wanted to have another one. I signalled to the hostess and asked her for another beer. The man beside me quietly left his seat and went to the washroom. I knew he was running away from another beer shower. I managed to get it open without splashing it this time. He stayed away until he was sure that I had finished opening the beer. If he'd come back earlier, I could have proved to him that he had nothing to worry about. That would have kept him in his seat if I ordered a third beer.

I was not in the mood to read or even to glance at a newspaper. I was thinking about my young family that I had left behind and the new world out in front. I was also thinking about Emaye's life without Abaye. I was sure she would think about us and see us in her dreams. Abaye, her lifelong friend had left her forever, against his will, but I had gone voluntarily. I comforted myself by hoping that Wondime would stand by her. I was also anxious to reach my destination.

Finally, the plane landed at Mirabel International Airport in Montreal. Conrad picked me up at the airport and took me to a hotel in Ottawa. He told me that someone would pick me up the next morning and take me to their office. Then he wished me goodnight and went to his place. From my fifth-floor hotel room I looked out at the city. It looked very beautiful at night. I was excited but had nobody to share my feelings with. I left the hotel and walked around but didn't see much because it was dark. I had a good supper and some cold beer and then went to my room to watch television. The TV had many channels – we had only one back home and only a few people were even lucky to have TV. Ninety-nine percent of the households don't have it. I changed channels one after another without really watching the programs. It was amazing.

The next morning, Conrad picked me up and took me to their office. They gave me pocket money and told me to buy clothes, especially winter clothes. They also invited me to have lunch with them in a revolving rooftop hotel in downtown Ottawa. I looked out at the city while we were having lunch and it was very exciting. Conrad invited me to his place for supper and his wife greeted me warmly and served me a good dinner. They lived on the

Quebec side of Ottawa and they spoke French between themselves. I knew he had emigrated from Poland and spoke many languages. I thought that his wife was French Canadian. They had two young sons and they were very friendly too. It was my first time to experience the Canadian way of life. It seemed a big house for four people and I thought they were affluent. Mrs Studnicki-Gizbert offered to help me do some shopping the next day. She took me to a very big shopping mall. I had never seen such a place – it was ten times the size of any shop back home. There were clothes everywhere and nice ones too – I would have bought them all if I'd had the money. I did buy some summer and fall clothes and some clothes for winter too. I bought a winter jacket that turned out to be too long and too heavy. I bought a fur hat with flaps to cover my ears. I couldn't imagine what kind of winter it would be.

I left Ottawa for Fredericton and arrived at the Fredericton Airport – it was very small –sometime that afternoon. Dr. Frank Wilson, the dean of engineering at the university, was there to meet me. As we drove to the university, he described the dormitory he had reserved for us and said that it was where mature students stayed. He took me to his office, made some telephone calls, and then drove me to the dormitory. I was assigned to the same room as Teressa. He had come earlier. I thanked Dr. Wilson and he left. His kindness and simplicity impressed me. I went to the cafeteria for supper – the food was varied and abundant. I had been at a university where students queued for hours to eat and drink not so sufficient. A lot had been demanded from us, but we had no good food, not enough books, and didn't have enough experienced professors. It was like expecting a lot of milk from cows without properly feeding them.

I saw a young student carrying his tray from the serving area to the dining hall. Another student came rushing in from opposite direction and collided with him, the tray fell on the floor and juice splashed all over his clothes and eyes. The student who had been rushing said, "I'm sorry," the other one said, "It's okay," then they went their own ways. I was impressed. I would have fought to the death if that had happened to me when I was a young man at university. I would have done it to prove my manhood.

I went to class the next day. My field of study was transportation planning and it was offered through the department of civil engineering. There were quite a few graduate students – 17 in all –and there were six professors, including Dr. Wilson. Professor Barry Bisson was the coordinator of the program. Our classes included class discussions, report writing and presentations and a final exam. We Ethiopians felt very uncomfortable during class discussions. We were used to one-way education, from professors to students. As well, our culture had not prepared us for open discussion. As children, we had to keep quiet while grown-ups talked. If a father and son collided in the doorway, the son would be scolded for not having paid attention. The professors tried their best to get us involved in discussions, but it was difficult for us. We were also reserved because we didn't have enough English. I was worried about doing badly and remembered the terror I had felt at Addis Ababa University. Many first-year students flunked the first semester – it came to be known as "Christmas Graduation." Many good students got very nervous. Class grades had to have a normal distribution, with as many As as Fs and as many Bs as Ds. The majority were supposed to be C. I thought it would be the same at UNB. However, the professors there were concerned about our participating and learning and not about our grades. In Ethiopia, few students graduate with good grades and most face serious problems in getting into graduate schools abroad.

The students in the transportation group were extremely nice. They were kind and always willing to help. I was more impressed with them than with the professors. The professors had travelled to many countries and had seen and appreciated many cultures. However, most of the students had never left Canada; what they knew about other places was what they had heard on the radio, or watched on television, or read in newspapers that were usually biased against other cultures. The students were much younger than I was and were respectful. I found them exceptional. I always remember students Keith Bonnyman and Margaret Gallagher who comforted me to feel at home all the time.

Each of us Ethiopian students had a tutor. We met with them once a week and discussed on our academic performance and any problems we might be having. Dr. Wilson called us to his office once a week and asked us about personal problems. I was the only person with a family and he usually asked me about my wife and children; I appreciated his concern and compassion. Professor Bisson was exceptional too. Whenever we visited the professors' offices they would say, "Come on in." They pulled up chairs for us and asked how they could help. That was very kind of them and quiet strange from back home.

The transportation group arranged get-together parties frequently, sometimes at a professor's place and other times at a student's apartment. Everybody would bring something to eat or drink. We were not used to that since back home all the responsibility lies with the host. We got slowly accustomed to it though. The professors would serve everyone drinks and would stand while the students sat down and that was very strange to us. In our culture, we always give our seat to an older person. As well, when an elderly person comes in the house, everybody stands up. We are proud of that and I believe we will do that for generations to come.

I walked around Fredericton to see what life was like in the city. Houses were not fenced. I was surprised since houses back home have fences all around to keep unwelcome persons and pets away. At King's Place, downtown, I saw a young woman and a young man kissing each other. I walked a little further and saw other couples kissing each other. On campus, I saw boys and girls kissing each other. I was amazed. I had never seen such open expressions of love in public places in Ethiopia. When I was going to Wondirad Elementary School, I used to see a white couple that was teaching at Haile Selassie I Secondary School kissing in a car and that was quite the talk of the school. The Oromos are one of the few tribes in Ethiopia that express love in public. When returning from Saint Michael's Church on holidays, young Oromos would sing and dance in the streets and sometimes the young men would gently pull the young women to them and they would kiss, but it wasn't as open as it was in Fredericton. Back home, I had heard that Ethiopians who had studied abroad and come back with foreign wives were having problems when their wives asked for a kiss in public – their husbands would have to refuse because it was culturally unacceptable. I now understood why the wives were doing that.

One of the professors in the department of civil engineering invited the three of us Ethiopians to an international banquet at the Brunswick Street United Baptist Church. We went there and a host family, the Wayes, had been arranged for us. The Wayes were younger than I was and had two children, Nicholas and Marisa. They were about the same age as my children – Nick was about four years old and Marisa was about two. I felt like I was with my own children whenever I visited them. I would carry around on my shoulders and toss them up in the air just like I used to do with my children. They liked it and whenever I went to their place, they were all over me. The Wayes invited us to dinner many times afterwards and we always enjoyed going there. Canadian desserts were not to be missed.

A few days after my arrival in Fredericton, I bought some clothes for my family and for Emaye. I packed them separately and shipped them home. When I received the first letter from Shewaye, six weeks after my arrival, I found myself teary-eyed before I opened it and Teressa asked me if I was crying. I couldn't help it. After a while, I opened the letter and read it again and again. She told me that she had received the clothes and that my son had said, "Canada seems a good country." They were doing fine and growing like weeds. Emaye was recovering from losing Abaye, which pleased me. However, Emaye's package has not arrived. I checked with Canada Post to find out what had happened to Emaye's package and was told that it had arrived at the local post office in Addis Ababa. Wondime checked with the post office and was told that it hadn't arrived.

One night at the end of October, I couldn't sleep. I was worried about everything. I worried what would happen to my family if anything happened to me. I was especially worried about my children. In the middle of the night, I slipped out of my room while Teressa was in bed and went to the balcony and tried to get some fresh air. I couldn't sleep. The next morning, I went to Professor Bisson's office – he was the program co-ordinator – and told him that I hadn't slept the night before and I had to get some sleep. He agreed and I went back to my room and slept. However, my sleep was even more disturbed than it had been at night.

At ten that morning, Teressa came to my room and told me that Dr. Wilson wanted to see me immediately. I went to his office and he asked me how I felt. I told him my fears and he arranged a meeting for me with Dr. Tingley, the university's doctor, and I went there early that afternoon. Dr. Tingley invited me into his office and asked me to grab a chair. He sat nearby and listened to me without any interruptions. It took me about half an hour to tell my story. Finally, he gave me some tablets and told me to take one whenever I had trouble falling asleep. I took only one tablet and the problem was over.

One day in November, I saw something that looked like ash falling on the ground. I asked someone what it was and was told that I was seeing snow, which was completely different from our snow back home. I learned that what we called snow was really hail. Our hailstones were large and occurred rarely. Back home, our precipitation was rain and hail. But in Canada I would see snow, rain, freezing rain, and more. I never really knew the difference between snow and ice until I came to Canada.

One evening, my Ethiopian friends and I saw a professor teaching while wearing a skirt. We were amazed and asked ourselves, "Do men wear dresses in this country?" We walked across the room two or three times to make sure. Later, we met a Canadian student in the hallway and told him of our surprise. He went into the room, looked at the skirt and then laughed. "He's wearing a Scottish kilt," he told us. We said, "It is a skirt anyway and skirts are supposed to be for women." He left us without responding.

December came with snow and ice, which scared us to death. We got bundled up with every piece of clothing we could put on and ran from one building to another. The professors teased us about our hats and said that we'd brought them from home. The washroom at the dormitory was right in front of my bedroom. Even on cold days, Canadian students usually opened the windows in the hallway and I ran to the washroom every time I went.

I felt like I was in my grave. The worst part was the slippery ice – how could people walk on it? Political democracy and walking in winter seemed diametrically opposed in Canada. I concluded that it was not the place for me and decided to finish my study and run home.

I learned a lot about Canada and the Province of New Brunswick as well. Canada is a very large country with, about 10 million square kilometres of area but only about 26 million people – less than three persons per square kilometre, which is much lower than many countries in the world. At the time, there were ten provinces and two territories. New Brunswick was one of the smallest provinces. It has less than one percent of the area and about two percent of the total population in Canada. New Brunswick is also part of the Atlantic Provinces, along with Newfoundland, Nova Scotia and Prince Edward Island, and part of the Maritimes. New Brunswick is one of the oldest parts of Canada. It entered Confederation as one of the founding provinces. New Brunswick had three major cities: Moncton, Saint John and Fredericton, all with populations of less than 60,000. Fredericton is the smallest of the three cities. New Brunswick also had a lot of snow and bitter winters.

Canada is also one of the richest countries in the world and one of the most peaceful places to live. The snow that fell in large amounts was cleared from streets in no time. Streets were always open to traffic; buildings were warm in winter and cool in summer. I was amazed how much money was spent on energy. Ethiopia is naturally air-conditioned, with an average high of less than 30^0 C and an average low of about 10^0 C. Ethiopia's energy costs are insignificant compared to Canada and yet the population is always facing starvation.

Winter was not friendly to newcomers and it certainly wasn't friendly to us. Berhanu fell on the ice and broke his hand. It was not serious, but he made it an excuse for delaying his assignments and wore bandages for many months. Berhanu was eccentric and he always took contrary positions. Back home during the surveys, he would travel with a colleague, Fekadu. When Fekadu wanted to have lunch at noon, Berhanu would say that they should eat at one, and when Fekadu suggested one in the afternoon, Berhanu would say it should be noon. Finally, Fekadu came to understand Berhanu very well and whenever he wanted to have lunch at noon, he would suggest that it be at one and so on. No more problems.

The three of us went to K-Mart one day. We finished shopping and had agreed to leave when Berhanu decided that he wanted to leave through the emergency door. We told him that the door was meant for emergencies only, but he insisted. He opened the door and the alarm went off. People started running here and there while Teressa and I hid behind some clothes. One of the employees went to the emergency door and saw our poor friend fixed there like a statue. The employee calmed people down by saying it was just a man acting strange.

Sometimes that winter, we would go for a beer in the nearby pub. The bouncers were huge and scary. Once, a Canadian tried to create nuisance in the pub and was picked up and carried out like a little boy. We learned we had to behave although it was a place for entertainment. On the way back, Teressa sang Oromo songs and was jumping up and down in the snow. He said he was expressing his bitterness against it.

We completed the first semester with good results. Dr. Wilson called us to his office and asked us if we wanted to continue our education and get our master's degree. We all said that we would be happy to do that but ERA and the World Bank would have to agree. He called a man at the Bank to discuss the matter but the man said that he was too busy to talk to him. Dr. Wilson was angry and never called him back. We were very disappointed.

Christmas came and the Wayes and some other Canadians invited us to their places. We didn't know what gifts to take to them. They usually invited us while shops were closed and we were embarrassed to go without taking anything. I remember being asked by an inviter in surprise whether we exchanged gifts back home. We were embarrassed. Gradually, we managed to handle it though.

The church organized skiing and other winter outings and the transportation group organised skating, which was tough for me. I tried skiing and rolled down the hill – that was quite fun – but skating was the most difficult exercise I ever tried. Keith and Margie held me up. I couldn't even stand by myself, never mind skate. I was astonished that hockey players managed to play on ice. However, I was not a fan of hockey – it had a lot of fighting. The sport I liked best was figure skating – it was beautiful and there was no physical confrontation, just individual excellence. Football was another sport that was too scary for me. The size of the players and the equipment they used made me think they had prepared for confrontation. Soccer was not popular in North America. One of our professors told us, "It would take time to make soccer popular – the scores are not there. After 90 minutes play, they could finish in a draw. North America wants high scores, like in basketball and football." I recalled what a Briton once said: "Americans want to become billionaires and so took off three zeros from the actual 12." He meant that the number one billion has 12 zeros in the United Kingdom and only nine in the United States.

In January 1984, there was a transportation conference in Washington D.C., co-ordinated by the Transportation Research Board of the United States. All the students in the transportation group had been booked for the conference. We went by car, crossing the states of Maine, New Hampshire, Massachusetts, Connecticut, New York, New Jersey, Pennsylvania, Delaware and Maryland. The road infrastructure in the United States is a combination of art and science. From a distance, bypasses resemble buildings. The number of lanes and the traffic flows are designed for maximum efficiency. The safety devices amazed me. And the suspension bridges and the tunnels astounded me. I remembered the fanfare by the military government after completing a 305-metre bridge back home. As we drove through Harlem in New York City, our professors hid behind us, for fear of being attacked by the African-Americans who lived in the area. One of the students with us was from New York and had told our professors that they would be in danger. We laughed at our professors and sometimes moved so that they were exposed. My broad chest helped Dr. Wilson and Professor Bisson to hide comfortably behind me. The journey to Washington D.C. took us two days.

We spent five days stay in Washington D.C. It was very difficult to attend all the presentations I was interested in – sessions ran concurrently and time was limited. I had intended to visit friends in the city as well. The group visited one of the Ethiopian restaurants in the city and enjoyed it. We Ethiopians showed the Canadians how to eat and how to do *gursha* – to put a mouthful of *injera* into a friend's mouth. We explained that one *gursha* means a fight, but two means love. At mealtime in some parts of Ethiopia, the first thing a husband does is to give his wife a *gursha* before he takes one for himself – it's an expression of his love and commitment.

In the meantime, Dr. Wilson and Professor Stevens, the most senior professor in the group, visited the World Bank to seek an extension for us. The Bank had no objections, but our government would have to start the process. After our return from Washington D.C., Dr. Wilson wrote a letter to the ERA's general manager, Keleta, and stressed the advantages for Ethiopia and for us if we completed our master's degrees, which would take another six months. After few days, we learned that the general manager had agreed but the executive body had not. Berhanu had decided not to return to Ethiopia if the extension wasn't granted. However, I missed my family and had decided to return whatever the outcome. Later, we heard that Mengesha, our boss, had taken the letter straight to the minister of construction and the minister endorsed our extension. The general manager faxed the good news to Dr. Wilson and he gave me a copy. Our boss Mengesha had his first degree but fought so that we could get our second degree – few Ethiopian bosses would do that and I heard that some people had called him a fool. Many scholarships had expired in the desk drawers of Ethiopian bosses and many of them believed they could curb the brain drain by refusing to let Ethiopians study overseas. Of course, that only encouraged intellectuals to flee. Mengesha was especially good to me. Whenever he phoned us, he would let my wife to speak to me first. I was very grateful for his concern for my family and for his interest in my education.

March was over and April had arrived. I found March even more depressing than January and February – just when I thought the snow would soon be over, we would get another heavy snowfall. Although it was getting warmer, the ice was becoming more slippery. April looked much better with melting snow and improved temperature. Very soon, the snow and ice were gone and I felt like I had climbed out of my grave. I felt like jumping up and down.

We finished the second semester successfully. Now we needed to pick topics for our research. I had revised the ERA's manual on vehicle operating costs. Delcan was developing a new one and I would be comparing the two and then recommending which manual the ERA should use. Dr. Wilson and Professor Stevens were my thesis supervisors and I started as soon as the semester was over. I was determined to complete my thesis as soon I could and go back to my family.

It was Saturday afternoon. I was in the attic, working on my thesis. Dr. Wilson slipped into the room and sat on a chair at my side. We talked about my thesis and he then asked me about the political situation in Ethiopia and about the drought. I told him both were man-made and could not be fixed by outsiders – only we could do that. I also told him that I was not sure whether we intended to change direction even if we had the will to do that. He asked me about my family and I told him they were fine. He told me that if he were around when my children were ready for university, he might help them. I thanked him very much for his concern.

Summer in New Brunswick was hot but short. The temperature had dropped to -30^0 C that winter and now it was reaching 30^0 C in summer, a difference of 60 degrees. I thought that Canadians had to be tough to stand such cold and such heat. I didn't mind the heat since I had lived where it was 48^0 C. However, cold can be challenged while heat is difficult. When it's cold we can put on heavy clothing, but when it's hot even taking off all our clothes doesn't help.

The transportation group organized a golf tournament in Alma at the Wilsons' summerhouse. I had never heard of golf and it was my first time to play. I had played field hockey at home. Golf uses various clubs while hockey uses just a hockey stick. My Ethiopian friends and I played golf as though we were hitting a field hockey ball. The Canadians laughed and said we were playing "Ethiopian style." We never missed though and we became famous for our shots.

The Wayes begot another son, Jordan, in August 1984. Their older children, Nick and Marisa, would still play with us when we visited their place. The Wayes invited us for weekend barbecues that summer and their church arranged an outing to a lake nearby. Fredericton is very beautiful in the summer – the streets and sidewalks are clean, trees line the roads, and there is lots of green space. The city is peaceful and quiet and safe for walking. The people are exceptionally friendly. Fredericton is ideal for the way I want to rear my children.

I finished the draft of my thesis in September 1984 and submitted it to my supervisors. In the meantime, I needed to have minor surgery and Dr. Tingley arranged a date and time at the Dr. Chalmers Hospital in Fredericton. I stayed in the hospital for two days. It's a good hospital and the staff was kind and helpful. Patients ordered food in advance for the next day and toast and snacks, including milk and juice, were available at any time and in any quantity we wanted. I was amazed and compared everything to medical facilities back home. We had good doctors back home but extremely poor medical equipment and inadequate rooms for both in-patients and out-patients. The most important difference is that doctors in Canada are accountable for their actions and doctors in Ethiopia are not. Doctors in Ethiopia cannot be prosecuted for negligence.

While I was in the hospital, I shared a room with an elderly man. He told me that he was a plumber and that he watched cable TV at home, with news and movies from Europe and South America. He had a private pool at home. I thought that Abaye would have been rich if he had been born in Canada – he was very good at woodcutting. I left the hospital on the third day and felt healthy. It didn't cost me anything. What a blessed country! However, I was surprised that nobody except my friends had come to visit me in the hospital. Dr. Tingley had come twice to check on how my surgery had gone and Mr. Waye visited me once – his wife Bonnie was at home with their new baby. It was different back home. After I left the hospital, nobody at the university – except Dr. Wilson – even asked me how I felt. I asked myself whether it was cultural.

Some cultures in Canada are completely different from what we have back home. Some Canadian students told me that most working parents save their money in three separate accounts – each has an account that the other spouse doesn't know about and the third is a common account. That would be rare even among the rich in my country. Marriage in Ethiopia is a long-term commitment and so divorce is very rare and money belongs to the whole family. I came to know that divorce was very common in Canada.

I remembered what Gregg, the Delcan transport economist, had told me when we were working together in Ethiopia. I had asked him how long he had been married. He said, "Thirteen years, a record in North America."

I finished my thesis by first week of November 1984. I had started shopping for clothes for my family and relatives beginning that spring and had bought the best I could for my wife. My wife was and still is a special person in my life. She is an extraordinary woman. She hadn't demanded jewels and a fancy wedding as many women do in Ethiopia. She had even managed gold rings for both of us and had bought sofa for our house. She is meticulous in managing our house and has been selflessly devoted to our marriage and our family. I knew that after spending 14 months in Canada it wouldn't be easy for me to go back home. Relatives and close friends would be expecting gifts, especially clothes or shoes. It would be an embarrassment for anyone to go back home from Canada with empty hands to meet relatives.

Dr. Wilson had arranged for a supper with the deputy minister of the New Brunswick Department of Transportation. We talked after supper and the minister was very frank. He gave us good advice and finally said, "The consultants that come to your country are not different from your classmates here. They have the same education you have. You have to be confident in what you do." That was very kind of him.

The Wayes invited me for dinner. My Ethiopian friends hadn't got their visas to Belgium yet since they had applied late. The Wayes were like relatives to me, very concerned and compassionate. We had a very good evening. Bill and Nick dropped me at the Fredericton Airport while Bonnie stayed at home with baby Jordan and Marisa. Nick felt sad with tears in his eyes when he wished me bon voyage. I felt very sorry for leaving them.

Brussels was a good place to buy used cars and electronic equipment. It took me three months to get a visa from the Belgian Consulate in Montreal. I was supposed to arrive in Brussels on November 12, 1984, but didn't arrive until the 13th because I had to add some documentation to my thesis. Because I was a day late, the customs officer at the Brussels airport refused to let me in. I explained why I was late and why I had come to Brussels and showed him traveller's cheques. He was adamant, but I pleaded. Finally, he checked on the next flight to Addis Ababa and gave me three days for shopping. I thanked him and left his office. After a few seconds, I heard him yelling. He came out of his office and called me back and said I had taken something from his desk. I told him I didn't know what he was talking about, but he yelled and called me many bad names. If it had been my country, I would have reacted. His colleague from the office next door called out that he had the stuff with him, whatever it was. Then the man looked at me in contempt and told me to get out of his office. That was too much. I was there only to shop and had Canadian $8,000 worth of traveller's cheques. I bought a used Toyota Corolla, a refrigerator, a television, a camera and a recorder. The Canadian and US Dollars were very strong that time against the European currencies and that helped me buy many stuff. I left Brussels after ten days.

I wished that I could have bought those goods in my country with respect and decency. Unfortunately, there was none.

I took Lufthansa from Brussels to Frankfurt and was sitting by the window. An Italian was sitting beside me and a German by the aisle. The Italian asked me about myself and about my travel. I told him I was Ethiopian and was travelling home from Canada. I asked him the same and also asked him how many languages he spoke. He said he spoke Italian, English and French. I asked him if he spoke German and he said he didn't. We continued talking until Frankfurt. The plane landed at Frankfurt Airport and the Italian and I stood up to leave, but the German was sitting and reading a magazine. He didn't pay any attention to us. The Italian turned to me and said, "That is why I don't speak German."

I continued my trip and finally landed at Bole International Airport in Addis Ababa. It was a Saturday in late November 1984. Wondime was inside the terminal and helped me check out. My wife and children, other relatives and friends had been waiting for me outside since early that morning. My son had lost weight, not from lack of food but from not having my love. My wife had also lost weight because of family responsibilities. My daughter looked fine – she had been too young to notice that I was gone. Relatives and friends looked desperate and helpless. I felt very sorry for my family, my relatives and my country. We went straight home and Emaye was there, waiting for me. She looked fine. I embraced her. She kissed my forehead three times, thanked Saint George of the Lydia and kissed the ground that I had come back home safely.

CHAPTER NINE

I reported to the office the next Monday. All my colleagues were there and they congratulated me on getting my master's degree. My boss said he was very proud of us. Delcan had finished the study and it turned out to be one of the best ever done by foreign consultants. I was very happy since I had initially recommended them for the job. I very much wanted to see the study implemented. It had cost the country nearly one million US Dollars, not counting our training.

The monitoring and evaluation branch had not been set up yet. The ministry was not interested and the World Bank was not pushing as it had before the study. As time went by, I felt rather unutilised and wanted to leave the ERA. I started looking for a job and found one at the freight transport authority, part of the ministry of transport and communications. The ERA refused to release me. At the time, Ethiopians could be jailed for changing government jobs without a release. I had no intention of going to jail, so I kept quiet.

In the meantime, I wanted to know what had happened to the parcel that I sent Emaye from Canada. I had mailed it the first month I was there. I had contacted Canada Post before I left and had been told that it had been lying in the Addis Ababa Central Post Office for many months. I wrote to inquire and a person there went through the registrations for the last 14 months and discovered that the parcel had been there for more than a year. Since it hadn't been claimed, it should have been returned to Canada long ago. It was no more a surprise to Emaye.

There were no interesting projects at the office. I got a part-time job lecturing in statistics at the Addis Ababa University and I also got a job with ULG Consultants of the United Kingdom to study coffee processing, storage and transportation in Ethiopia. It was very well paid and I learned a lot. I worked as the local counterpart to a very kind and highly skilled transportation engineer from London, England, Dr. Philip Cornwell. We were the same age and it was quite an experience to work with him. He told me that he had read Dr. Wilson's Ph.D. dissertation while he was studying at the University of Birmingham in the United Kingdom. I knew Dr. Wilson had studied there. Philip came to Ethiopia only twice, the first time to brief me on my assignment and the second time to evaluate my work. However, he was so unassuming, understanding and helpful that I felt I had worked with him for years.

I met Gugsa, a local agricultural economist working on the same study. He was from Harerghe Province. People from there were known for being jolly, friendly and mixing well with others and Gugsa was not different. We talked about work, life and politics. One day he told me a story about his friend Taye, who had studied in the United States. "Taye had a close friend, Damena, here in Addis Ababa and he came from Taye's native area in Harerghe Province. Taye's father died and he came back to visit his mother and relatives. When he went to Harerghe, he left $8,000 US with Damena in Addis Ababa. Damena gave the money to his wife to put it in a safe place. Taye returned to Addis Ababa after few days in Harerghe and asked Damena for the money. Damena asked his wife for the money but she told she had lost it. Damena got furious but his wife insisted that it was lost and that is what Damena told Taye. Taye didn't say a word, but he left for the United States very soon – he had no money and couldn't stay any longer. A few months later, Damena's wife travelled to the United States for medical reasons. I knew where she got the money. After treatment, she returned, looking healthy and perfect. Less than a year later, she was travelling inside the country, on a military plane, and the plane crashed and she died. Damena lost his wife and his best friend within a year." It reminded me of something Abaye once said to me, "It is better to cheat a person in the presence of others than alone while God is witnessing it."

I completed my contract with ULG and used what I was paid to add a room to my house. It had been 54 square metres and was now 72 square metres. We had a television and a recorder and beautiful curtains. We had a car too and our children were growing up fine and I felt very grateful to God. My son was four years old and my daughter two. When I got home from work, my son would run and bring my sandals to me – he didn't want me leave home again. I played with them like I had with Nick and Marisa in Canada. My son never got tired first. Life was good except for the office. We were also thinking about our son's school since he was now four years old and the right age to start. However, it would be very difficult to get him into a good school without help.

The Catholic schools in Ethiopia provided the best education in the country, but it was difficult to get a place in one. The officials that discouraged the establishment of private schools were the very ones that sent their children there. I decided to try for my son as much as I could. My sister- in-law was a Catholic, so I approached her husband, Kirubel, to see if he would talk to the director of the Lideta Cathedral School. Kirubel was in his 70s and liked my son very much for my son's name was the same as Kirubel's late brother, Surafel.[21] Kirubel did talk to the director and was promised a place for my son. In the meantime, Kirubel got seriously ill and died. The family was devastated for he was very kind and helpful. After a month, I went to the director and reminded him about my son. He recalled that he had promised Kirubel and felt very saddened for his death. He did admit my son and I felt very blessed.

My son started pre-school and he was lucky because a car was available to transport him. There were 100 students in a class, or more than three times the number that would be appropriate by Western standards. I had to check on him at noon to see whether he had eaten his lunch. Sometimes it was difficult to identify him since they all were of a similar height and weight. It was even worse at the end of the day – all the students left at the same time. Lost lunchboxes were common and those who lost theirs would go home

---

[21] According to the Bible, Kirubel and Surafel guard Heaven.

with somebody else's lunchboxes. They had homework and parents had to check to see that the children had done it right and then to sign off on the homework before the children handed it in. We appreciated it, however.

I got another consulting job at the Industrial Projects Service and a part-time teaching job at the economics department of Addis Ababa University. I used my office for preparing notes and reports – there was no real work at the ERA at the time. Monthly salaries of 600 Birr and over had been frozen by government decree. Changing jobs without the consent of the government led to shaved heads and prison. Cadres controlled government offices and pushed people to join the government party, Seded, which means Wild Fire. People joined to protect their jobs and their lives – many who refused were jailed and even killed. People that had been jailed for being "anti-revolutionary elements" switched sides and became prominent cadres in the government political machinery and sought revenge on their former allies. Some opposition leaders who encouraged youths to die for their beliefs then joined the government and caused their compatriots got killed. It was despicable.

Uniforms became mandatory at government offices. There were two uniforms for workdays and one for political occasions. Those who didn't comply were harassed. The uniform for political occasions looked disgusting because of its colour. Fortunately, I never had to wear that one for political occasions – I was neither a party member nor an official and. eventually, I gave it to the man that guarded my house. I had no time and no place to wear the clothes I brought from Canada. The chief cadre at the ERA had organized a meeting in the main hall and told us, "From now on, no more English wool and Italian shoes!" The only time I could wear my suits was on weekends and so I wore them to weddings and feasts.

The government also issued a decree that no one could sell a house. No one could import a car either – except for people in the upper echelons of the government party. I was very lucky that I brought my car in when I did. Afterwards, those who studied abroad and came back with cars had them confiscated. Then party members bought them for a nominal sum. Sometimes, officials bought the cars cheap and sold them at exorbitant prices. It was state vandalism of private property. Farmers worked in groups said to be organized in accordance with the Marxist dictum, "From each according to his ability, to each according to his needs" but the lazy ones earned as much as the diligent. Those who produced efficiently on private farms had their harvest confiscated. Survival itself depended on one's relationship with the cadres. It was very disappointing.

Metish, my best friend's wife, got sick. She was Wondime's friend's sister – the one I met while our brothers were in prison in Addis Ababa and the one who organized my marriage. While I was in Canada, she had been to London, England, for medical treatment and had returned to Ethiopia after me. I had sent her flowers from Canada and wishes for her fast recovery. She was very compassionate and very caring. She was fine when she came back from London, had brought a car on the way back, and was looking towards a better future. She had a three-year-old daughter and her husband was a professor at Addis Ababa University. She started feeling ill again after a few months, mostly from fear of poor medical care in Ethiopia if she got sick again. She got seriously ill as time went by and eventually required surgery. Her husband would wake up early in the morning, check on their daughter's well-being, take food to her at the hospital, drive to the university, lecture and administer his department. After work, he would go to the hospital and then home to his daughter. He did that for six months. I admired his strength, dedication and commitment to his family. She lost too much weight. The operation did not work and she died in agony at the age of 28. Her mother had died when Metish was three years old and now the same had happened to Metish's daughter. Emaye was devastated and said, "Saint George of the Lydia, I wish you had done that to me instead." It was one of the saddest times of my life. Why do good people die young?

Mengesha, my boss, had gone for graduate study at the University of New Brunswick. He had a family with two children and I visited them often – he had delegated me to receive his salary and pass it on to his wife. I also wanted to help out since he had been good to my family while I was abroad. He was alone and felt very uncomfortable and sick. The family was getting constant calls from an Ethiopian at UNB who would tell them that Mengesha was seriously ill. We were very worried about his heath – health care is much better in Canada than in Ethiopia, so we thought it was a hopeless case. I heard that Dr. Wilson had been at his side all along. We expected a call telling us that Mengesha was dead. His family, relatives and friends were very disturbed. Finally, he finished his studies and returned. I saw him when he arrived and he looked sick and tired. However, he recovered dramatically and looked fine and healthy in one week. I concluded that he hadn't been sick at all but had missed his family even more terribly than I had missed mine.

In the meantime, I had become completely dissatisfied with the ERA and applied to the general manager for release. However, he angrily denied my request, arguing that I had been educated to serve the ERA, which was totally pretentious. I tried and tried but with no success. Finally, I decided to go abroad again to further my education. Dr. Wilson had told me that if I found myself in trouble, he would help my family and me. He was excellent to me. I wrote him a letter saying that I had decided to go for my Ph.D. He asked me to send him two reference letters and a third letter to be prepared by Mengesha while he was in Canada. It wasn't long before Dr. Wilson sent me a fax saying that I had been accepted. I wrote a letter to the ERA, saying that I intended to go abroad and further my education and asking to be released. By then, the general manager had gone to the United States and the planning and programming division had an acting head. The acting general manager advised me to wait until the general manager returned from the United States. However, he did not return as expected. The acting general manager finally agreed but not the acting planning head. He was afraid that Mengesha would take action against him after his return from Canada. I appreciated his concern; but, Mengesha was a referral to me. I had a good friend, Woldeselassie at the ERA and the political cadre there was also good to me. They pressured the acting planning head to agree. He did.

But it was not over yet. I still needed permission from the ministry of construction. The ERA's previous personnel manager had consistently blocked my release and he had been transferred to that ministry. I approached him through his closest colleagues before the letter from ERA reached him. He said that he would refuse my release and I knew he would. I don't know what happened, but my letter didn't go to him and the ministry did approve my going for my Ph.D. studies. I had crossed the major hurdle. Next, I had to get the agreement of the commission on higher education. I went to their office with the fax from Dr. Wilson and the letter from the ministry, but they refused to accept the fax and questioned its authenticity. I asked them why they were so worried – after all, if the Canadian government issued me a visa, there would be no problem. I was told, "We don't want you to suffer in a foreign country." I smiled and left.

I wrote Dr. Wilson that I needed an official letter of acceptance. He was always willing to help and very quickly sent me the letter. I submitted that letter to the commission. Then I was told to get a letter from my community association, stating that I hadn't been involved in any anti-revolutionary activities. I would also have to produce a letter from the ministry of defence, stating that I wasn't needed for the militia. By then, I was 41 years old and the militia were under age 30. I couldn't understand why the hell I was being given such a hard time. I didn't know the man at the commission and

I didn't know anybody who knew him. There was nobody I could ask for help. I persisted. After many delays, I got the letter from the commission. I submitted everything with my visa application to the Canadian Embassy in Addis Ababa. The Embassy designated a doctor to do my medical examination and I had no problems this time. The Embassy sent the application and the medical results to the Canadian High Commission in Kenya. I knew it would take some time for the Commission to act and so I waited patiently.

In the meantime, I went to the Municipality of Addis Ababa to get an official birth certificate. I submitted the necessary documents and waited outside, reading posters and notices. My eyes landed on a notice that interested me a lot. It advertised a vacancy with the following educational requirements: Ph.D. in civil engineering, or an M.Sc.E in civil engineering and two years of work experience; or a B.Sc. in civil engineering and four years of work experience, completion of the 12th grade and eight years of work experience, or completion of the eighth grade and 16 years of work experience, or completion of the sixth grade and 24 years of work experience. I asked myself, "Am I facing all these bureaucracies to go back to grade six?" It was clear who the vacancy was for. I was astonished that someone would in any way compare a Ph.D. in civil engineering with a sixth grade education.

I got my visa. I felt very sorry for my family. My son was six and my daughter was four years old. Being away from them would be the most painful thing I would ever feel. Both were in school, meaning more responsibility for my wife. Emaye was ageing. It was not the right time to leave her. However, our survival meant a lot of sacrifice. I had resigned from the ERA and would have no salary to support my family. My wife and I had to arrange something, so we decided to sell our car. We had paid about 14,000 Birr for it and had used it for two and half years. At the time, the government was still blocking the importation of vehicles and prices had shot up. We sold our car for 45,000 Birr – more than three times what we paid for it. We paid in two years of our mortgage in advance, set aside 4,000 Birr for our mothers, and bought a smaller car for my wife for 22,500 Birr. I bought my plane ticket to Canada, although Dr. Cornwell at the United Kingdom had offered to pay for it. I thanked him and told him I could manage it. My wife would have 10,000 Birr and that would augment her salary enough to keep the family going for two years. I was content and determined to go.

I wanted Emaye to have a check up before I left and was hoping that she would live at least until I returned. Wondime and I took her to a heart specialist and the doctor told us that her heart had been growing larger as a result of her sedentary life. Then, I took her to the Black Lion Hospital for blood tests and x-rays. The x-ray technician asked her to take off her clothes above her waist. She stood naked from waist up and said "Alemye, I have few years to live – why are you worried so much?" I couldn't control my tears.

Families and friends invited me for farewell parties. It was a very emotional time for me. My departure was set for May 13, 1987. I had said goodbye to Emaye and my sister the previous night. When the day came, I hugged and kissed my children. My wife, relatives and friends went with me to the airport. At last, I kissed my wife, embraced my relatives and friends and said goodbye. They wished me bon voyage and good luck while Wondime escorted me into the terminal. Wondime and I have never given each cheek kisses and didn't embrace often either – our relationship was beyond that. He had two children by then and was doing well at the Ethiopian Airlines. We had built our houses about 50 metres apart and shared our problems and our good times. Because of him, I was always comfortable about leaving my family behind. I finished checking in my luggage and ticket and filled out my boarding card. Finally, I said goodbye to Wondime and headed forward without looking back. It was very painful for me to leave my young family and ageing mother behind.

In the developed world, children normally live 18 years with their families. In Ethiopia, they usually live with their families up to 30 years because of limited opportunities to settle on their own. In my case, I was going to be without my children for more than three years and had already been separated from them for 14 months during my master's program. These years would be the best in their lives. At the time, leaving a family behind was like leaving bail for Ethiopians travelling overseas – it was expected that they would return for their family's sake. It was very rare for a single person to return and thousands had left never to come back.

A joke making those rounds in Addis Ababa said that Mengistu, the president, was told that people were leaving the country and not returning. Truly, there were many people at the immigration office, struggling to get exit visas. They would wake up at four in the morning so they could get a place in the queue – it's strange, though, for a country to require that its citizens get a visa to leave. In this case, the president disguised himself as an ordinary person and went to the immigration office and queued for a visa. Of course, people knew he was the president. Slowly, everybody left for home, leaving the president behind. Mengistu asked why they had left and was told that they had changed their minds. They had decided to leave the country because of him and if he was leaving then why should they?

CHAPTER TEN

The plane for London took off from Bole International Airport early in the afternoon on May 13, 1987. I was not excited. I didn't care if the plane was called back for any reason. Thoughts of my young family haunted me all the way to London. I didn't talk to the people beside me and don't even remember if there were any. I thought about the trouble I had getting an exit visa and said to myself "Why do people create traps for one another?

The plane landed at Heathrow Airport about nine that evening. The Ethiopian Airlines office in London had arranged a hotel for the night and I was taken there. The hotel was a poor one compared to the one I had stayed in during my last time in London. I thought the airline was penny-pinching, or maybe losing money. I had a good sleep, though. When I woke up the next morning, it was raining. London was the point of no return and I was ready for Canada.

My Air Canada flight left London Heathrow about ten on the morning of May 14, 1987. The flight was excellent and the food and drink abundant. I remember that a man drank too much and fainted and when the hostesses tried to help him, he refused. He was troublesome the whole way. I arrived in Montreal about five that evening and called Dr. Wilson. He promised to pick me up at the airport in Fredericton as soon as I arrived. However, the connecting flight was delayed and I didn't get to Fredericton until after 11:00 that night. Dr. Wilson still picked me up. He took me to the Lady

Beaverbrook Hotel, one of the top hotels in town. He arranged for my food and room and left for his home after midnight.

I had a good night's sleep at the Lady Beaverbrook Hotel and I wished I could have another night. Dr. Wilson picked me up the next morning and took me to the university's housing office. It was a beautiful day in May – the trees on campus were covered with green leaves and the ground with green grass. The university is on a hill. It's built of red brick and it looked gorgeous. A room was arranged for me at Rosary Hall; it was downtown and had many foreign students. I didn't like the first room and after three days went back to the housing office to get a better one. I didn't like that one either and went back again. I gave them a hard time, but they never complained. I was missing my family dearly and they had no way of knowing that.

Fredericton had changed a lot in the last three years. K-Mart had closed down and a Canadian Tire store was in its place. Zellers had moved from downtown to bigger quarters uptown. Regent Mall had just been built. The university had added more buildings to its Fredericton campus. There were other development activities going on in town too. Nevertheless, the population hadn't grown. Development was taking place to serve the existing population. I imagined other cities in New Brunswick and elsewhere in Canada had expanded similarly. In my imagination I went back home. When I was a child, my family was extremely poor and we rarely had three meals a day. However, Ethiopia did have the rule of law and people could peacefully struggle for survival. We had enough schoolrooms and they were clean. We had textbooks and competent teachers. Government officials were respected, even though they didn't fully discharge their responsibilities. Now, it was upside down. No one respected the leader of the country. Government officials were thought of as hoodlums. For many households, life was much worse than it had been when I was a child. The country had gone unimaginably backward.

Dr. Wilson arranged for me to meet with Professors Stevens and Brander to select a topic for my thesis. They suggested a topic and asked me to prepare a proposal about how to go about it. Some Canadian graduate students were collecting data for their own work and were prepared to share that data with me. They were fine young men and women and, as usual, friendly and helpful. I added Shaun Landers and Garry Hogg for my remembrance as my closest and helpful classmates.

I visited the Waye family. The children had grown and Nick was now eight years old, Marisa six and Jordan almost three years old. The children were still playful and Jordan was the craziest of all. Whenever they came to visit me, Jordan would climb up my fridge, on my table and on everything climbable. Their mother Bonnie and their father Bill were excellent human beings and had an enviable family. I was extremely happy for them.

Tegene, my old friend from Addis Ababa University, was getting married in the United States and had asked me to be one of his best men. He was a professor at the University of Wisconsin in Milwaukee. Nebebe, another friend of ours, was also invited and he offered me a ride. He is a professor at Concordia University in Montreal. I travelled to Montreal by bus and then to Milwaukee by car. The roads were excellent and the traffic signs so perfect that we reached our destination without any problems and without having to ask anyone for directions. Tegene had invited all his old friends. His first best man, Kassa was a lifetime friend born and raised in the same village. His second best man, Gurmu had been a friend since they were in high school and had graduated from Addis Ababa University with him. I was his third best man. The fourth was Teklu, a colleague and a friend from Addis Ababa University. Other friends came from different parts of the United States. Four of us had been among the six who feared for our lives that afternoon in the bar in Addis Ababa. The wedding was held in a Greek Orthodox Church – that was the closest to the Ethiopian Orthodox Tewahedo Church. We played traditional songs and danced. Afterwards, there was a gift opening ceremony at Tegene's house and that was quite an experience for me since we did not have that occasion back home.

In keeping with Ethiopian tradition, the bride's family invited us for dinner on the third day. That was a time for the families and relatives of the couple to get to know one another. Traditional Ethiopian foods were served, including raw meat and local wine. Had we been in Ethiopia, the best men would have slaughtered a sheep in front of the family's house and the bride and bridegroom would walk over the carcass as they entered the house. Then, the best men would roast the meat and serve the guests.

Typically in Addis Ababa during my youth, on the day of weddings – Sundays – guests would arrive bearing money, have their names registered, and then sit down in the hall and wait for the bridegroom to come. While they waited, the guests would be served a meal. The bridegroom would come with his best men and his friends and they would sit together. The bridegroom and his best men would go to the bride's room and take her to the hall. Then the main ceremony would begin, with feasting, singing and dancing. After the feast while the bride and the bridegroom are leaving, the family of the bride would take a large loaf of bread, specially prepared for the occasion, and toss it to the crowd. The young men would fight for a piece of the loaf.

In modern Ethiopian cities, marriage feasts have been turned into film sets except for few. Guests are invited to be videoed but not to enjoy the feast. Food is scanty and soda pop is the most common drink. I had been to many such weddings and returned home without eating anything except what I provided myself. The worst happens when the guest is invited as part of the team that accompanies the couple the whole day. On the other hand, the Gurage still hold good wedding feasts – I would never miss a Gurage wedding when invited. Close friends and relatives help with Gurage weddings; some come with drink, some with live animals for slaughter, others with foodstuffs. At the end of the feast, guests are fully satisfied and the two families have surplus food and drink. It is an enviable society.

I returned to Fredericton and the university in August 1987. I was expecting that my friend Woldeselassie would be arriving from Ethiopia – he was supposed to be coming for his master's degree and to be part of the transportation group. We were very close friends back home, worked in the same office and went on the same field studies. Our families were also very close. At the time, I had moved to a family-style apartment with two bedrooms.

I had met another Ethiopian student, Gelan, at the university. He had been sent to Cuba to study while the rest of his family stayed in Ethiopia. Cuba was very strange for him and he felt very uncomfortable. Leaving his family behind had made him especially uneasy. Gelan and some of his fellow students couldn't go along with their Cuban teachers and they were sent home, as prisoners. When the plane landed in Montreal for fuel, they asked their guards if they could relieve themselves and were given permission. As soon as they entered the washroom, they started shouting for help. Airport security came and let them out and they asked for political asylum. Afterwards, the Canadian government granted them permission to stay and after a few years Gelan's family joined him.

Gelan's son Daniel was handsome and energetic and about the same age as my son. His mother, Alemitu told me a story about him. The two of them were alone back home and Gelan was in Cuba. They were surviving by selling contraband clothes, travelling between Diredawa, the major eastern city, and Addis Ababa. There was a customs officer named Eshetu who was highly feared by the traders for he was merciless in confiscating even petty amounts of clothing. People smuggling lots of clothing were easily identified – they wore several garments and looked like heavily loaded draft animals. Daniel had heard about Eshetu and one day he was travelling with his mom from Diredawa to Addis Ababa. In the middle of the journey, Eshetu got on the train; people began to talk about him and to try to hide their belongings. Daniel stood up and said, "Where is Eshetu? Bring him on!" Eshetu was embarrassed and scolded the people for making small children like Daniel hate him. He called Daniel and kissed his cheeks. Thenceforth, Eshetu had never bothered Daniel's mother, even when she carried more contraband clothing.

Woldeselassie arrived from Ethiopia in late August 1987. He had brought some local food with him and letters from my wife, children and Wondime. My daughter was supposed to go to pre-school in September. I had talked with some people who had contacts at the Lideta Catholic Girls School and they had promised to secure a place for her. The school was adjacent to the boys' school where my son went and it would have been ideal for Shewaye in dropping and picking them. However, I learned that she had not been admitted and I felt very sad. Woldeselassie cooled me down and promised to help her get in next year, through his father-in-law who was working for the Catholic Church at the time.

Classes began and the campus was flooded with young women and men. The bookstore, libraries, classes, cafeteria, dormitories – and even the athletic fields – were all crowded with young women and men and the university was at full speed again. I remembered what a staff at UNB said once, "Students leave campus in April when I am fed up of them and return in September when I am happy to see them back." Students in the transportation group started our first class. Dr. Wilson was there and he was famous for overloading students; he really enjoyed keeping students busy. I registered to take four courses and my friend Woldeselassie five. My friend had a master's degree in civil engineering from the Soviet Union. A lecturer in transport economics was teaching part-time at night. We had a class with him. During his first class, he asked us to introduce ourselves and when Woldeselassie and I introduced ourselves as Ethiopians, he stared at us for few minutes. He had never expected to see such healthy and strongly-built Ethiopians and had thought we were all skinny and impoverished. It made me think of a story a friend in Montreal had told me. Once he was taking a taxi and two more people got in. One complained about his obesity and the other advised him to go to Ethiopia to lose weight. Ethiopia's image has been negatively changed after the 1973-74 droughts and the media is the major contributing factor.

Ethiopia covers one million square kilometres. More than 75 percent of it is suitable for agriculture, but less than 20 percent is under cultivation. There are many rivers flowing into neighbouring Sudan, Egypt, Somalia and Kenya. The problem with us is war: we fight with neighbouring countries and amongst ourselves. A country cannot develop if it is always at war. Countries that exploit our rivers also benefit from our suffering. So do aid agencies because our problems mean employment opportunities for them. Ethiopia has lost thousands of good minds to other countries. There are many Ethiopian professors in American universities and Ethiopian scientists in research institutes. There are other well-educated Ethiopians in Canada, the United Kingdom, Australia and many African countries. The country doesn't lack resources; it lacks good governance. Governments are not the only ones to blame – everybody in the country is responsible as well.

We completed our first semester with no trouble. At Christmas, the Wayes invited us to visit and Dr. Wilson also invited us to his place. Sharon Cody, a staff at the university bookstore invited us too. We enjoyed Canadian dishes and most importantly the deserts. Winter was not easier for me than it was the first time, three years ago. Woldeselassie had lived in the Soviet Union for six years and managed it better than I did. One evening, I was bundling up to go to my apartment and Garry Hogg; the Canadian student looked at me and said, "It seems you are heading for space." I said, "Yes, from my grave to space." That Saint Patrick's Day we went to the bars. Woldeselassie had a badge on his chest that read "Kiss me, I'm Irish," and people looked at him strangely. One person said to me, "He's Irish?" I said, "Yes, he's Irish and I'm Scottish." It was fun and we enjoyed it.

The academic year was over and I completed my course requirements and was concentrating on my dissertation. That summer, Dr. Wilson arranged a golf tournament in Alma County, by the Bay of Fundy. Woldeselassie and I travelled with Dr. Wilson and he took us to his birthplace and showed us the old house he was born in. He told us that his father had had enough money to feed the family but not to pay for a university education. "But," he said, "There was a man in Alma who was close to me. When he found out that I didn't have money to pay for university, he lent me the money that he had saved for his daughter who wasn't interested going to university. I worked in summers to pay back my debt and again in September, I borrowed for the next year. That was how I completed my university education." It reminded me of my childhood when Abaye didn't have enough money to feed us. One evening, he said "If I could manage 20 Birr per month, I would sleep much better."

Next, Dr. Wilson took us to his elementary school. It was a two-storey building with a tube fire escape. He said that during fire drills he had stood outside the tube and helped students get out of it. When he saw students he didn't like, he would trip them and they would flip over. Some young men in our village did such funny things all the times.

The night before the golf tournament, we made a campfire by the Bay of Fundy and boiled shellfish. I liked shellfish but had never eaten such things back home. In general, Ethiopians are not fish or seafood eaters but meat eaters. Our rivers and lakes have lots of fish, but they are not marketed well, either domestically or for export. We all enjoyed the evening. The Canadian students and professors joked and laughed and made us all enjoy ourselves. The next day, we golfed Ethiopian-style at the tournament and made Canadians laugh in return. The tournament ended with a party with steak and beer and the handing out trophies at the Wilsons. We Ethiopians got trophies too. It was one of my most memorable times.

The Wayes invited us for barbecues that summer. The kids were lively as usual and played with us happily. Bill told us that the family had been once to Toronto for wedding and there were black children at the party. The kids played well with them while most white Canadians from other areas shied away from them. People were amazed at how comfortable the Waye children were. The Waye children had crossed the colour barrier. Jordan was four years old and was getting crazier everyday. Gelan's family was friendly to us as well. They invited us for lunch on the weekends and we ate *injera bewot,* a traditional dish at home. His wife Alemitu was expert at making that. We played with Daniel, their son, and that was good for Woldeselassie – he had left three children back home, the oldest 11 and the youngest less than four.

The summer of 1988 was over and September arrived. Nothing changed for me. I was still working on my dissertation. Woldeselassie was finishing his studies and was planning to leave by the end of October. Another Ethiopian engineer, Duressa, joined us and he too was studying for his master's degree. I knew him back home, but we weren't close. He was much younger than us and had no family. We gave him one of our bedrooms and the two of us slept in the same room until Woldeselassie left.

Woldeselassie was Gurage, the most industrious ethnic group in the country. They are very business-minded people and were called money-lovers. One early morning, Woldeselassie told me about the dream he had the previous night. He felt that he was back home. Many black lions came to attack him, but he had chased them away with a stick. I didn't comment but thought he had been a beast during the night. Another night, I heard him groaning in his sleep. I got out of bed, woke him up and asked what was wrong. He said, "A lot of thieves came after me to take my money." I said, "You chased the lions away with a stick but groaned because of thieves. Is it because of the money?"

Woldeselassie finished his studies and shopped for clothes for his family and friends. I was his consultant on the sizes because I knew his wife and his children very well. I shopped for my family too since he had offered to take things for them. He left for home and I was very sorry that I was staying behind. We had so many things in common to talk about and we had been together through good and bad back home. Through his father-in-law, he had helped my daughter get into the Catholic school. I missed him like a brother when he left.

I didn't know much about Duressa and we didn't have so much in common, but he was interesting and had a sense of humour. One day he told me this story: "Once, a man had an affair with another man's wife. That man was a bully and scared everybody in the village. The woman had told her husband about the affair, but he was scared of the bully himself and the wife always mocked her husband for his cowardice. Finally, the husband decided to face him and husband and wife went to the market together. The bully had come to the same market, with a sheepskin for sale. When he saw them, he put the skin on the ground and asked the wife to come with him. Then he told her husband, 'Watch this sheepskin. If any flies get on it; you're going to be in deep trouble.' The bully and the wife left together and came back after some hours. The bully took his sheepskin and left. The wife said to her husband, 'Are you a man? You can't even stand up for your wife. You'd be better off dead.' The husband said, 'You didn't see what I did. There were flies all over his sheepskin and I didn't touch them at all.'"

I advised Duressa how to act and told him it was good to take part in student gatherings and the golf tournament at Alma. Mixing with the group was as important as his academic achievement. I told him that Canadians at the Group want to know about other people and their culture and to share their own. Initially, he didn't seem to take my advice seriously. As time went on however, he learnt from his experiences and tried to cope with the system.

The group was to go to a Transportation Research Board conference in Washington, but I decided not to go because I was saving money to pay a typist for my dissertation. At the time, I was not good at word processing. Dr. Wilson told me that I should go and not to worry about the money. I agreed. During our trips, Dr. Wilson, Professor Bisson and I shared a room. They were very kind to me. We went to an Ethiopian restaurant this time too and enjoyed the meal and did *gursha* for one another. Duressa met a girl there, Almaz who later became his wife. He was the only guy among the Ethiopians at UNB who benefited the most from the Transportation Research Board Conference in Washington, D.C.

Once again, we had the transportation group's golf tournament at the Bay of Fundy. I went as usual, played "Ethiopian style" and came back with a trophy.

The Wayes invited us for dinner at Easter and for barbecue during the summer. I travelled with them to their parents' places in Miramichi, about an hour drive from Fredericton. I also went with them to Moncton and Saint John. Gelan's family also invited us for lunch on the weekend. All the same, the longer I stayed in Canada, the more I missed my family. They wrote me letters and sent me photographs taken on their birthdays. I could see that they were growing fast and missed them dearly. I fixed their pictures on the bulletin board in my office. Dr. Wilson came by and, after looking at them with their soft drinks and birthday cakes, said, "Are they getting enough to eat?" He sat down on a chair and said, "Would your government let your family out?" I said, "I don't know but I can try." I asked Shewaye to check with a friend who worked at the ministry of internal affairs and he told her it would be impossible.

The summer of 1989 was over and another academic year began. I submitted the first draft of my dissertation in early October 1989 and got it back, with many corrections, at the end of November. I finished the corrections by the end the month and submitted the second draft. The professors gave it back with some more corrections; I did the corrections and submitted the third draft at the beginning of January 1990. The first date for presentation was set for early January. The presentation went well, with some corrections. I did the final draft and it was sent to an external examiner. The examiner accepted it, with a few corrections. I did the final presentation on January 26, 1990, and got my Ph.D. I called my family the next week. I asked Shewaye about Emaye and she told me she was fine. I asked her to bring her to our house next time so that I could talk to her and she said she would.

I had dedicated my dissertation to my family and in the acknowledgements, I wrote, "I feel grateful to be able to acknowledge those people who directly or indirectly gave me support during my studies and during the preparation of this thesis... Finally, my thanks travel across the ocean to Ethiopia to my brother Negussie Ambo and to my wife Shewaye Feyissa who always encouraged me to go on with my studies with great enthusiasm and determination. My deepest thanks go to my wife not only for the encouragement she gave me but also for the responsibility she carried on in taking care of our children during my absence."

A Somali student, Jamma had come from Turkey and was looking for a room. We asked him to join us. Since I would be leaving soon, I gave him my room and slept on the sofa in the living room. Somalis and Ethiopians are neighbours but usually adversaries. There are Ethiopian Somalis as well. We know each other very well, through war and peace, so we understand how to live together. Once I heard a story about a Canadian-Somali who had gone back home to visit his relatives. A friend there asked him what kind of country Canada was. The visiting Somali thought about how to explain Canada. Somalis are Muslims and the women cover themselves from head to feet. Women in Canada wear very short clothes in summer. So the visiting Somali said to his friend, "Canada is a country in North America where the trees are naked in winter and the women are naked in summer."

It was early in the morning at the beginning of February 1990 and I was dead asleep on the sofa in the living room. Duressa woke me up and I saw him and Jamma standing there, looking terribly sad. I wasn't fully awake and was confused. I asked Duressa what had happened and he said, "Your mother has passed away." I couldn't believe it. I bowed and looked at the floor. Memories of her flooded my mind. I thought she might have called my name many times before she died. I cried, cried and cried. I was alone even though they were standing in front of me. I wished I was back home at her funeral, crying with my brother, sister, nephews, relatives and friends. I pleaded her spirit to forgive me for not being there when she needed me most. It was the darkest time of my life. Gelan and his family came that day and spent some time with me, but it wasn't enough for a man who had lost his dearest friend. I developed stomach trouble that would haunt me for a long time.

It would have been different back home. Food and coffee would be prepared for the mourners. The news of a death is almost always broken early in the morning. Friends and neighbours would wake up early in the morning and be alert. Some would be standing by the bereaved's gate. Immediately after hearing the news, they would come into the house and mourn with the bereaved. They would eat lunch and supper together for two or three days, and the closest family members and friends would continue that for few more days. The loss of a family member weighs heavily in our culture and we believe sorrow is eased if shared with friends. I called home and talked to my wife. She told me that Emaye died on January 26, 1990, the day I was granted my Ph.D. I wished that she had lived few days longer and that her vision had come true.

I finished the documentation for my dissertation at the end of February 1990. I didn't know what to do next and thought of moving to Toronto to look for a job. In the meantime however, the transportation group granted me a post-doctoral fellowship for six months, up to October 1990. I finished my post-doc, got ready to say goodbye to friends and colleagues. The group organized goodbye party for me, with students, professors and staff members. They gave me gifts of money to buy things for my family on the way back. I felt very grateful for their gifts and sorry for leaving them. The Wayes invited me to their place. It was sad to leave that blessed family. Gelan and his family had moved to Halifax and I had to visit them before I leave. I went to Halifax and said goodbye.

Then, I went to Toronto at the beginning of November and stayed with Tsadik and his family while looking for a job. One morning, I went to one office and talked to a secretary about job opportunities. She said that they had been looking seriously for a transport economist and may be I would be lucky. I gave her my resume and she took it to her boss, but then returned quick to tell me "sorry." Another time, I was taking a bus, on my way to another office and was sitting by the window. I hadn't noticed whoever had sat down in the aisle seat but later felt constant push from that side. I turned to look and saw an old woman. She looked uncomfortable, but I couldn't see how sitting by an old woman could be a problem since I had done it many times in Fredericton. I stayed in my seat, but the pushing never stopped. Then, I slowly edged towards her and pushed back. She angrily jumped up from her seat and moved to another.

I lost hope of getting a job in Toronto and decided to go home. A consulting firm in London, England, had asked me to stop by their office on the way back to Ethiopia. In addition, my friend Philip had invited me to stay at his home in London. So I applied for a visa, but it was not easy to get it. Philip had asked the British Home Office in London to co-operate on issuing a visa for me. I waited for three weeks and decided to abandon it. I called the British High Commission in Ottawa and told them to forget about my request for a visa and send back my passport instead. In three days, I had my passport and the visa. I flew to London. Philip was flying there from Washington, D.C., the same day. We met at Heathrow Airport and took a taxi to his place at Park Hill, Kent. He lived in a gorgeous three-storey building lied in a beautiful compound that was even more beautiful inside. His wife Wendy, two daughters and his mother lived there. Their son lived someplace else by himself. They gave me a beautiful room on the second floor and fed me well. With two friends, he had a small consulting firm. Each worked from his home and so Philip had a nice office. Wendy tutored high school students in maths. I visited London and the consulting firm that invited me. They had no job at hand but promised something for the future. I took the tube to and from the Cornwells' home, using Victoria Station. I visited Hyde Park, saw Westminster Abbey from the outside and saw other places too. London is a very beautiful city, but life is very expensive there.

I finished my visit to London and headed for Brussels. I had had such a bad experience the last time that I didn't feel comfortable there. I wished I hadn't gone there but had no choice. I stayed at Kebede's place – he was a diplomat at the Ethiopian Embassy in Brussels and had been in the bar that frightening afternoon in Addis Ababa. I had stayed with him last time too. He had two children then and has three now. I didn't shop much this time because I was short on cash. I left Brussels and travelled on Lufthansa to Frankfurt and then on Ethiopian Airlines to Addis Ababa, arriving at Bole International Airport on December 29, 1990.

CHAPTER ELEVEN

Wondime, his daughter and my daughter came to the terminal to meet me, but I didn't recognise my daughter. I kissed them and we left the building. Families and friends were waiting for me. I kissed and hugged everybody and then asked for my daughter. Everybody laughed at me because I hadn't recognised her in the airport. She had grown tall and slender. On the drive home I wanted to visit Emaye's grave first, so we went to the graveyard at Saint Michael's Church. I had arranged for her to be with Abaye and I walked straight to her grave. I bowed and cried, asking for her forgiveness for betraying her in her time of trouble and for not sharing her sufferings. Emaye and I had always stood together, had always shared our losses and our triumphs. I knew she had always wished to die before us, but at least I should have shared her pain. It was a very painful moment for me.

Before, I had always gone to my parents' place when I came home. This time, I went to my place. Seven years had gone by since Abaye had passed away and now Emaye was gone. Their home had been a place of a fierce struggle for survival. This time, although my sister lived in my parents' home, I felt that I would be going to a haunted house. I didn't want to see the place at all, at least for some time. Relatives, neighbours and friends had gathered at our house to console me for Emaye's death. That is our tradition, even if years have passed since the loss. The visits continued for a few days afterwards. My children had grown tall – my son was now nine years old and my daughter seven. I felt that they weren't close to me any more. I understood their distancing themselves – by then I had been away continuously for 40 percent of my son's life and for half of my daughter's. I had to spend more time with them this time.

When I left for Canada, I had resigned from the ERA, so I had to look for a job. I decided not to look for work in any government office – under the military government everything had gone wrong. There were few consulting firms in the country and the most recognised management-consulting firm at the time was Shawel Consult International (SCI). The owner and the manager of the firm, Ato Hailu Shawel, had been a prominent government official and an entrepreneur. He had been the general manager of the ERA just before I joined it in 1976 and had also been the first Ethiopian general manager of the HVA (Ethiopia) Sugar Factory after its nationalisation. Later, he was minister of state farms and had done well. I called SCI and made an appointment to meet with him at his office. He worked from his home in western suburb of the city. His home lay in the middle of 7,000 square metres of land, with his second-floor office looking out over a beautiful landscape with hills and forests. The garden at the back was filled with flowers and greenery. It looked like an ideal place to work. I had heard his name but had never met him. He was a tall man with a striking personality. He welcomed me in and gave me coffee served in beautiful cups engraved with "Ethiopian Airlines." I gave him my resume and we discussed the restricted business opportunities in the country. He told me that he had no vacancies, but was expecting work soon and asked me to call him often.

In the meantime, I met Dr. Abebe Aderay, who was working at the United Nations Economic Commission for Africa (UNECA) in Addis Ababa. I had known him when I was at Dejazmach Wondirad Elementary School. He was a close friend of Tadesse Mengesha, who was himself an inspiration to young students in our village. Both were older than I. After they finished elementary school, Tadesse went to the Haile Selassie I Secondary School while Abebe went to the Commercial School of Addis Ababa. After high school, Tadesse enrolled in the Haile Selassie I University in Addis Ababa and Abebe went to India. Finally, Tadesse earned his Ph.D. in economics and settled in the United States. Abebe went to work for UNECA in Addis Ababa. It had been a long time since I had seen Abebe. He had almost forgotten me, but someone who knew us both reintroduced us.

One day, Abebe called and told me that a new research post had been set up for a post-doctoral fellow. The candidate had to be a recent Ph.D. graduate. I submitted a research proposal and my curriculum vitae. He called me a few days later to say that I had been rejected because of my age. How could someone 44 years old be too old to do research? I knew that even if I had lowered my age and dyed my hair, I wouldn't have got the position – another candidate had contacts more powerful than Dr. Aderay did.

At the end of the month, I called Ato Hailu Shawel, the general manager of SCI. He asked me to come to his office. When we met, he told me the work had not yet materialised, but he was ready to hire me. We discussed my salary and I told him I was not asking much at the moment but might ask for more in the future. I was hired as of February 1, 1991, as a senior transportation economist. At the time, there were seven permanent and three contract employees. He had had more staff earlier, but some had gone to start their own firms. At the beginning, I was not busy.

The car that I had bought in Brussels had arrived at the port of Asab. However, the rebels fighting to topple the government were advancing towards Addis Ababa from north. Eritrean rebels were also surrounding Asmara and the ports of Massawa and Asab. If the Eritreans took control of Asab, my car would be gone, so I arranged for a driver to clear customs in Asab and drive the car to Addis Ababa – before the Eritreans took the port and confiscated everything in it. Now that I had my car, my colleagues at Shawel Consult requested *fintir* from me – that I buy them lunch. Buying new goods, including clothes, commonly meant that *fintir* would be expected. We finished our lunch at one that afternoon and were ready to leave the restaurant when the radio announced that President Mengistu Hailemariam had run away to Kenya. He had said that he would fight until the end. We were alarmed and had no idea who would take power next. For the second time, I was seeing an Ethiopian leader leave a power vacuum. General Tesfaye, the defence minister, temporarily assumed power. However, the rebels were moving on Addis Ababa from all sides.

Within few days, government soldiers had fled the battlefield and come to Addis Ababa. They were confused and pitiful. They were armed and could have taken whatever they wanted, instead they asked for food and for money to go home. Some sold their weapons at a very cheap price, just to get enough money to get home. People fed them and paid for their transport. The people of Tigray had suffered the most under the military government, but even they fed the soldiers, clothed them, paid their transport, and showed them the safest routes for escape. It was sign of the strength of Ethiopian culture. The Ethiopian rebels did not harm them either. However, the Eritrean army mercilessly killed and mistreated the Ethiopian soldiers and robbed them of their belongings, including their gold teeth.

Within a few days, rebels surrounded Addis Ababa. Government forces collapsed and the president's bodyguards – men who had terrorised the people of Addis Ababa – began to loot their own garrison. Members of the Derg had been torturing and killing Ethiopians for the last 17 years and now urged that northerners be attacked. That was rejected outright by the rest of the Ethiopian people. Diplomats and other foreigners left the country. The people of Addis Ababa were left alone and hopeless. We were very scared. My wife and I slept on the floor, with our two children lying between us for safety. Some people died from bullets shot through their roofs.

Looting began in the countryside and to some degrees in Addis Ababa. Schools were robbed of their corrugated iron, clinics of their drugs and offices of their furniture. The rebel force that called itself the Ethiopian People's Revolutionary Democratic Front (EPRDF) swiftly took power, which kept Addis Ababa from falling into chaos. If they had delayed a little, things would have spun out of control in Addis Ababa – a bloodbath would have been inevitable. We later learned that thugs in our village had lists of houses to loot. Formerly respected people were caught stealing community property.

There was an attempt to set Addis Ababa ablaze. An ammunition store in the centre of the city was set on fire. We lived five kilometres away, but our house shook from the blast. My mother- in-law lived near the site of the explosion and Shewaye cried terribly for her mom, which disturbed the whole family. Haile – my neighbour – and I went to check on his father-in-law and my mother-in-law. Debris was still flying. We reached my mother-in-law's place first. She had run to the nearest church. Flying rocks had destroyed the door to her house. Except for a very few people acting as watchmen, the area was abandoned.

Major fuel distributing stations were located nearby. The oil depots for Mobil, Agip and Total were half a kilometre away and the depot for Shell was only a kilometre from the site. It was a calculated attack and it was thought that the Eritrean Peoples Revolutionary Front (EPLF) had been behind it. They were suspected because of their hatred towards the people of central Ethiopia. That was completely wrong – the two groups had lived amicably and inter-marriages were very common. Moreover, no matter what some people boasted, nobody could tell the difference between Eritreans and Ethiopians. We are the same people and had lived separately for only 60 years, after Eritrea was colonised by Italy. The Tigreans in Ethiopia and the highlanders in Eritrea are the same people, speaking the same language and sharing the same culture. The only difference in language is that the Eritreans include some Italian words and expressions.

Unfortunately, this time there would be two countries: Ethiopia and Eritrea. I wished the two governments sat down and discussed foreign debt, citizenship, the border, the appropriation of assets, and more before separation was declared. However, the United Nations was keen in having one more member country, Eritrea and so encouraged it. The UN's secretary-general was Mr. Boutros Boutros-Gali, an Egyptian whose country had been supporting the Eritrean rebels for 30 years, in order to destabilise Ethiopia and exploit its water resources. Such a debacle had never before happened in the Ethiopian history.

Many Ethiopian nationalists were disappointed with the US government too. They saw this as the second time that the US had betrayed Ethiopia. The first time, it was believed that the Carter administration refused to give arms to the military government during the Somali invasion of eastern Ethiopia, although the Haile Selassie government had paid for them. As a result, the military government had been forced to go to the Soviets for aid and consequently, Ethiopia lost many of its young and dear sons and daughters. This time, the Clinton administration watched quietly as the country was falling apart. A previous US administration had supported the annexation of Eritrea by Haile Selassie government.

At present, Ethiopia is divided into regions based on ethnicity. I had never imagined that the idea would be supported by northerners – they had been at the centre of nation building and the source of Ethiopian civilization. The US ambassador to Ethiopia in the early 1990s backed the plan and commented that Ethiopia could be a model for other African countries. Some in the government have tried to exacerbate ethnic tensions, although Ethiopians have lived together for centuries, with northerners settling in central and southern Ethiopia and centralists and southerners travelling north to fight against foreign invaders and similarly settling there. This has been the case for a very long time and it is my dream to continue for centuries to come.

Similarly, Eritreans had also lived elsewhere in Ethiopia. When I was in Mendefera, Eritrea, during my national university service, I had heard people in the village of Debarwa saying that their forefathers came from central Ethiopia in the fifth century. Similarly, I have known of people in Asmara who claimed to have come from Gondar, northern Ethiopia. Despite this sharing of space and history, my generation has failed to maintain the relationship and instead led the two peoples to unrelenting enmity. I believe that the sovereignty of Eritrea should be decided by the Eritreans themselves. Patience and prudence should have prevailed for good neighbourhood. Eventually, however, I hope that the two countries will live as good neighbours and the people as brothers and sisters.

The general manager of SCI called me to his office to tell me that there might be a short-term assignment for a transport economist at the African

Development Bank (ADB) in Abidjan, Ivory Coast. He knew that I had recently returned from Canada and asked me if I would be interested in the work. It was painful to leave my family so soon, but I had no choice because of limited opportunities in the country. I left Addis Ababa for a three-month stint at the ADB. Ivory Coast is in West Africa and in a time zone of three hours behind Addis Ababa. At the time, only Ethiopian Airlines flew along the route. The plane landed at three airports on the way, it took 13 hours and was very boring.

Abidjan was a very beautiful city with modern streets and bypasses, quite different from home. The elegant ADB building is in the heart of the city. The building's interior is even more impressive and unlike what I had seen anywhere. There were north and south towers, each with its own group of elevators. I was confused about which was which. Although the ADB served only African countries, its staff came from all over the world. Financing was coming from 74 countries, 50 of them within Africa and the rest all over the world. Offices were shared, except for senior officials. Consultants did not have fixed office space but instead used that of staff who were away on missions. I was assigned to work with Balram, a transportation engineer, who was Asian. The work was routine – I evaluated the bids submitted by borrowing countries.

I met many Ethiopian professionals and they arranged a studio apartment for me. Many of them lived in the building and it was within a walking distance of the ADB. They invited me to visit, especially when fresh *injera* came from Ethiopia. The city itself is on the Atlantic Ocean, hot and infested with malaria. Ethiopians in Abidjan were vulnerable to malaria – most had lived in highlands, where there are no mosquitoes.

Ivory Coast was a colony of France and French remains the official language. It was to my disadvantage that I do not speak the language. French was offered as a subject when I was in high school and the teacher would give us the exam questions ahead of the time so that we could prepare. Our marks were in the 90s, but we had no knowledge of the language. I regretted that and found that without French it was very difficult to find out about the people. I understood that Ivorians regarded French very highly – talking to a Frenchman was different from talking to an Englishman.

The three months went fast. One day, Balram came to my office and gave me a hand-written draft to type. It was a notice about recruiting someone in my position for the next assignment. I typed it and gave it to him. I noticed that the fee was quoted as US $400 per day, while my company was being paid US$ 250 per day and I thought I could have continued at that fee. I had no idea why Balram wanted another person at such a high fee. I was puzzled and so talked about it with an Ethiopian friend who had been at the ADB for many years. He was also amazed and in turn contacted another Ethiopian who was quite a bit senior. The senior Ethiopian took the matter to the director of the department and had it changed in my company's favour. Balram came to my office to have me re-type the letter. He looked sick. He hated me and harassed me. I knew why and kept quiet. Eventually, the SCI got the new assignment and my stay was extended. I would be appraising a road project in Ethiopia. It was a very good opportunity for me to visit my family. Balram was the team leader and had a meeting with other experts in the department to discuss future reports and the kind of data to be included in the report. He told me nothing of that before we left for Ethiopia.

We travelled to Ethiopia and I stayed with my family. Our local counterpart organisation was the ERA, my home office for 12 years. I knew everybody in the planning and programming division and they made available whatever data I required. The subject road was Chida-Sodo and I had done the original economic feasibility study for it. It was also Emaye's birthplace. Balram, two Ethiopian counterparts and I went to the site and drove along the road. Most of the trip was at night and we didn't see much of the surroundings – it seemed to be a formality rather than real visit to the area.

I visited SCI and found that its work had dropped off drastically. The manager had recently gone into politics and the government of the day was denying it work, which was not surprising since no government provides firearms to its enemies. Even in the developed world, most private companies contribute money to all parties, directly or indirectly, for the sake of securing government contracts. It was clear at the time that a prominent company like SCI would be an easy target for the government. We returned to Abidjan after two weeks in Ethiopia. The next day, Balram came to my office and gave me a copy of the paper that they had discussed before the mission. That paper should have been given to me before we left for Ethiopia. I knew that he was sabotaging me? Fortunately, however, I had worked on the project and had all the information with me. Even if I required more data, I could call my friends at the ERA and have what I needed within a few days. Nevertheless, it was very difficult for me to understand Balram's actions: he was a senior engineer, was earning enough money, he was nearly 60 years old, and we had never met before. Humanity manifested to me its unkindness.

One day, Balram told me a story about his travel to Brussels, Belgium. His wife and his son went with him. They had arrived in Brussels from India and were to take a subway to a hotel. He gave his briefcase to his wife and went to buy the tickets. A man had touched her shoulder from behind and when she turned towards his touch, he took the briefcase and disappeared with travellers cheques worth US $10,000, a cheque for more than £1,000 and his passport and other documents. He was devastated. Three days later, the briefcase was found empty. He should have learned a lot from that.

We prepared the report and submitted it. There were to be two meetings, one at the division level and another one at the department level. When we had the division meeting everybody attacked the report. I had written many reports before and most were accepted with comments. I became very tense and could only think that the ADB had a completely different approach. We revised the report and submitted it for discussion at the department level. Another kick in the head. Surprisingly, this committee told us to include what the division had told us to leave out. I said to myself, "There is a new technique practiced here; you have to learn it."

Next, Balram and I were assigned to prepare the terms of reference for a road in Ghana, which borders Ivory Coast. He would be the team leader. We travelled to Accra, the capital, by air. The city was not as sophisticated as Abidjan, but Ghanaians spoke English and I felt more at home. They were kind and friendly people and the staffs at government offices were very helpful. We went to the project site and found a road that was unnecessarily curved. We asked the local counterpart engineer why it was built like that and he said it had been done for a minister who came from that area. I had heard a similar story in Addis Ababa: a member of the city council had arranged for a road to cross his property so that he could collect compensation.

Ghanaian officials treated us well, briefed us on the project road and on social and economic activities in the country. They also organized lunch for us. They promised to send us any additional information we required and we returned to Abidjan after two weeks. We prepared the terms of reference and I completed my assignments successfully. All the same, it was quite an experience to work with Balram.

Before I arrived at the ADB, it had advertised for a transport economist. Mengesha at the ERA was among the six short-listed. However, he had been too busy to come for interview. There were going to be two groups of interviews. An Ethiopian was the deputy director of the department I worked for and he told me to get prepared for an interview in case Mengesha didn't come. I did prepare. The first group had its interviews and one professional was selected.

Mengesha did come for the interview. I gave him all the documents I had prepared and he did very well at the interview. Immediately after the interview, the division head said to me "Your man did very well." I was very happy for him. We heard that the division head had written a letter of recommendation to the human resources division. The Ethiopians working at the ADB advised Mengesha to stay in Abidjan so that he could follow the matter closely. They said that anything could happen. However, Mengesha decided to go back home and do his follow-up from Addis Ababa. The outcome was different. Mengesha spoiled his chance and mine. It would have been a very good opportunity for me and my children.

Fikru, my Ethiopian friend at the ADB, gave me a ride to the city of Yamoussoukro, a two-hour drive north of Abidjan. It was the birthplace place of Houphouët-Boigny, the first president of Ivory Coast. He had built a famous basilica, Notre Dame de la Paix – Our Lady of Peace. The basilica is a huge domed structure and said to have more than 7,000 individually air-conditioned seats. The stained-glass windows are magnificent. It is said that it is one of the world's largest Catholic churches, to be larger than Saint Peter's in Rome, and is in a large compound with a beautiful garden. We went inside and it is very beautiful. However, it was too much of an expense for an African country with limited resources. The country's president claimed to have paid for it from his own pocket. Nevertheless, it is difficult to believe that he had so much of his own when the country was struggling to survive. It seemed that he was a typical extortionate African leader.

I finished my assignment and returned to Ethiopia. I met very good people at the ADB, Ethiopians as well as other Africans. I learned in life that good friends are not acquired but delivered. I have lifetime friends who are as close as Wondime and my family. I also learned that the best thing in life is to do good without expecting reciprocity. I understood that the establishment of ADB would significantly contribute to the economic, social and environmental development of African countries.

I continued to work for SCI. A Kenyan firm asked us to join it on a construction supervision project in Ethiopia. The project was to be financed by ADB. We prepared a joint technical proposal and submitted it to the ERA. Through my friends at the ERA, I was closely following the matter. In the meantime, I met a close friend of mine who had left the ERA and we talked about the project. I gave him all the details without knowing that he was working for a competing firm. As I found out later, he was passing on everything I told him. I new that SCI-Kenyan was one of two finalists and that we were sure to be on the lower side of the cost since the other firm was European. I thought we had a better chance of getting the job.

In the meantime, I heard that the results of the analysis had been reversed in favour of the European firm, by throwing us out of the range. Fortunately, the division head I knew at the ADB was visiting Addis Ababa at the time. I met him at the Hilton Hotel and told him everything. He promised to request the documents from the ADB's headquarters in Abidjan and evaluate all the proposals again. On my way out of the Hilton, I met the agent of the European firm – he was Ethiopian, Akalu – and he alleged that I was interfering through my friends in the ERA. He also told me that he got the information from the man I had shared the proposal with. I was really shocked since he was one of my friends I trusted and respected most. I told Akalu that I had the right to follow up – it was in my company's interest. And I asked him what my friend was doing with the European firm.

We made an appointment to talk at Ethiopia Hotel. When we met, Akalu told me that my friend had been working for the European firm and had prepared the technical proposal. He also told me in detail the information he had provided him. He said, "I have spent more than 200,000 Birr to renovate an office – I am expecting to win this project. If I lose the project, I'll go after his life." I told him that was too much. The documents were sent to Abidjan for re-evaluation and Akalu travelled there to follow up. Later I was told that the proposals had been re-evaluated and that we were competitive. Eventually, however, the European firm got the project for US $2.3 million against our bid of US $1.5 million. With the difference, the country could have built at least ten kilometres of road or maintained hundreds of kilometres of roads. It was an expensive lesson for me.

The work at office was not encouraging. My salary was meagre, but I felt ashamed to ask for a raise. I started to do some work with other firms. In the meantime, Dr. Philip Cornwell sent me a fax from London about a job at the World Bank. Someone at the Bank's human resources office had written to him and asked him to recommend a reliable transport economist. He said he had given my name to a woman and asked me to send her my curriculum vitae. The Bank's letter stated that it was seriously looking for a qualified transport economist. I called Washington, D.C., and talked to the woman. She said she would put my curriculum vitae in the roster and let me know if an opportunity came up. For the first time, I was disappointed with the world's biggest institution.

In the meantime, the Kenyan firm asked me if I would be interested in working on an engineering and economic study of two roads in Uganda. I asked the general manager of SCI, Ato Hailu Shawel for a leave of absence and was granted it. It was a five-month assignment and I travelled to Uganda. The capital city, Kampala, was recovering from the damage done by the two previous presidents, Idi Amin and Milton Obote. I was informed by intellectuals in Kampala that Idi Amin (1971-1980) had launched a campaign of persecution against the Ugandan people murdering more than 100,000. He murdered ordinary citizens, government officials, educators, medical practitioners, church officials, prominent figures and a number of foreigners. He had wiped out entire villages. So many corpses were thrown into the White Nile River. Idi Amin was also alleged for so many bizarre rumours and myths - stories of cannibalism and keeping of victims' heads in his freezers at his home. He had condoned the actions of Adolf Hitler and planned to build a statue for him in Kampala. After his overthrow, he ran to Saudi Arabia. Milton Obote returned to power for the second time (1980-85) from Tanzania and killed more people than his predecessor did. After his overthrow, Obote ran to Tanzania and then to Zambia. The worst happened when those butchers were accepted and protected by foreign governments.

Uganda is known as the 'Pearl of Africa' for its variety of landscape, wildlife and culture. It's a country with about 17 million people and more than 40 ethnic groups. I was informed that there were four kingdoms in ancient times – Buganda, Bunyoro, Toro and Ankole. There are traces of Bantu ancestry in the south and Nilotic in the north. At the time, Uganda was a republic ruled by President Museveni.

A Kenyan and a Ugandan firm jointly managed the work. My living quarters and food were provided and two young Ugandan brothers served as cooks. The house was very large but was located in a shabby compound with an untrimmed lawn and a ramshackle fence. I guessed that the rent was cheap. I worked and slept there and took a daily one-hour walk round the town. Along the way to the main asphalt road was a fence with a dog behind it. The dog would always bare its teeth and growl at passers-by. Once, an engineer working with us got angry at the dog and tried to kick it through the fence and the dog grabbed his shoe, pulled it off, and dragged it inside the fence. The engineer came with one shoe. He did recover the other one the next day, but it had been destroyed. The dog looked dangerous and sometimes got out. I had a big stick and carried it with me whenever I walked that route.

One consultant was an expatriate transport economist from the United Kingdom. His input was brief. As informed, he had been included to win the project. It was not easy to win a project with an exclusively African staff. That was because the clients wanted it that way – they lacked confidence in their fellow Africans, even when a foreign consulting firm had hired them. The project manager was a Canadian engineer with Asian background and was not friendly at all, especially with the Ugandan cooks. He reminded me of Balram at the ADB.

When I was in Kampala, foreign residences were heavily protected, some hotel rooms had double doors, and elevators had heavily protected bars. Stores in Kampala had heavy doors and remained locked until those who wanted to enter were checked. Car hijackings and house robberies were also common. One of the cooks told me a story about theft in Kampala: "A foreigner was driving in the city with his wife by his side and a baby in the back seat. Behind the child was a briefcase. The foreigner parked the car and went into a shop, leaving his wife and the baby behind. Immediately, a local man – he had looked like a passer-by – opened the back door and took the baby away. The mother got out of the car and followed him. The man, after carrying the baby a little distance, put it down by the side of the road and left. The woman picked up the baby and put it back in the car. When the husband came back, she told him what had happened. He looked for his briefcase and it was gone. He got mad, took off his jacket and tore his shirt to pieces. Everything was gone." While the man was carrying off the baby, his friend had taken the briefcase.

I had heard about a similar incident in Addis Ababa. During the Derg Regime, there were many military experts from the Soviet Union in Addis Ababa. One day, two of them went to Merkato, said to be the largest market in Africa. It was very crowded and very noisy. As they were trying to park their car, a man with a fresh cigar came up and poked it at the sidelight, as though to light it. The Soviets were surprised by this "miracle of the fool" and stared at him. In the meantime, his friend slowly opened the car's back door and took everything. The man with the cigar saw that the mission had been accomplished and left. The Soviets checked to be sure the doors were locked before they went to shop and were shocked to find that the back seat was empty. The fool had fooled them.

The cooks complained a lot about the project manager. When I asked what the problem was, they told me that he had instructed them not to eat the leftover food but to keep it instead. Once the food had spoiled, he would tell them to throw it out. They showed me some of the spoiled food. I could hardly believe he had come from Canada. He was there to enjoy their resources and yet denied them his leftovers? Some human beings are cruel for no reason whatsoever – they are that way by nature.

The study comprised two roads, one in the east, and the other in the west. I travelled from Busia – a town in the east on the Kenyan border – to Lake Albert, on the western border with the Democratic Republic of Congo. Uganda is green with all kinds of crops and plants and was famous for its coffee, tobacco and forestry products. It shares Lake Victoria, the source of the White Nile, with the neighbouring countries of Tanzania, Kenya, Burundi and Rwanda. The most popular foods were *matoke*, a porridge made with banana, and *ugali*, a porridge made of maize. Different varieties of banana are used as fruit, for chips, to make *matoke*, and so on. The porridges are served with goat meat stew and eaten with the hands, as in Ethiopia.

A Ugandan engineer and I were on our way to Hoima – a village in the western part of the country – to conduct traffic surveys. We started our journey at six o'clock one evening, with the engineer driving. We travelled through dense forests, with neither cars nor animals to be seen on the way. About nine that evening, the car stopped unexpectedly – the engine was dead. We could see nothing and we had no flashlight. I asked the engineer if we would be able to spend the night in the car and he said it would be dangerous. Then I asked him about the nearby bushes and ditches and he said that would be even more dangerous. I was scared and so was he. It took us some time to do anything and we sat in the car. Finally, he lit a match, then seemed to be trying to figure out something. After a while, he managed to start the engine. I thought that something similar must have happened to him before. That was one of the scariest moments of my life.

We continued our journey, but I wasn't at ease until we reached our final destination. It reminded me of an incident in Ethiopia. At the time of the Somali invasion in 1977, a livestock team was conducting cattle surveys and doing vaccinations in the eastern part of the country. After a long day, they decided to pitch their tents close to a big city. But the driver insisted on going to the city and renting rooms – it would be dangerous to sleep in a field. However, the others didn't take him seriously. The driver refused to sleep in his tent and instead slept in a nearby ditch. In the middle of the night, rebels came. The driver escaped. The others were butchered.

AIDS was killing thousands in Uganda. Our counterpart engineer died while I was there. He had a family. Later, a secretary in our office died. She had no family. AIDS was not a serious problem in Ethiopia at the time. The engineer who went with me to Hoima said, "You have heard of AIDS, but we have seen it. We have seen our relatives and friends shrinking until they die." It was very scary. A foreign geologist was supporting more than 20 children whose parents had died of AIDS. He had rented a hut and was sleeping on the floor, surrounded by kids. He manifested the good side of humanity.

I travelled to Kapchorwa, a town in eastern Uganda, near Kenyan border. The people there claim to have come from the highlands of Ethiopia many generations ago. I talked to some of them and they told me, "We hear a lot about the drought in your country. Our hearts bled but we had no way of reaching you." That was very kind of them and amazing too – they were far away but still considered themselves as part of us, while in Ethiopia we were destroying one another through civil wars and the mismanagement of our resources.

During my time in Uganda, I thought seriously about my future at SCI. It was not getting enough work and my staying there would only cost the company while I would be idle. I had set up my own consulting firm, Alem Consult, while working for SCI, but had not made use of it yet. Finally, I decided to quit the SCI and sent a letter of resignation. I finished my work in Uganda and returned home. I had a reasonably big compound with 500 square metres of land and three rooms, including a washroom, for an office. I bought three tables, a photocopier, a computer, a printer, two shelves and accessories as necessary. Then, I began working with expatriate and with local consulting firms. Immediately, I got a contract with the European Union to work on four studies dealing with the management and financing of roads in Ethiopia. I hired three professionals and produced solid studies and a book. Subsequently, I worked with many European and North American consulting firms and I made good friends.

Once, I went in a group to Bahir Dar City on a water supply project financed by the Finnish International Development Agency (FINNIDA). We travelled throughout the area to assess the condition of the people living there and to determine their water management capacities. They were living in appalling conditions. I went to the historic town of Debre Tabor, the capital of Ras Gugsa Mersa, and also the capital of Emperor Tewodros II in 1860. It was sad to see Debre Tabor with no potable water, poorly clad school children, unclean hotel rooms – everything was in shambles. Many well-educated and successful people come from this area. Those still living in the country and with those in the Diaspora could have contributed a lot to their region, like the Gurage have done in the south.

We finished the project and submitted the report to FINNIDA, but they didn't like it. They had no room for professional evaluation and wanted everything their own way. That is the problem with many NGOs that operate in the country. In the first place, many of their "experts" are not specialised in their areas of assignment. Second, they have no knowledge of the place and the people. Third, they are there because it is a job and they don't much care about development. Ultimately, a substantial part of aid money is spent on overhead when it should have benefited the target population. In some NGOs, the salary of one expatriate could be greater than the sum of the earnings of all its local employees. Aid money should not be exploited. I felt deeply sorry for the donors in developed countries and for those who dreamed of help in my country.

Through the Ethiopian Orthodox Tewahedo Church, we had got two consecutive jobs from the United States Aid for International Development (USAID). The jobs would bring trouble. We had two contracts, for different times. During the negotiations, the Church asked us not to include surcharges in the project costs – the government had decreed that there would be no surcharges, we were told. We did as requested. However, when we went to settle our taxes, we were told to produce the decree. The Church didn't have it, but refused to pay the surcharges. We were fined and the total costs came to more than 40,000 Birr. They finally paid the surcharges but refused to pay the fine. The case has been waiting to be heard by a court in Addis Ababa since 1998.

I travelled to Kenya on a transport project. I had been there before. I remember going to a hotel for lunch. I sat there for an hour and the lunch had not appeared. A foreigner came half an hour later and was served before me. I wondered what had happened to Kenyans. The country was doing well in agriculture, with well-managed tea and coffee plantations. A few big officials owned most properties, and most shops and businesses in Nairobi were owned by Indo-Kenyans. Robbery was common – even a small shop in rural Kenya would have heavily protected windows with small openings to accommodate transactions. In Nairobi, it was not safe to walk alone in sparsely populated areas.

I stayed with the Bangs throughout my assignment. Mr. Jens Bang was an employee of Carl Bro International of Denmark and I was working with him. He had been in Kenya for more than 30 years and his wife Anni was a lovely person who was always smiling. They had three children, two daughters and one son. All the children were in Denmark – one daughter was a medical doctor, the other an economist, and the son was a university student. The house in Nairobi was their own and had a beautiful compound and well tended coffee bushes. Jens told me that they harvested more than

100 kilograms – or 2,200 pounds – every year and took it to friends in Denmark. They loved Africa. Jen said he wouldn't leave Kenya unless he was forced out.

I came to know more about Kenyans this time. They were good people, with more than 75 percent of them coming from the five major ethnic groups – the Kikuyu, Luhya, Luo, Kalenjin and Kamba. The Kikuyu were known for their industriousness and money-loving. I travelled with a Kikuyu engineer and he told me jokes about them. He said that when a Kikuyu woman is in hard labour, the sound of coins would be used to motivate the child to come out and that a similar technique is used to confirm the death of a Kikuyu. He told me that when the Kikuyu slaughter a goat, an ear is given to the wife so that she can hear her husband's orders. He also claimed that a wife is allowed to have one child from another man – without anyone knowing about it –in order to keep hereditary diseases out of the family. He said that adults in rural Kenya keep sticks with them that signify their age. In case a man wants to have an affair with another man's wife, he plants the stick in front of the house. When the husband comes, he checks the stick. If it's a man of his age, he turns back but would create havoc if it were otherwise. I have heard similar stories in Ethiopia. I finished my job in Kenya. I enjoyed my stay at Bangs.

In June 1997, the ADB hired me to prepare the terms of reference for a road in Eritrea. At the time, the governments of Eritrea and Ethiopia had good relations. It was four years after Eritrea got its independence from Ethiopia.

I took an Ethiopian Airlines flight from Addis Ababa and landed at Asmara International Airport. There I met Sam, the team leader from the ADB. He had been on the same flight but in business class. A man from the ministry of construction received us warmly and the people at the airport looked happy and were pleasant to us. I saw Eritreans from the Diaspora coming to visit relatives. They would kiss the ground after disembarking the plane. We took rooms at Embasoira Hotel in the heart of the city. I had been to Asmara before and so I recognised the streets, bars and restaurants. As usual, the city was very clean. The centre was crowded with young men and women, but the suburbs looked deserted and I saw only a few elderly people. The restaurants were filled with Eritreans from the Diaspora. The food was good and reasonably priced. We visited shops full of merchandise at reasonable prices and often heard Ethiopian music playing. Shops were open until late. We walked around the city in the middle of the night. It was very peaceful.

We visited government offices the next day. People were friendly and ready to help. They asked me about the well-being of Ethiopia and about Addis Ababa – Eritrea was benefiting a lot from Ethiopia at the time. Exports from and imports to Ethiopia were largely coming through the Eritrean ports of Massawa and Asab. Addis Ababa was crowded with Eritrean sweaters and shoes. Eritrean businessmen imported goods from Kenya through Ethiopia and were not taxed by the Ethiopian government. Goods ended up in the markets of Addis Ababa and Ethiopian firms could not really compete. In Addis Ababa, I had bought four Michelin tires for my car from an Eritrean tradesman selling from a container – he charged me one-fourth of the price

I would have paid in the markets. Why shouldn't Eritreans be happy and feel goodwill towards Ethiopia? I remembered a magazine illustration I had seen in Ethiopia – it had a cow with her mouth in Ethiopia and her teats in Eritrea.

The Eritrean minister of finance was forceful, while the minister of construction was an unassuming person. I thought that the former had been in bush for a longer period of time and that the latter had been an 11th-hour comer. The minister of finance tried to interpret the ADB's rules as if he were a lender instead of a borrower. He thought that winning the war against Ethiopia meant that they had won against the whole world. We visited a manufacturing site near Asmara where seven crushers were busy producing construction materials. Sam asked the Eritrean engineer where the crushers came from and he said that they had seized four of them from Ethiopia. We travelled to western Eritrea, where the major road leading towards the project site was under construction. They worked from six in the morning until nine at night and were doing a great job. I met a surveyor, Habtay who had worked at the ERA. He had been very vocal about Eritrean independence and here he was deeply involved in building his country. He was a man of his commitment.

We reached Barentu Town, the centre of the Kunama people, one of the nine ethnic groups in Eritrea. The town is in the remotest part of the country, 245 kilometres from Asmara, yet Amharic songs were dominant in bars and hotels even after independence. The two countries still have strong cultural ties, but the area had not fully recovered from the war for independence. We visited the project area near the Setit River. It had irrigable land but was a long way from being developed. We finished our field trip and got ready for Abidjan.

Our flight to Abidjan was through Addis Ababa. I wanted to spend two nights with my family and Sam wanted to visit his friends in Addis Ababa. He was a Nigerian but had worked there for three years at the Economic Commission for Africa. So both of us directed our luggage to Addis Ababa and landed at the Bole International Airport after a 55-minute flight. Airport security refused to issue a temporary visa to Sam, arguing that there was a flight to Abidjan the same day. That flight was taking off in 15 minutes. Sam didn't have enough time to transfer his luggage and pleaded for a visa. However, Sam was insulted and abused instead. He had a diplomatic visa and deserved courtesy. I tried to explain the matter but was lambasted by the security man and threatened to bash me. The man looked 25 years old and I was 51. He should have respected me, at least on cultural basis. However, he had acquired a wrong culture and his behaviour was even worse than I had experienced with the customs officer in Brussels. I wondered whether I was home or in Belgium again.

We approached the man's boss. He seemed to be a decent person and was more selective with his words. He explained the situation to us, advised Sam to come with a visa next time, and then gave him permission to stay 48 hours. Sam had reserved a room in a hotel near my home and I invited him to dinner at our place. My wife had prepared delicious Ethiopian food and the unique national coffee ceremony followed. Sam enjoyed it.

Sam and I flew to Abidjan the next day. I met my Ethiopian friends in Abidjan. My good friend Fikru was there, ready to leave on vacation with his family. His wife Melkam had worked at the Ethiopian Airlines before her husband began to work for the Bank. She knew Wondime very well. They left the whole house for me, complete with food and drink that lasted the whole three weeks. At the time, Ivory Coast was not politically stable and, as in many African countries, soldiers were creating disturbances. I was scared since I didn't speak French to search my way out in case serious troubles occurred. Fortunately, I finished my assignment before anything bad happened.

In October 1997, I got a job in Kenya with Carl Bro International of Denmark again. The funding was from the Danish government but through the World Bank. Initially, the Bank's transport economist refused to give me the job, preferring Mengesha, my ex-boss at ERA. I didn't mind, provided Mengesha got the job, but he refused and the Bank insisted on him. Finally, he demanded a fee higher than the budget allowed and the job was given to me. I was grateful to Mengesha who was always helpful to me. I travelled to Nairobi and met the project manager and the Bank's transport economist, who never liked my being there. A British transport economist was joining me from South America. The next day, the Danish project manager and I were sitting in the hotel restaurant, having breakfast. The waiter brought us bread and I was puzzled because the project manager had been given twice as much as I had. He said, "Does he take me for bread lover?" I responded, "I think he expects a higher tip from you and I am safe."

The British transport economist arrived after we had finished collecting the data. He was a gentleman and very professional. We finished our work and submitted the report. After few months, the team leader told me that he had met the Bank's transport economist, who criticised the report and degraded my work. When he told him that the chief transport economist was the British, then the Bank's man stopped talking any more. I considered it to be character and professional assassination. I have met many good World Bank people, but this one was very arrogant.

In November 1997, I was hired as a transport economist by Sheladia Associates of the US and Metaferia Consulting Engineers of Ethiopia to carry out an economic feasibility study of the 235-kilometre-long Gondar-Humera road. Gondar City, in northern Ethiopia, is one of the oldest and most historic cities in Ethiopia and was founded in the 17th century by Emperor Fasilades as the country's first permanent capital. It has some of Ethiopia's most important historical sites and is famous for its castles and palaces, the Emperor Fasilades's bath, Emperor Johannes I's library, and the remnants of many ancient Ethiopian churches. Gondar had been the site of the oldest public health college, which had become the present medical school. I travelled to Gondar to study a road that was envisaged to join the city with the town of Humera, in the middle of vast agricultural lands.

The road from Gondar descends towards Humera. There are many rivers and agricultural lands along the way. Marzeneb, meaning Rains Honey, has great agricultural potential but was unexploited. The bulls were so huge that they could hardly walk and the trees and rivers made it ideal for raising livestock. However, there was serious market inaccessibility. After Easter, weddings were very common in the area. Farmers would have saleable commodities but no access to markets. So bridegrooms and best men would resort to robberies for dowries for the brides. I witnessed a bus robbery at the time of the study, but I hadn't known the motive. The end of the project road, Humera Town, was surrounded with lands that could grow soybeans, cotton and sorghum. The Tekeze River that feeds Sudan and Egypt flows adjacent to the town and also marked the border between Ethiopia and Eritrea. The agricultural potential of the area had been partially realised since the time of Emperor Haile Selassie I. But there was still a vast area that remained unexploited. At the same time, the houses were ramshackle, the hotels dilapidated and the streets unplanned and unsurfaced. The development of urban centres at the expense of the hinterlands has been the case throughout the country. It deprives the latter, unnecessarily expands the former, and draws rural Ethiopians to the over-stressed cities in search of a better life.

After completing the study of Gondar-Humera Road in December 1997, I went to Nigeria to work on a study on a national road rehabilitation project. I was stationed in Abuja, the capital city. The heat was scorching, the area dry and with little green space. The development of Abuja as an administrative capital was underway. The previous capital had been in Lagos. There were several uncompleted private homes in town and I was puzzled about whether the owners had died or had run out of money. I had travelled to the northern cities of Kanu and Kaduna. Nigeria was a very rich country, well endowed with natural resources and with a population of more than 120 million. The land provided was suitable for all kinds of crops and the country was rich in oil, exporting a huge volume of crude oil. The resources and the markets were all there. However, the mismanagement was clear. At the time, there were three oil refineries and none functioned. The country was importing refined oil. Nigeria had been a British colony, but vehicles drove on the right, while the former colonies of East Africa drive on the left, like in the United Kingdom. I asked a Nigerian why they changed and he said because they thought that was the right way. I jokingly asked him, "Do you think the United Kingdom will shift to driving on the right?" He responded, "Yes, after everybody has changed to the left." Nigerians were very pleasant people and looked happy. I stayed there for four months.

My son was finishing high school in March 1999. It was very difficult to find the right place and area of study in universities in Ethiopia. The Ethiopian population had reached more than 60 million, but there were only five universities in the whole nation. Even those universities lacked sufficient professors, books, laboratories and computers. Every year more than 200,000 students sit for the high school leaving examination, but fewer than 20,000 will qualify for higher education. Those who complete high school successfully are not assigned university places in accordance with their choices but by the will of the administration. Students who qualify to study for degrees should score B and above. Of those, about a quarter will flunk out by Christmas. Addis Ababa University was famous for its "Christmas Graduation" in my time and still is at the moment.

Given all that, I had started contacting universities in the USA, Canada, South Africa and India. Once, I visited the South African Embassy in Addis Ababa and talked to a diplomat there. He told me about the educational opportunities in his country and in the middle of our discussion he said, "Ethiopians have become professional asylum seekers." He was telling me that I was trying to get my son out of the country under the cover of education.

I knew many young Ethiopians had gone to South Africa for better opportunities. I remembered a young Ethiopian man who had travelled with me by plane from Malawi to Addis Ababa and had started his journey in South Africa. He was telling another Ethiopian, sitting beside him, about the harassment, beatings and imprisonment he had experienced in South Africa. He said, "I better die in my country rather than go back to South Africa. I will never do it again." Ethiopians had many sad stories to tell. Many young Ethiopian girls go to Arab countries such as Lebanon, Saudi Arabia and Yemen to work as maids and nannies. Their dead bodies get shipped home after they were assaulted and raped by the men and thrown out of windows by the women when the girls are found pregnant. Their employers confiscate their passports on the day of their arrival in the host country and thenceforth they have no way out. It is a modern way of slavery.

I had been in touch with Dr. Wilson at the University of New Brunswick ever since I returned from Canada. My time with the transportation group and the people of Fredericton were always in my mind. I have been sending Christmas cards to the professors in the group, the Wayes and other close friends every year since 1983. Similarly, Dr. Wilson had been writing to me. In 1995, I had a letter from him, telling me that things were fine with the group and with him. In addition, he wrote, "The good news is how well your children are doing in school. I will be a contact for them. Also, I will try during the year to work a Post Doc or some other arrangement for you but cannot be totally sure. I'll try hard. Keep up your spirits..." He was our family man.

Consultancy work got scarce in Ethiopia and the fees were getting low. Corruption had spread rampantly. The government insisted on minimum costs, irrespective of the kind of project. My experience was that there was a threshold cost, especially for construction activities. Below that threshold, the infrastructure would not be physically viable. I remember a bid on a management project for which one bidder quoted a cost of 65,000 Birr, while another bid 5,000 Birr. The quality of the staff had been deteriorating in government offices and thus reports submitted by consultants were not challenged. Anybody could produce a report and get paid the money.

My office was in my house. I would have had rented an office if I hadn't my own. I wanted to settle my firm's taxes, but first I wanted to discuss the matter with a professional accountant. The accountant suggested 800 Birr per month as office rent, or 28,800 Birr for three years. After the financial report was prepared, I went to settle the matter, but the revenue administration refused to consider the house rent and I knew they wanted me "to travel by airplane instead of on foot," as that woman at the municipality had advised me long ago. This problem was even more serious. It took me long to convince them and have it settled.

My son had successfully completed his high school. At the time, Dr. Wilson asked me if I would be interested in becoming a post-doctoral fellow at UNB if I were offered the opportunity and I had responded positively. On July 26, 1999, I got a letter from the vice-president for academic affairs. It read, "On behalf of the University of New Brunswick, I am pleased to offer you a Postdoctoral Fellowship which will provide an opportunity for you to further your research under the guidance of Dr. E. D. Hildebrand and Dr. F. Wilson, Department of Civil Engineering..." It was very good news for my son. My daughter was finishing grade nine and was doing pleasingly at school. I thought it would be an excellent opportunity for her too. The government of the day, the EPRDF, had loosened restrictions on leaving the country, but exit visas were very expensive. I submitted the letter and applied for a visa at the Canadian Embassy in Addis Ababa. The final say rested with the Canadian High Commission in Nairobi, Kenya. I knew the commission would take some time, but wouldn't reject me without proper justification. We received our visas to Canada on October 6, 1999, and decided to leave earlier so that my son could start classes as soon as we got there.

We didn't have time to organise a party for friends and neighbours. Instead, we concentrated on important matters. We sold our car, signed our house over to Wondime and bought our plane tickets. However, my mother-in-law had been living with us for a while. She has four daughters, including my wife, and two sons. We had cherished her time with us and she had wanted to be with us too for she was deeply attached to my wife. She had her own bedroom, her own kitchen, and hosted her guests and visited friends as she wished. She was a church goer and never cooked food or prepared coffee on the weekend. Everything was ready by Friday. She would fire housemaids for not keeping food and utensils clean. One evening in 1998, she was watching the TV news as war broke between Ethiopia and Eritrea. When she saw the damage done by the Eritrean air attack on school children in Mekele City, in northern Ethiopia, she had a stroke. She had been in bed ever since and my wife was taking care of her. She was 88 years old and we felt very disturbed at leaving her behind. Finally, we left her with one of the daughters, with some money for her food. She was the most beloved person in the family.

We decided we would leave Addis Ababa on October 17, 1999. Friends invited us to visit and also took us to restaurants prior to our departure. The day was a special one. Relatives, friends and neighbours gathered in our compound. It was one of the happiest and the saddest days of my life. I was very happy that my children would have a better future but sad for that they were abandoning their country. I knew that they wouldn't come back. I knew the country was exhausted from drought and war. How can a country survive when its best hope – the young – must leave it?

We were very sorry to be leaving our neighbourhood. We had been members of seven associations and had participated in the social and environmental development of the community, standing together in times of prosperity and hardship. We sold our lifetime possessions at cheap prices, gave some to relatives and friends, and hastily stored some. We would have stayed had the future not looked so doubtful for our children. We embraced and kissed everybody. The compound was full of crying and sobbing. Some people came with us to the airport. The last person I said good bye was my sister. I embraced her warmly and she kissed me and said, "Are you going away without burying me?" She wanted me around in case anything bad happened to her.

CHAPTER TWELVE

We had arranged to fly Ethiopian Airlines from Addis Ababa to Newark, USA, and then on Continental Airlines to Toronto. We had planned to buy tickets in Toronto for the flight from Toronto to Fredericton. The plane left Bole International Airport at seven that evening. It was the first flight for my wife and children and they were very excited. The in-plane service was quite good and the flight was excellent. I didn't worry about the flight being called back since political situation was less tense by then and EPRDF wasn't nervous as Derg used to be. The plane landed at Rome International Airport for fuel and stayed there for 45 minutes. The next flight was straight to Newark and was very long and tiring. Magazines and newspapers were distributed and films were shown, yet it was boring. Flying is more boring than travelling by bus – there is no sightseeing and no getting off and relaxing. After a 17-hour flight, we arrived at Newark International Airport at six the next morning. The flight to Toronto had just left and we had to wait until noon for the next flight. We didn't have transit visas for the US and so had to be closely watched by the airport guards. We couldn't freely move within the airport – security would follow us into the washrooms and canteens. It felt like a temporary jail.

We took Continental Airlines to Toronto and arrived there in about two hours. Tsadik, a friend of mine in Toronto, had bought tickets for us and we flew direct to Montreal. Once in Montreal, we had to wait for more than three hours for a connecting flight. I called Dr. Wilson and told him about our situation and he promised to pick us up at the Fredericton Airport. We arrived in Fredericton after midnight, 36 hours after we left Ethiopia. Mistre, my daughter, was totally exhausted and Surafel was tired too. I called Dr. Wilson again on our arrival. Dr. and Mrs. Wilson each drove a car to the airport, then took us and our luggage to the Howard Johnson Hotel, across from the Princess Margaret Bridge. They didn't leave for home until about two in the morning. We were very grateful to them. They are a very kind couple.

The next morning, Dr. Wilson came back and arranged everything with the hotel. Surafel was late starting his classes. I took Mistre to Fredericton High School on the third day and had her registered. She started classes the next Monday. The school was the largest high school in the Commonwealth until it split in two in 1998. It is very large and the arrangement is complex, so it took Mistre a few days to find her way around. The school has also three levels in each class with Level I at top and Level III at the bottom. She was put in Level III and would also have tutoring. Classes have few students, not more than 35, and the facilities are good, in fact, they are amazing compared to good high schools in Ethiopia, where there are 100 students in a class. Well-equipped laboratories, libraries and gyms are almost non-existent back home.

The Waye family visited us shortly. Nicholas was now 20, Marisa 18 and Jordan 15. Nick had started work as a cook at the Sheraton in Fredericton; Marisa had entered university in Moncton, two hours drive from Fredericton, and Jordan was in grade ten, the same as my daughter. Bill was still working at the department of natural resources and Bonnie was doing some work at the Brunswick Street United Baptist Church. They were happy to see my family in Canada and promised to help us whenever we needed it. They have always been very helpful and compassionate and are part of what attracted me to return to Canada again and again.

We stayed at the hotel for two weeks and then moved to two-bedroom apartment within a 20- minute walk from the university. There was a free bus to the high school for Mistre and books were free. Surafel got registered for second semester to study computer science and started getting a sense of the Western world through television. I went to the university and shared an office with my former transport economics professor, John Brander. A few days later, Dr. Wilson suggested a topic for my research and I was soon at work.

I had met an Indian family in Fredericton. The wife, Gangu, worked at UNB and her husband, Vittala, worked for the New Brunswick Power Company as an electrical engineer. They had two smart daughters. The eldest was specialising in heart surgery at McGill University in Montreal, while the youngest had become a journalist. I had known Gangu very well while I was studying for my Ph.D. and she had invited me to their house and comforted me when my family was not around. This time again, they provided us with a bed, a mattress and utensils. Others provided us with additional utensils, sheets and a couch. We felt very welcome in our second home. I enjoyed being close with my family – I had been away from them for most of the last 16 years. We had never spent a full year together and now I could share my children's problems and closely follow their studies. However, Shewaye faced a problem with the food – she was a traditional Ethiopian and for her, food meant *injera.* No rice, pizza, pasta, hamburgers or hot dogs. There was no *injera* in Fredericton. She was also worrying a lot about her ailing mother. We tried to reduce her distress by calling home as often as we could. The children and I didn't have problems with Canadian food, so it was easier for us.

Mistre was shocked by the behaviour of the students in her class – they bluntly asked questions and challenged their teachers. She found that unusual since teachers back home were serious and in most cases dispassionate. However, students here asked their teachers on personal questions and wanted to know about their preferences and dislikes. She felt both were extremes but was interested in mixing with Canadian students. It took her long though. I was a bit concerned but not too much for she had strong ties with her mother and Shewaye was here for her. The first semester was over and Mistre had excellent marks and was transferred to Level II. We were even busier the second semester because Surafel had enrolled at UNB and I was working on my research. However, Shewaye was alone at home and worrying about her mom. We called her family every month to find out how her mother was. Her mother was lucky to have such concerned children. Her daughters nursed her in shifts, while the sons helped out in other ways. Shewaye's food problem and her worry about her mother concerned me though.

Winter was underway and it was a new experience for my family. The children adapted easily, but Shewaye couldn't take it at all. She didn't want to leave the house and always stayed indoors. Surafel and I had to walk to the university, carrying our lunches. He kept his lunchbox in my office and at lunchtime, he would come to my office, we would warm up our food in the microwave, then take it to the student lounge and sit side by side to eat. Evenings, I would wait for him until he had finished his assignments and then we would head to our place, on foot or by taxi, depending on the weather. Mistre briefed me on her days at school and we discussed her assignments in the evenings and weekends. I had missed that closeness and sharing for a very long time.

Dr. Wilson would often come to my office, grab a chair and sit down beside me, and say, "How is the family? How is Mistre making out at school? How is the young fellow doing? How is your wife? How is your brother back home?" He was a wonderful human being, very concerned for people of other continents and race. The staffs at the transportation group and in the department of civil engineering were all good to me too. Professor Brander, my officemate, was very kind and helpful. Gangu would call me at my office and at home and ask me on the wellbeing of my family. Dr. Wilson invited Shewaye and I for Christmas dinner at King's Landing and the department of civil engineering did the same on campus. The Brunswick Street United Baptist Church invited my family to a Christmas banquet. People were wonderful and my family was impressed with that.

There is no Orthodox Tewahedo Church in Fredericton which we attended back home. And there was no Greek Orthodox Church either which is the closest to our church. Nevertheless, Bill offered us transport to the Brunswick Street United Baptist Church and I started going there on Sundays. Shewaye wasn't daring enough to go there during her first winter.

The second semester was now over. Surafel did very well and so did Mistre. She received various certificates of outstanding achievement, a certificate of achievement and a certificate of merit. She was transferred to Level I in grade 11. Her background at the Lideta Cathedral School in Addis Ababa prepared her for the challenge and I was reminded that the fight to get her in that school had been well worth it. The school had contributed to Surafel's achievement as well.

What surprised Shewaye and I most was that after arriving in Canada, our children began to identify with Africa. Back in Ethiopia, they had always listened to Western music, watched Western films and left the living room whenever Ethiopian songs were aired on television. Within few months after coming to Canada, however, they started listening to cassettes from home and from other African countries as well. Pictures of Nelson Mandela, Haile Selassie and Nkrumah were on in their bedroom walls. They also covered their walls with cultural posters purchased from the Ethiopian Tourism Commission. Their screensavers were Ethiopian landscapes, including the obelisks in Axum, the rock-hewn churches in Lalibela, the

Castle of Fassillades in Gondar and the Tis Isat Falls on the Blue Nile. They were adding to the Canadian mosaic.

In July 2000, I was invited by the African Development Bank to do a road appraisal in Mauritius, an island east of South Africa. I talked with Dr. Wilson and he agreed to give me leave for 35 days. I needed transit and entry visas for countries in Europe and Africa. I was given very short notice and was advised to go straight to Mauritius instead of going through Abidjan, Ivory Coast. I called the French Consulate in Moncton for a transit visa, but they said it would take at least three months. Next, I called the Italian Embassy in Ottawa and they weren't willing to issue me a transit visa either. I called the British High Commission in Ottawa and they required visas to Ivory Coast and Mauritius and I would have to provide a record of employment, a bank statement and proof of my Canadian status before they would issue a transit visa. It wasn't easy for an Ethiopian even to pass through a country. It reminded me of the South African diplomat in Addis Ababa who said that Ethiopians are professional asylum seekers.

I travelled to Ottawa for a British visa, then on to London, where they never asked me to produce any document. I flew direct to Mauritius from London, on Air Mauritius. The plane was an Airbus and the flight took 13 long hours, but it was very comfortable – one of my best flights ever. The flight was at night, so the plane landed early morning. Mauritius is a beautiful island in the Indian Ocean and is very small, about 25 kilometres in radius inhabited with 1.2 million people. As informed, Mauritius was discovered by the

Portuguese in the 16th century and was subsequently held by the Dutch, French, and British before it gained independence in 1968. Industry, finance and tourism are the dominant economic sectors. Sugarcane grows on about 90 percent of the land. It is a tourist destination for European vacationers and has a per capita income of more than US $10,000, the highest in Africa. Ethnically, it comprises Indo-Mauritian, Creole, Sino-Mauritian and Franco-Mauritian. The capital city, Port Louis, is very crowded but clean and beautiful by African standard. The project road was designed to keep traffic from crossing the city running between southeast and northeast.

We visited government offices and travelled all over the country. Mauritians look well nourished and are well dressed, testimony to the economic success of their country. Very few countries in Africa have used their resources as well as Mauritius has. Many of them keep themselves busy fighting one another.

We finished our work in Mauritius and flew on South African Airlines to Johannesburg, a three-hour flight. The outside of the airport in Johannesburg was crowded with taxi drivers fighting for passengers. Luckily, I managed to get a hotel taxi and avoided trouble. We spent a night in Johannesburg, a very modern city with elegant buildings and large malls with good merchandise at reasonable prices. It was like any Western city. I took South African Airlines again from Johannesburg to Abidjan, through Accra, Ghana. The flight to Ghana was very crowded, with luggage in the cabin and no place to put my briefcase or even to stretch my legs. I thought that

Ghanaian traders were likely transporting merchandise from South Africa, to sell at exorbitant prices at home. South African Airlines seems to be busy along that route but oblivious to the comfort of its passengers.

I arrived in Abidjan in late afternoon and stayed at a friend's house, Woudneh – he was away on vacation. Abidjan was politically volatile at the time, with soldiers seeming to be ready to butcher the civilians. In addition, the ordinary people had grudge with the Bank's employees because of the latter's affluent lifestyle and thought that they benefited from the country's resources. Most Bank workers had left Abidjan for other missions or had gone on vacation to avoid trouble. I didn't speak enough French to talk my way out of an emergency and it was difficult for me even to take taxis. The taxi drivers demanded exorbitant fares from non-French-speaking passengers, especially between the airport and the city centre. Gregg, the Canadian consultant, had told me that he had been travelling from the airport to a hotel when the driver parked his taxi somewhere along the way and demanded more money. Gregg had no choice but to comply, though he did negotiate for a little less. Most of the taxi drivers were from neighbouring countries of Burkina Faso, Guinea, Senegal and Mauritania and were very violent when their demands were not met. In Ivory Coast, car-jacking and house robberies were daily events. I thought that some of the police were collaborating with the criminals. While I was there, looting was frequent, the civilians and soldiers raiding banks and shops. The soldiers who were supposed to protect the people and public properties ransacked instead. It was very scary for me. Offices were closed for three days and the town was very tense. I was lucky that I was at my friend's house – I had plenty of food and would have starved if I had stayed in rental accommodation. Fortunately, my assignment was completed before the worst happened and I escaped to Canada.

Initially, when we left our country for Canada, my wife and I had planned for our children to stay in Canada. Canada is one of the best countries in the world for opportunities and we wanted them fulfil their aspirations. Consequently, we applied for landed immigrant status by the middle of 2000. Dr. Wilson, Professors Stevens and Bisson, and Mr. Waye wrote supportive documents to the immigration office on our behalf. The process was lengthy, but I was used to it and did as requested. I was summoned to go alone to the Canadian immigration office in New York for an interview that lasted only 20 minutes. I thought they wanted to see me how old I was – age is one of the major factors in admitting immigrants into the country. Finally, they granted us landed immigrant status in March 2001. In order to fulfil our final obligations, we had to leave the country and enter again. We had no car then and so I consulted our man, Dr. Wilson, and he agreed to take us to Houlton, a border point between Canada and the US on December 31, 2001. The day was stormy, with masses of snow and driving would have been very difficult had it not been for Dr. Wilson, who had been on the road for many years. We reached Houlton, made a U-turn about 20 metres into the United States, entered the Canadian immigration office and completed the requirements. The officers said "Welcome to Canada!" Now we were landed immigrants.

In celebration, the Wilsons had organized a small party at their place. Mrs Wilson had prepared food and drinks by the time we were back. Professor Albert Stevens and his wife, Ena, and Professor Barry Bisson and his wife, Mary Ann, were also there with gifts for us. Professor Bisson gave me a T-shirt with I AM CANADIAN written on the back. They are wonderful people. We started life in our second home.

In May 2001, a professor at UNB informed me that there was a vacancy at Transport Canada in Ottawa. I called the director general for economic policy analysis and also faxed him my curriculum vitae and he referred me to the chief of aviation forecasts. The chief told me that he wanted to see me in Ottawa and I travelled to Ottawa to talk to both of them. We had a good discussion and they told me that they had positions in other offices as well, but the chief said that he wanted me to work with him. We discussed salary; I suggested an amount and they expressed no objection. They wanted me to start as soon as possible.

After my return to Fredericton, I told Drs. Wilson and Hildebrand and both agreed that I should start in early July 2001. I called the chief at Transport Canada and told him that I could join them on July 1, 2001. He agreed and said that he would start processing my application as soon as possible. I filled out the forms that came from the human resources office and faxed them back to them. After few days, however, the chief told me that the human resources department had rejected my application. That was quiet a disappointment since I had confidently expected otherwise.

I continued working at UNB until March 2002, when Dr. Hildebrand came to my office and told me about a temporary post at the New Brunswick department of transportation (NBDOT). I called the manager of passenger services and she told me that they were looking for someone to fill in for a woman on maternity leave. I met with the manager, Mrs Margaret Grant-McGivney, at her office and briefed her on my education and experience. She was very friendly and welcoming. She then got a promotion and moved to another office. She deserved it and I congratulated her and said good luck. The man who replaced her, Mr. Don Mason was another wonderful person. My office there was good compared to the one at UNB – it had much better chairs and other facilities. I asked myself, "Why so much here but so little there?" The job was research-oriented and I was used to that. There were some more good people there, especially Claudette, who would come to my office and say good morning and make small talk. She would ask about my country and appreciated other cultures and I was impressed with her keenness. She was one of the best people I met at NBDOT. In general, however, the atmosphere was quite different from that at UNB. I never felt comfortable when one of the secretaries by the door would turn her face the other way every time I passed her desk.

People at UNB have been exposed to foreigners and so most of the staff was very friendly to outsiders. The professors had travelled to other parts of the world, had experienced many cultures and were keen to know more. NBDOT looked a bit different to me. It was not like meeting Dr. Wilson or Professor Bisson in a hallway at UNB – they would be full of jokes and laughter and would tease me and I would tease them. At NBDOT, however, sometimes I never spoke a word the whole day. I am a quiet person by nature to a new environment, may be that also contributed to the silence. In general though, the work was so challenging and satisfying that I was oblivious to the chilly personalities at NBDOT, compared to UNB.

One afternoon, I was looking through some documents in the records management office at NBDOT. Bernita, the manager, greeted me and asked if there was anything she could help me with. She always did that whenever I visited her office. After some conversation, she asked me where my home country was and I told her it was Ethiopia. After hearing the word Ethiopia, she stood motionless for about a minute. I imagined that she was counting my bones. I thought that the name "Ethiopia" brought to her mind the starving people she'd seen on television. It was a very sad incident for me.

While I was at NBDOT, I was invited by a transport consulting firm in Ottawa for a job interview. I travelled to Ottawa and talked with the chairman and the president. The company had not fully started in road sub-sector yet and they required someone to help them get started. We discussed many points, including getting work in developing countries. They frankly told me that I might be a liability for them because getting jobs under my name in developing countries would be a challenge. They told me that they had

had that problem when another professional from a developing country was working for them. I appreciated their point and they were absolutely right – I had found that many African countries believed in colour rather than expertise and that is the path to advancement in developed countries. Some of them won't pay their own experts half what they pay foreign consultants with the same qualifications. Despite that, I thought the company was intending to recruit me but with low salary. I appreciated their frankness and returned to Fredericton.

The World Bank had advertised positions for transport economists and senior transport economists, under job posting R200209E003. It read, "Candidates from Sub-Saharan African countries are strongly encouraged to apply for these positions." I was very motivated and so applied in October 2002. I got an e-mail from Rose Gordon in January 2003 that read, "Thank you for your interest and applications for the above mentioned position. We are pleased to inform you that you have been short-listed for this position. During the weeks of January 13th & 20th, we will be conducting preliminary (half hour) telephone interviews. Kindly let me know your telephone number on which you would prefer to be contacted."

I was excited – the Bank was the biggest lending agency in the world – and felt very happy to be short-listed and in no time responded by e-mail as follows, "Thank you very much for letting me know that I have been short-listed for the position of a Transport Economist. I can be available for the preliminary telephone interview on 20th January, 2003 through my home telephone number. In this regard, I want to know the time since I have to leave office early. I prefer 4:00 pm Washington, D.C. time. However, I will accept any time that is convenient to you." Fredericton time was one hour earlier than Washington, D.C. time. She responded, "Thanks for your response. I now realise that January 20th is a pub holiday here and so our offices will be closed. Please let me know which other date is convenient for you and I apologize for not informing you earlier." I responded to the second e-mail by saying, "I can manage on January 13, 2003 at 4:00 pm Washington, D.C. time. Please let me know on your final decision." Next, she wrote, "Thanks, will let you know something definite the week of January 6th."

The fourth time, she sent an e-mail that said, "Is it possible to do the phone interview on Wednesday, January 15th @ 4:00 pm? I know your preference was the 13th but we are not able to do it then." I said okay, but another e-mail came and said, "Sorry for the inconvenience, but we would like to change your appointment to 5:00 p.m. on Wednesday, January 15th." I wrote back that I had no problem at all.

I talked a lot to friends about the interview and was ready at home on the appointed date and time. I told my family to be quiet and not to touch the telephone. I waited for the call with anxiety. The telephone rang at five that afternoon, Washington, D.C. time, and when I picked up the phone, the secretary said, "Richard will be half an hour late. Please wait for him." I said it was okay. The second call came 45 minutes later. Richard was on the phone. He said his colleague would join him for the interview shortly. He told me that he was a landed immigrant in Canada and had lived in Toronto but had moved to London, England. Then, he said, "Let's start until my colleague comes." He began with, "Tell me about yourself." That is a standard question, so I told him about myself. He then said, "That's enough. We'll let you know on the result in two weeks." Quietly, I left the room. My son said, "What happened?" I said, "It is finished." He said again, "What kind of interview is that?" I didn't respond - what could I say to that kind of interview? That was the last I heard from him. I believed his arrogance didn't represent the Bank.

I finished my contract with NBDOT on March 18, 2003, and started applying throughout Canada and to international organizations as well. Nobody responded. I was surprised because I had never seen any Canadian who had been a student at UNB's transportation group who had any problem in getting a job. Some of them even took jobs before completing their thesis and never returned for their diplomas. I have M.Sc.E and Ph.D. from UNB, Canada and twenty-five years of international work experience. I said to myself "May be age is against you in getting work here?" I kept on looking for a job with more surprises.

In May 2003, I was asked by the Louis Berger Group (LBG) of the US to join them in competing for a transport study – "East and Central Africa Global Competitiveness Hub" – to be financed by the United States Agency for International Development (USAID). The assignment would be at least two years and the office would be in Kenya, so I was very pleased. They submitted the proposal and LBG got the job and they informed me to get prepared. I was very happy and ready to go. However, LBG called me again and told me that the USAID has suggested its person to replace me. And that was after the firm had won the job on my qualifications and experience. What can a rabbit do when an elephant takes its food? Up until then, I had believed that education is the only thing that could not be expropriated and had stressed the point to my children. USAID disproved my theory.

Life has been a challenge. I started with only the love of my parents. Abaye sweated in the forest for minimal return and Wondime and I laboured like a pair of oxen, Emaye behind us firmly holding the harness as we all struggled to make sure the family survived. With love and through tenacity, we withstood everything. I fought to help my family and accomplished the highest academic achievement. I have travelled half the world, as my name implies. I am blessed with an excellent wife and very smart children. I am happy with what I have achieved.

However, all aspects of Ethiopian life continue to deteriorate. The country has faced three famines in 30 years and a most brutal military government during the 1970s. Many of our best and our brightest perished. Those who got lucky escaped to the West. Ethiopians are now scattered all over the world – found even on the smallest islands. Some perished at sea or in the desert along their journeys to a better place and a better future. Some of my sisters who went to the Middle East for a better future returned not with fortunes but as dead bodies. Right now in Ethiopia, people are fomenting ethnic tension domestically and with our neighbours and no peace is in sight. The rich history of the country is being replaced with poverty, starvation and deprivation. It is very painful to behold.

In Canada, however, my family and I have seen that people can do more than satisfy their basic needs – Canadians also have quality health care, education, and social services, effective and efficient transportation systems, and a peaceful environment. In Canada my family and I have enjoyed the fruits of peace and real development.

I know that Ethiopians can create a peaceful environment and sustainable development. I see Ethiopia where each citizen gets a fair share and each does its part in keeping the country safe and secure. I hope that Canada's prosperity continues and that it continues to work for peace elsewhere.

ABOUT THE AUTHOR

Born and brought up in Ethiopia and educated in Ethiopia and Canada, Alemayehu Ambo is a transportation planner by profession. He has worked for the Ethiopian Roads Authority in Ethiopia and for the University of New Brunswick and the New Brunswick Department of Transportation in Canada. As well, he has worked as a transport consultant on projects funded by the World Bank, the European Union, the African Development Bank, the United States Aid for International Development and for non-governmental organizations.